WHAT OTHERS ARE SAYING...

Sam Certo is a man who is successful in life and love and faith. He is also a great family man who, as you will read, has integrated the business acumen he shares with us in his relationship with two of his sons. He is an elder in our church and I enjoy learning from him as he has learned from his own experience and Scripture. You will be glad you read this book, and others in your life will be glad you read it as well!

—Dr. Joel C. Hunter,
Senior Pastor
Northland—A Church Distributed

Chasing Wisdom is easy to read. Chapters carry a message. It is very practical. Most importantly is the clear path to transfer the subject matter into your business.

—Dave Whitten
Sales Manager
Toshiba

This book includes real world dilemmas that every manager is likely to face. Case studies help the reader to discover and apply timeless wisdom in Scripture. I highly recommend *Chasing Wisdom* to everyone who wants to improve skills at managing employees and grow a solid, profitable company.

—Tom Starnes
Chairman & CEO

Chasing Wisdom is an excellent tool for professionals from all walks of life, and focuses on the individual encountering different cultures and situations, and provides key insights into developing oneself to gain wisdom from all aspects of their career.

The book opens with a specific charge for wisdom: "Chase wisdom vigorously—the way you would chase the stars on a summer night. Feel it in your bones the way you feel the wind. Fly with it. Sleep with it. Dream with it." Having not only the tools to *chase wisdom*, but also the biblical and social definitions, is imperative for future growth in today's society and this book provides just that.

I would highly recommend *Chasing Wisdom* to professionals in all stages of their careers and life as it specifically outlines key aspects and provides *valuable tools* to becoming more effective as a leader, a colleague and most importantly a wiser person.

—Andrew Robertson,
Realtor
Sotheby's International Realty

I really liked *Chasing Wisdom*! The combination of eternal truth and best business practice came through loud and clear. The real life examples made it come alive. Personally, I most appreciated the chapters on good and bad pride, listening and the wisdom marathon track. If you need a short quote to summarize my thoughts, here it is:

Chasing Wisdom has given us timeless truth and practical, timely application. It has given us real world business examples brought to life, showing how it works today. I most appreciated the *Active Listening* and *Wisdom Marathon* applications. This book is for any serious business leader who is willing to pursue God's wisdom for a lifetime.

—Bill Wolfe
Director of Strategic Partnerships
Jesus Film Project
Cru–Campus Crusade for Christ in the United States

With all of the media coverage on Ponzi schemes, insider trading, tax evasion, and shady behind door agreements which make a few wealthy while costing others their livelihoods (think Enron), it is invigorating to read about how one can be successful in business while doing the *right things*.

Chasing Wisdom offers a fresh look at the duality of business life and Christian beliefs. It shares insights into the relevance of Christian teachings in today's business world by using Biblical passages to help the reader navigate real world business challenges. Each chapter embarks upon a new trial; providing discussion, real world examples, and a path for the individual reader's quest. Intelligent people are as numerous as stars in the sky, while those able to amass experience and knowledge, and apply them along with Christian principles to their business & personal lives are indeed the rarest of gems. This book provides a means through which rough-hewn stones can become those rare gems.

—Mary Kay Williams
Sr. Director of Business Process Innovations
ADP

I am struck by many things in *Chasing Wisdom*. Dr. Samuel C. Certo has written a book to be read by all leaders in any organization – profit or nonprofit. It is also a book to be read by pastors, ministry workers, and persons of any other faith. It is academically profound because this work reflects his genius, years of studying, teaching his sons and college students, his consulting work, leading leaders, his faith journey, and observing and understanding everyday life experiences along the way.

Dr. Certo has also committed to us words of wisdom from the Bible as he has personally encountered those truths in his own life marathon. In each chapter he integrates God's truth with practical principles from true-life stories and examples of everyday issues. Overall, this book is filled with a wellspring of knowledge based on Wisdom from God for business adventure.

I highly recommend this book as an equipping resource for chasing wisdom in life, ways of building up yourself and others, and acting on truths for doing business the right way! Be committed to learn, grow, and serve.

—Gus Davies
Pastor
Northland—A Church Distributed

I wanted to thank you for having the courage to write *Chasing Wisdom*. A powerful book jam-packed with truths that will only make our lives more successful on every front! I can tell you that I really enjoyed it and believe you are striking a chord with a needed resource for the workplace. I could see this book as required reading by employees of many, many companies. My opinion is that close and careful reading of this book and its exercises will be a tremendous help for many as they live out their professional lives.

—Bob Minotti
Vice President of Sales and Marketing
Snapt

Chasing Wisdom is great! I have a number of people that I need to give it to as soon as it's published.

—Doug Fudge
Vice President
P. Fudge and Associates Insurance Agency

Chasing Wisdom has good content. This is wonderful for developing leadership. It reframes and reinforces lessons in a Biblical context. I liked the examples that brought concepts into concrete scenarios.

—Melody Giacomino
Chief Operating Officer
US Phytotherapy

CHASING WISDOM

2/3/17

To Miguel,

Enjoy you chase!

God Bless Your
Wisdom Efforts,

Sam

CHASING WISDOM

WISDOM

Finding Everyday Leadership in Business and Life

Samuel C. Certo, PhD
with Donna Peerce

TATE PUBLISHING
AND **ENTERPRISES**, LLC

Published by Tate Publishing & Enterprises, LLC
127 E. Trade Center Terrace | Mustang, Oklahoma 73064 USA
1.888.361.9473 | www.tatepublishing.com

Tate Publishing is committed to excellence in the publishing industry. The company reflects the philosophy established by the founders, based on Psalm 68:11,
"The Lord gave the word and great was the company of those who published it."

Book design copyright © 2014 by Tate Publishing, LLC. All rights reserved.
Cover design by Joseph Emnace
Interior design by Gram Telen
Illustrations by Wyndelle Remonde

Published in the United States of America

ISBN: 978-1-63063-882-5
1. Business & Economics / General
2. Business & Economics / Leadership
14.03.24

DEDICATION

My wife, Mimi, and I have been blessed with four fantastic children. Two of these children, Sarah and Trevis, have chosen academic careers. Trevis is a professor of business administration at Arizona State University. Sarah is a professor of psychology at the College of Charleston. Each reminds me of earlier times in my life—both personal and professional. Through their own intensity, they inspire me to keep improving. I love them both very much and dedicate this book to them as a small token of appreciation for the vast enrichment that they have brought to my life.

You will learn more about our other children, Brian and Matthew, as you read this book. Of course, my love for them is undeniable and vast, as well.

AUTHOR'S NOTE

The authors have changed the names of some individuals and modified identifying features of other individuals and some places in order to preserve their anonymity. The goal in all cases was to protect those people's privacy without damaging the integrity of the manuscript, and any similarity is purely coincidental.

ACKNOWLEDGMENTS

Needless to say, I am very pleased with *Chasing Wisdom : Finding Everyday Leadership in Business and Life*. Reviews have been very positive and extremely encouraging.

Any author knows, however, that taking an idea for publication to its final book form is impossible without the encouragement, commitment, and dedication of many other people. Many friends and colleagues made immense contributions, sometimes unknowingly, to making this book a reality.

Chasing Wisdom focuses on how to become a wiser leader in business and life by better understanding and applying Biblical principles to solving problems. I would like to thank two people in particular for preparing me over the last twenty years for this book journey by helping me to better understand and clarify Biblical tenets. Donald Bjork, a retired Baptist minister, has been my personal Bible teacher for close to two decades. Don has always been available to help me better understand God's Word. In addition, Dr. Joel Hunter has been my pastor and friend for almost twenty years at Northland—A Church Distributed. His excellent teaching and personal clarification of Scripture, even from time to time via email, have been invaluable.

I'd like to extend a special *thank you* to my fellow writer, Donna Peerce, for her important and significant role in making this book a reality. Donna was my confidante and sounding board for all important facets of book development. She took my starchy, sticky, staid academic writing style and gave it new life—*heart and soul*. Together, Donna and I produced manuscript that neither could have produced individually—a true, fruitful writing partnership. She was always cheerful, competent, and cooperative. I'm very grateful for Donna's vital contributions to *Chasing Wisdom*.

I'm also very grateful to my colleagues at Rollins College for help in making this book a reality. It starts at the top. Our president, Dr. Lewis M. Duncan, was always very encouraging about my treatment of wisdom. Dr. Craig McAllaster, dean of the Crummer Graduate School of Business at Rollins, was also very supportive. I also want to acknowledge my fellow professors for creating a professional climate of innovation and creativity that encourages and supports projects like *Chasing Wisdom*. Special recognition for Steve Gauthier, my associate dean, for helping me to adjust my teaching schedule in such a way that it enabled me to focus on this project. Lynda Boyce, my administrative assistant was indispensable in managing practical issues needed to move this project forward.

We're blessed with fantastic students in the Rollins MBA program. Several of my graduate student assistants helped in doing much of the legwork for this project. Jessica Fornasier, Ellen King, Brendan Richard, and Shannon Walsh deserve special thanks. Others students who provided useful thoughts and ideas about the book and its publication: Ian Scott, Chris Enger, Autumn Sheridan, KC Normont, and Kate Gordon.

Many others have invested much time and effort throughout my writing process to help make my book the best possible. Those who deserve special thanks are Bill Wolfe (director of Strategic Partnerships, Cru-Campus Crusade for Christ), Mary Kay Williams (Sr. Director of Business Process Innovations, ADP), Pastor Gus Davies (Northland—A Church Distributed) and Bob Minotti (VP of Sales and Marketing, Snapt).

Then, there's my family. My wife, Mimi, has been my constant and most important source of personal encouragement for this project. She is a strong Christian whose excitement for this project kept me going. She was even one of the key manuscript reviewers. Thanks, Mim! Thanks also to Brian and Matthew, two of our sons, for allowing me to interview them about their companies and helping me to make decisions about what material to finally include. Sarah and Trevis, our other two children, were very encouraging over the life of this project. I much appreciated the *How's that wisdom project going?* questions.

Andrew Robertson also provided sound advice on how to make the manuscript more relevant. Thanks, Drew!

Most of all, I want to credit God for any skills that I might have in making *Chasing Wisdom* a reality. This book, and anything else that I might be able to accomplish in life, are due to the gifts He has given me and my faith in Him to help me use them in the right way.

CONTENTS

FOREWORD

There are many sources of wisdom in this world, but my two favorite sources are the successful person who shares effective practices with others, and the Bible with its timeless truth for every area of life. Wisdom is not mere knowledge—it is a lifestyle of truth embedded in love that improves the lives of many people in practical ways.

Wisdom is especially needed and grows as we deal with our closest relationships. When we talk about any endeavor, especially business, we need the kind of guidance that will produce not only effective products or organizations, but the kind of guidance that will produce fulfilled lives. All organizations, not only nonprofits and churches, can be in the business of improving lives—not just making money.

In these pages you will get reoriented toward what is really important in life. And you will learn practical lessons in creating a better relationship with God and people. The most successful people I have known are perpetual students. They are always learning. They don't see themselves as experts, but as pupils of productive practicality who share what they are learning with others. It is in that servant-leader spirit of humility that Sam Certo writes the Biblical wisdom found in these pages.

Sam Certo is a man who is successful in life, and love, and faith. He is also a great family man who, as you will read, has integrated the business acumen he shares with us in his relationship with two of his sons. He is an elder in our church and I enjoy learning from him as he has learned from his own experience and Scripture.

You will be glad you read this book, and others in your life will be glad you read it as well!

—Dr. Joel C. Hunter,
Senior Pastor
Northland—A Church Distributed

PREFACE:

EVERYDAY LEADERSHIP ADVENTURES WITH TWO SONS

For over thirty years, I've devoted my entire professional life to helping people become better at business. As a business professor, behavioral scientist, consultant, entrepreneur, and author, I've been on a lifelong quest to explore and better understand business processes myself and to share this information with others.

In my opinion, a trend exists today toward people needing and craving a deeper, *more spiritually-based* foundation for understanding, surviving, and thriving in the business world. In fact, *spiritually-based* business principles seem to be suggested and incorporated into the business world more and more every day.

More broadly, this trend seems in existence for virtually all areas of life. The trend is evidenced by the many spiritual themes hitting the covers of top news magazines and the fact that books on spirituality now appear regularly on the bestseller lists. Americans of all ages, cultures, and socioeconomic environments, it seems, are looking for something bigger than themselves— bigger than the Beemer in the driveway, the weekly pedicure, and the one hundred dollars CK pants—something bigger to handle their daily troubles and challenges.

As further evidence of this societal interest in spirituality, Wall Street now sees *spirituality publications* as a growth industry with annual sales reaching upwards of $8 billion per year. In an newspaper article in *The Tennessean* newspaper on October 28, 2011, Anita Wadhwani reported that although it may seem like it's all over for some booksellers, religious book publishers are more than optimistic. Sales skyrocketed in 2011 and continue as more and more people turn to books about faith for guidance. The Christian publishing industry is a $2 billion industry. And the potential growth rate is staggering.

Mainstream books are crossing spirituality with everyday topics—business, entertainment, travel, and adventure—and numerous publishers are taking notice of this hunger for spiritual understanding.

Walk down the aisle of any bookstore and see how many titles include the words *soul* and *spirit*. More than fifty million Americans will purchase inspirational, business, and self-help books this year. Why? Because people are hungry for something *bigger than themselves* to help them better maneuver in life.

Likewise, in the business world, people are exploring more and more the impact of spiritual factors on seemingly every facet of business. Popular press business books reflecting this trend include recently published titles focusing on the leadership genius of Jesus or Jesus's management methods.

Too, in the academic world, a stream of fresh articles focusing on spirituality and business has also appeared and is growing. These articles explore subjects like management and the prophets, Biblical principles as guidance for lending money, and comparing servant leadership in different cultures.

Complementing these academic reports, more and more college professors are exploring spiritual issues and business by joining groups like the *Christian Business Faculty Association* or *Management Spirituality and Religion*. Growing membership in such groups seems a sure-fire indicator that our society's interest in the relationship between spirituality and business is alive and well, and will be growing for some time.

Closer inspection and study of the link between spirituality and business for over two decades, leads me to an exciting conclusion: *Biblical principles are a primary vehicle for building business success.* When Biblical principles are the basis for developing business tactics, the tactics generally have a noticeable likelihood of leading to business success. And when people are more in tune spiritually, they become wiser, and thereby, more likely to demonstrate wisdom in business. What does this have to do with you?

The purpose of this book is to help you become wiser in business, by becoming better at employing Biblical principles to solve business problems. Throughout the book, I will illustrate the use of Biblical principles in running a business by reflecting on business experiences and everyday leadership adventures I've had with two of my sons, Brian and Matthew.

A theme that runs throughout the book is that Biblical principles *can* and *should be* the standards against which all business practices are evaluated.

These business experiences with my sons are based upon real events within their companies, Websolvers (the name Websolvers is presently in the process of being changed to Findsome & Winmore) and Eden's Fresh Company. Websolvers is an Internet services company started by one of my sons, Matthew, in 1995 out of his dorm room as a freshman at Rollins College. Matthew is now thirty-five years old. Eden's Fresh Company is a fast-food, casual salad and wraps restaurant started by another of my sons, Brian, in 2007. Brian developed the business model for his company while a student at the Crummer Graduate School of Business at Rollins College. Brian is now twenty-eight years old.

Upon graduation, both Brian and Matthew decided to start businesses rather than work for someone else. Both businesses operate in Orlando, Florida. To date, the companies are surviving nicely and showing encouraging longer-term trends.

As a fatherly mentor and guide, I've had rich and far-reaching conversations with Matthew and Brian concerning the relationship of Jesus' teachings to virtually all aspects of business.

Discussion has focused on the same types of tough business challenges that you face in your business life. Topics have ranged all the way from hiring the right people to managing cash flow. Other topics have included building company identity, reacting to the fast-paced nature of business, controlling costs to permit company survival, dealing with fluctuating economic times, and continually producing high quality products.

As you read this book, remember that I am not a minister, a priest, or anything close to either. I cannot offer you worthwhile advice at all about complex spiritual issues like the significance of predestination or the difference between Reformed Theology and Black Theology. Additionally, I'm certainly not attempting to convert you to Christianity any more than I'm attempting to convert you to sociology or psychology as I tell you how those principles relate to successfully operating a business. However, please do keep in mind as you read this book that I am a business professor. As such, almost by reflex, I look for insights about how to improve business operations when I'm reading or studying almost anything. This book is a compilation of insights about how to be a wise businessperson based primarily upon what I've learned as a Christian from the Bible, as I've pursued daily Biblical readings and study over the last two decades.

Over my career, I've published over fifty business textbooks, several of which were translated into various languages and are used in colleges and universities throughout the world. These books are all based almost exclusively upon scientific investigations about business operations.

Chasing Wisdom is very different from all the other books that I've published. It's personal, but also opens the world of how the Bible can eloquently speak to people about how to operate businesses *wisely*. The Bible speaks to me very clearly in this regard. I hope that what it says to me makes sense to you, as well. I sincerely hope that *Chasing Wisdom* becomes an invaluable compass for guiding your business in successful directions.

Each chapter in this book opens with a real world business adventure that I've experienced with one of my sons. As an example, the adventure in the first chapter is Brian's *The Adventure of the Misfit Collars*. Each adventure is a commonplace business issue or problem of concern to either Brian or Matthew that could also be of concern to you in your company or workplace. Throughout the chapter, I've provided stories and examples as well as Biblical and other insights to illustrate how Brian or Matthew might react to the business circumstance they're facing. These adventures are all commonplace in today's work environment and reflecting on them should be of significant relevance to you.

Each chapter ends with a section called *You and Your Chase*. This section focuses on helping you to get practical advice from the chapter. If these adventurers and discussions of them help you to carefully consider your business problems and implement wise solutions for them, then the book will have served its purpose.

Study and enjoy this book with the goal of learning and benefitting from how a father and sons have together tried to become wiser businessmen by more clearly seeing that business practices and Biblical principles should be inextricably linked. I sincerely hope that you greatly benefit from studying this book whether you are a business owner, a supervisor/manager/leader, or an employee.

I've very much enjoyed writing *Chasing Wisdom* as a way to try to help businesspeople discover Biblical principles as a means to the end of business success. I sincerely hope that you enjoy your journey as you pursue your own chase for wisdom!

—Samuel C. Certo, Ph.D.
Steinmetz Professor of Management
Crummer Graduate School of Business
Rollins College, Winter Park, Florida

KNOWING WISDOM

Know also that wisdom is money for you:
> If you find it, there is a future hope for you, and your hope will not be cut off.

Proverbs 24:14 (NIV)

Before you can know how to *chase* wisdom in business, you need to know what wisdom is. It sounds simple and most people think they know what it is. *But do they? Do you? And can one really* chase *wisdom?* Answers to these and other wisdom-related questions begin with an understanding of one of Brian's real workplace experiences.

THE ADVENTURE OF THE MISFIT COLLARS

Brian clearly remembers his first job in a restaurant and some of the problems he encountered. Since he was new and at the bottom of the chain, he did jobs that nobody else wanted to do. Those menial jobs were not anything he'd want to discuss with brokers on Wall Street, but they taught him a lot about people and business. He knew he should put his best into everything he did, and so he promptly became the ace floor sweeper, window washer, and table cleaner.

Although he was fairly satisfied and comfortable in his job, he noticed that everyone else seemed to dislike the company with intense passion. His co-workers did everything they could to avoid work; they took lots of breaks, and even made fun of the restaurant's food and customers. He eventually became so upset at the general attitude of his coworkers that he decided to find out why they all felt the way they did.

He worked closely with two employees who had the worst attitudes, so he figured he'd start with them. During a break one day, he simply asked, "Why don't you guys like it here?"

The shorter of the two immediately spouted, "The Collars are such jerks. It's impossible to get along with any of them."

Brian responded, "Collars? Who are the Collars?"

"Just look around you," the short one said, glancing toward a couple of managers at the far side of the room.

And after taking a brief glance around the room, Brian realized who the Collars were. All of the managers wore different shirts than the other employees. The shirts the managers wore were *collared*, and the other employees wore t-shirts. Thus, the name, the Collars.

Somehow, the Collars created such resentment that the employees did whatever they could to avoid work as a way to show their dislike of management.

When Brian first opened his restaurant, he sat down with me one afternoon at the kitchen table and explained that he wanted to know how he could be different and more effective as a business owner and leader.

"I want to avoid becoming a Collar like those managers at the restaurant I worked at long ago."

"I remember," I told him. "All the employees hated them and they had a bad attitude."

"What if my employees hate me?" Brian asked. "How can I run a successful business, if they don't respect me and have a negative attitude?"

"You learned from your first restaurant job that it's important to get along with your staff and if you do this, you'll gain their trust and respect," I commented.

"I want my employees to be proud of the company and do all they can to make it a success. I want them to work with me and not against me."

"You have the right attitude," I told him. "I have no doubt that not one person will call you a *Collar*."

INITIAL REFLECTION ON THE COLLARS

Brian's story is an important one. It brings attention to many organizations that have leaders like the Collars. Brian probably didn't fully appreciate it, but asking how to avoid being a Collar is a critical question and one that many people should be thinking about in business.

As Brian described them, Collars are managers who do not get along with employees. When managers do not get along with employees, it limits the commitment and creativity of employees, making organizations much less likely to thrive. This kind of leader – a Collar – is not very wise. If you avoid being a Collar by getting along with employees, you'll have a valuable opportunity to build employee rapport and commitment, spark employee creativity, and thereby increase the likelihood that your restaurant will grow and prosper. It may seem like pure old common sense, but many people miss this principle altogether.

The rest of this chapter aims at explaining more fully what *getting along with others* means, why it is important to get along with employees no matter if you're a business owner, manager/supervisor, or coworker, and how getting along is one of the basic foundational elements of being wise in business.

WHAT IS WISDOM?

Many definitions of wisdom may seem too complex or abstract to be useful. Many people think that knowledge is wisdom. By itself, it's not. You can be the smartest person on the planet, but if you don't *possess* wisdom, you won't always make wise business and life decisions. There is an excellent line in the 2011 movie *Anonymous* spoken by the playwright and poet, Edward de Vere (played by Rhys Ifans), who some historians think actually penned all of William Shakespeare's plays and sonnets. "I *know* wisdom, but I have never *possessed* it."

This is very apropos. Many people intellectually know all kinds of wise *thoughts* but don't actually act wisely in business.

Some people believe that experiences in life build to a place of wisdom. By themselves, experiences are not *wisdom* either.

Think of wisdom in simple, straightforward terms. *Wisdom is insight about right and wrong in handling problems.*

Certainly, both knowledge and experience together can *contribute* to your insights about handling problems. But these alone will not make you wise.

This book focuses on helping you gain insights about right and wrong from the most important source of wisdom available to any of us, the Bible or *God's Word*. The major purpose of this book is to help you become wiser by employing Biblical principles as insights about right and wrong in handling problems.

From Brian's first job experience in a restaurant, he learned that something was drastically wrong with *not* getting along with others in an organization. His experience as a *low man on the totem pole* showed him that Collars were creating problems for themselves and the restaurant.

Not getting along with others in organizations is a serious problem that can actually lead to the downfall of a company. Wisdom—insights about right and wrong for managing people and interacting with people in organizations—comes to us directly from the Bible, from God. For example, *God's Word* tells us that leaders in organizations should strive to get along with others.[1] To get along with others, leaders should emphasize behaviors like fairness in dealings with people, showing respect for them, eliminating favoritism, and not being two-faced.

Leaders should be optimistic because they indeed can develop an organizational community that is robust and successful. This community, however, can only be built if leaders do the hard work of getting along with others. Treating others with honor and dignity will help leaders to establish such a community. Treating with honor means treating others with great respect. Treating with dignity means treating others as though they deserve respect.

Odds are that the Collars didn't treat employees with honor and dignity. Odds are also that the Collars didn't treat employees fairly. Had the Collars been wiser, and followed Biblically based insights about handling people, Brian would probably have experienced a much different group of workers. In addition, although we do not know exactly how successful the restaurant in which Brian worked actually was, it likely would have been much more successful with better relationships among managers and employees.

CHASE WISDOM: BECOME A WISER LEADER

Ultimately, my answer to Brian's question of how to avoid being a Collar may surprise you. *You avoid being a Collar by becoming*

---

[1] James 3:17, (*The Message*): Real wisdom, God's wisdom, begins with a holy life and is characterized by getting along with others. It is gentle and reasonable, overflowing with mercy and blessings, not hot one day and cold the next, not two-faced. You can develop a healthy, robust community that lives right with God and enjoy its results only if you do the hard work of getting along with each other, treating each other with dignity and honor.

a wise leader. You become someone that your employees will respect and embrace. If you treat your employees—as well as your peers—with respect, they will, in turn, treat you with respect. They will follow your lead. If you embrace wise principles in your decision making and business operations, employees will, in turn, embrace them.

Collars are the antithesis of *wise* leaders. They are much different than wise leaders. The Collars that Brian described most likely paid very little attention to trying to relate to employees. Their approach to management probably focused on instilling fear in their employees—on getting people to do their jobs because they were afraid not to and pushing employees into doing their jobs by threatening them, and likewise, punishing employees who didn't do their jobs. Employees generally end up fighting leaders like the Collars rather than cooperating with and being committed to them.

Wise leaders are much different than Collars. I know I mentioned this before, but it bears repeating: Wise leaders focus on people and try to build a workplace and culture that employees find personally satisfying, safe, and rewarding. Employees working in such an environment generally strive to be more productive and involved in organizational affairs. Employees working in such an environment usually make significant positive contributions to their organizations over time and help organizations achieve greater success over the long term.

Although it is quite easy to say that you should become a wise leader, it is very difficult to actually become one. Key Biblical insight that you'll need to grow in wisdom comes from topics like justice, pride, trust, foolishness, and anger. Chapters throughout this book cover Biblical insights from these and other topics to help you grow in wisdom.

CHASE WISDOM WITH VIGOR

Embrace your professional life firmly by building yourself into the wisest leader you can. This is not an easy task, but if you take the time to know and embrace wisdom, you will find that your life is more successful, and as a result, more rewarding.

Chase wisdom *vigorously*—the way you would chase the stars on a summer night. Feel it in your bones the way you feel the wind. Fly with it. Sleep with it. Dream with it. And pray for it in your quiet contemplative moments or whenever you read the Bible. Ask God continually for help and guidance. Never deviate in your laser-like quest for wisdom. Chase wisdom like an Olympian chases a world record. Be relentless, be dedicated, and never take your eye off it!

This book is a pilgrimage in many ways. It is a journey that engages our moral and spiritual beliefs along with our well-honed intellect. On this pilgrimage you will more deeply feel *chasing wisdom* and more deeply revisit it than ever before. You will be learning through study of the Bible and by *doing*.

Referring to drawing at the beginning of this chapter, how many rabbits should the boy chase in the garden? According to an old Chinese saying, if anyone chases two rabbits, both will get away. Think mostly of wisdom as the only *rabbit* that you should chase throughout your career and life. Stay focused on chasing the *wisdom rabbit*. Chasing other *rabbits* at the same time will only allow all the rabbits you're chasing to get away and you'll end up with nothing.

As your chase enables you to become wiser, you won't be disappointed with your one rabbit. Wisdom is the only rabbit you'll need. You will gain something more valuable than gold or silver.[2] With true wisdom, you'll have the key to solving any

---

[2]   Proverbs 3:13-14, (*New International Version*): 13 Blessed is the man who finds wisdom, the man who gains understanding; 14 For she is more profitable than silver and yields better returns than gold.

problem you face. You'll have insight to meet any challenge. Wisdom is more valuable than any of the possessions of the wealthy.[3] Wisdom is more valuable than private jets, diamond rings, or private islands.

THE BIBLE: HELP FOR THE CHASE

Rely on the Bible, on *God's Word*, to help guide you in your chase. Learning the wisdom of the Bible helps us to gain invaluable insights for discerning right from wrong. There is no better application for the wisdom of the Bible than to help us navigate through the problems that we all continually and inevitably face in our lives—personal as well as business.

None of us are perfect and often, we fail in using wisdom in business, as the Collars failed. Becoming wise does not come easily or naturally, but takes time and focus. It is in many ways a crusade to discover and improve our truest selves. It is usually easy to follow our less-than-wise impulses. The reward for acting with wisdom, however, is great.

Michell Cassou, author of *Point Zero, Creativity Without Limits*, wrote, "We live in a time in which most people believe there is not much inside them, only what teachers, parents, and others have put there." My experience says otherwise. If we study the Bible and try our best to apply the principles within, we will grow in wisdom, and as a result, become better problem solvers. And, in turn, the payoff in the business world *and life* can be greater than we ever imagined.

WHAT IS CHASING WISDOM?

Chasing wisdom is *pursuing* wisdom—doing what we can to become wiser. Can one actually take steps to become wiser? The

---

[3]   Proverbs 8:1 (*The Message*): ...For Wisdom is better than all the trappings of wealth; nothing you could wish for holds a candle to her.

answer is a resounding, *Yes!* God's Word, as it appears in the Bible is a solid foundation on which we can base our attitudes and actions in business and life. It is the primary key in helping us to gain insights about what to do when facing difficult business problems.

On one hand, think of *chasing wisdom* as receiving a gift from God. King Solomon provides an excellent example of asking God for wisdom. One night God appeared to Solomon and told Solomon that he could have anything he wanted. All Solomon had to do was ask. Solomon asked God to give him wisdom and knowledge so that he would be able to govern his people.[4] God granted Solomon's request.[5] As a result of God granting Solomon's request, Solomon has become known as one of the wisest men who has ever lived. Never be reluctant to ask God for wisdom because God gives wisdom generously to all.[6]

On the other hand, also think of wisdom as a characteristic you gain by listening carefully to God's Word and growing and maturing in your understanding of it.[7] In this sense, you chase

---

[4]   2 Chronicles 1:10, (*New International Version*): Give me wisdom and knowledge, that I may lead this people, for who is able to govern this great people of yours?

[5]   2 Chronicles 1:11-12, (*New International Version*): 11 God said to Solomon, "Since this is your heart's desire and you have not asked for wealth, riches or honor, nor for the death of your enemies, and since you have not asked for a long life but for wisdom and knowledge to govern my people over whom I have made you king; 12 therefore wisdom and knowledge will be given you. And I will also give you wealth, riches and honor, such as no king who was before you ever had and none after you will have."

[6]   James 1:5, (*New International Version*): If any of you lacks wisdom, he should ask God, who gives generously to all without finding fault, and it will be given to him.

[7]   Proverbs 1:1-6, (*The Message*): These are the wise sayings of Solomon, David's son, Israel's king—Written down so we'll know how to live well and right, to understand what life means and where it's going;

wisdom by improving your knowledge of God's Word, the Bible. The Bible is a manual that helps all live well and right and to gain a better understanding of the implications of life in business. The Bible is a guide for how to live wisely in virtually all imaginable situations. It teaches all of us, but can be of special value to the inexperienced as it helps them get a handle on the reality of business and life.

YOU AND YOUR CHASE

This book is all *about you* and how to become wiser in your business activities, which will benefit you in all areas of your life. If you are wise in business, you will most likely be wise in life.

What insights can you gain from this chapter about how to act wisely in business?

For one thing, remember that avoiding being a Collar is critical. As a leader, the last thing you want to do is limit the commitment and creativity of others in the organization. Build commitment of others for the organization by treating them with honor and dignity.

In more general terms, avoid becoming a Collar by striving to become wiser. Know that you must study God's Word and avoid being a Collar by becoming wiser. When you align yourself with God's Word, you cannot help but be wiser.

Don't push employees or coworkers by using fear, threat, and punishment. Instead, build a workplace and culture that others find rewarding and uplifting. This type of work environment will encourage employees to be productive and involved. As a result,

---

A manual for living, for learning what's right and just and fair; To teach the inexperienced the ropes and give our young people a grasp on reality. There's something here also for seasoned men and women, still a thing or two for the experienced to learn—Fresh wisdom to probe and penetrate, the rhymes and reasons of wise men and women.

such employees will make contributions that positively impact your company and make it more successful.

Always stay focused on becoming wiser. Think of wisdom as a gift from God and pray to receive it. Also, remember that wisdom is based upon respect for, and trust in, God's Word. Use God's Word as the standard for determining the right and wrong ways to handle issues, doing what is moral and avoiding what is immoral.

When you discover a challenging problem and find it difficult to know what is right in solving it, be patient. Thoughtfully reflect on God's Word for insights about what to do.

In trying to become wiser, be a little selfish. Focus on yourself, doing what you need to do to become wiser. Spend whatever time you need to transform into a wise being by sharpening your most important tool—wisdom. Transformation is available to anyone willing to pick up the Bible and use it for unfolding.

Fortunately, God's Word is your plainspoken source of knowledge about handling business and life problems. The Bible provides a wealth of knowledge, which if understood, can virtually guarantee that you will become wiser and wiser over your life as long as you continue to study, understand, and apply it.

Here are a few additional tips you can use to chase wisdom:

1. *Read the Bible regularly to gain insight into your business life and situation.* Establishing when you will read the Bible each day and for how long is critical. When you make that *appointment* with God to study the Bible, it will become something you look forward to. It is your spiritual tool. Also, think of reading the Bible each day as your daily vitamin for strengthening your wisdom.

2. *Spend quiet, contemplative, prayerful moments alone to reflect on your workplace, your decisions, and your leadership tactics.* Becoming wiser takes serious thought and focus. Think

about problems you face and the best ways to attack them. Don't be reluctant to ask Jesus for advice!

3. *Find a Biblically savvy business mentor.* This mentor should be someone you admire and respect. Someone who knows both Biblical and business principles. Someone who can help guide you in your business practices. Listen to the mentor, learn from the mentor, and apply what you learn.

4. *Join a Bible study group that focuses on developing a rich understanding of God's Word.* Joining such a Bible study will help ensure that you'll review regular doses of God's Word. In addition, it's always good to hear the thoughts and opinions of others. Listening to the perspectives of other Bible study members on what God's Word means will help open your mind to new interpretations of God's Word and how it can help make you a wiser person.

BRIDLING THE TONGUE

> If anyone considers himself religious and yet does not keep a tight rein on his tongue, he deceives himself and his religion is worthless.
>
> James 1:26 (NIV)

You've probably witnessed this many times. Friends or family members who speak their mind before *thinking*. People who *fly off the handle* and don't stop to think about the repercussions of their words. Especially if those words are cruel or accusing. I cringe when this happens because I know people are going to get hurt and later on, people will be sorry for what they said. But the damage is done.

One Biblical theme that should be particularly useful to people who are focused on becoming wiser involves watching what you say. This theme is often referred to as *bridling your tongue*. As the chapter opening quote from the *Book of James* indicates, one's focus on *bridling your tongue* is so important that without it one's religion is worthless.

Most of you will associate a bridle with a horse rather than a tongue since a bridle is well-known headgear used to control a horse. A rider uses a bridle to direct a horse to do such things as stop or turn right or left. You need the bridle to control the horse and in this same way, this chapter makes the point that people need to think about bridling or directing their tongues in the same way the rider thinks of directing a horse.

There are many valuable insights about controlling what you say that are discussed in the Bible and can guide you. Knowing and understanding these insights will help you to lead more wisely in organizations and life.

Learning better about how to bridle your tongue starts with reflecting on a real life adventure that Matthew once experienced, *The Flatter Chatter*. Read on and see if you recognize yourself or others in this adventure.

THE FLATTER CHATTER ADVENTURE

Early in the history of Websolvers, Matthew asked if I would facilitate a strategic planning meeting for his company. Previously, we had talked for some time about the potential value of such a meeting and he had decided it was time.

I looked at my schedule and decided upon a time that would be beneficial for both of us and I agreed to facilitate an all-day meeting to generate the plan. This was not to be a meeting where Matthew would explain his strategic plan to his employees. Instead, the plan was to be developed through the course of the meeting by integrating the thoughts and ideas expressed by employees, including Matthew. The goal was to have a working plan at the end of the day.

In preparing for the meeting, Matthew and I agreed on several important topics for discussion. These included categorizing competitors, developing a company mission statement, and establishing company goals and coming up with strategies that could be implemented to accomplish those goals.

The meeting began early on a Wednesday morning. All seven employees of the company, including Matthew, were present. Everyone sat around a large round conference table. In the front of the room, we placed a whiteboard for taking notes. Discussions started quickly with all participants contributing and firmly focusing on the purpose of the meeting.

Whether the employees were bored, tired, hungry, or whatever, over time, the quality of the meeting began to lose a bit of steam. Employees began parroting and accepting Matthew's accumulated contributions rather than focusing on their own original thinking. And at times, it almost seemed like employees were competing for who could flatter Matthew the most. After all, he owned the company and it was obvious there were quite a few apple-polishers, brownnosers.

Comments like these became more and more frequent:

"I liked what Matthew had to say about our strategy."

"Matthew is correct; we need to be more focused on our customers."

"I think that the pace of growth proposed by Matthew is just right."

After the meeting, Matthew and I agreed that the day was very productive. We also both agreed that the meeting could have been even more productive if employees had stayed focused throughout the day on making original contributions instead of trying to flatter the boss.

REFLECTIONS ON FLATTER CHATTER

In how many meetings held in the business world everyday does *Flatter Chatter* exist? Many more than the managers of those meetings would like. In how many of those meetings where flattery exists does the flattery play an important role in helping to solve problems or build organizational success? None!

Matthew and all other leaders like him need to recognize when flattery exists and take steps to eliminate it if they want to keep the focus on company improvement and success.

Flattery or flowery speech is often used to try to manipulate someone. The Bible warns us of flatterers. People who use flattery indiscriminately are up to no good and probably trying to take advantage of someone.[8] Granted, there are some people who flatter others in a sincere complimentary way. That's not what we're discussing here. It's one thing to say, "Mom, you're pretty smart." It may be an entirely different thing to say, "Mr. Boss, you are an extremely bright, effective leader." Complimenting a friend, or family member, or even a boss, can be genuine and sincere. Complimenting a boss repeatedly, however, often means you are brownnosing.

There are many reasons why people use flattery. One reason is to get ahead in the world. They think that by flattering the boss, the leader, for example, they can gain the leader's favor and move up in line to receive benefits like pay increases, better work schedules, or promotions. People in organizations need to problem-solve, not flatter.

Another reason that people flatter others is simply to gain another's approval. God's Word explains that there's trouble ahead for those who flatter to gain another's approval.[9] Relationships built upon winning approval are not authentic and do not meet the test of hard times.

Wise leaders understand the negative consequences of flattery and strive to eliminate it whenever they can. If the leaders like the flattery, and many do, then they let it boost their ego even when it's false.

Flattery, however, represents only one of the many problems that arise in organizations because of what someone says. The remainder of *this chapter* discusses not only the implications of flattery, but other types of messages that can cause organizational problems.

---

[8] Proverbs 29:5, (*The Message*): A flattering neighbor is up to no good; he's probably planning to take advantage of you.

[9] Luke 6:26, (*The Message*): There's trouble ahead when you live only for the approval of others, saying what flatters them, doing what indulges them. Popularity contests are not truth contests—look how many scoundrel preachers were approved by your ancestors! Your task is to be true, not popular.

SIGNIFICANCE OF THE TONGUE

Think of the *tongue* and what you say as an apparatus—a tool—that largely determines what your life experiences will be. When good things happen, what you say is an important catalyst in making them happen. On the other hand, when undesirable things happen, what you say is also a significant catalyst in making that happen. Think of your tongue as the rudder that steers the path of your ship. Being careful of what you say can help you minimize undesirable events in business and maximize desirable ones.

Physiologically speaking, it has been said that the *tongue* is one of the most exercised muscles of our body. I don't think many of us ever think about the tongue as being an exercised muscle. When we think of muscles, we think of our abs, our biceps, and our legs. Not our tongues. Businesspeople, like everyone else, talk a lot. That being said, it makes good sense that we take care with every word we say. Words are powerful things. This chapter emphasizes useful ideas for carefully thinking about what we say and how we say it.

THE TALE OF TWO JESTERS

There is a story in the *Jewish Talmud* that talks about a powerful King. Throughout history, we have read about court jesters or *clowns* as we would call them today, who entertained the Queens and Kings. In this story in the *Jewish Talmud,* the collection of Jewish law and tradition, a King invited two court jesters, Simon and John, to come before him. When they appeared, he said to Simon, "Go and bring me back the best thing in the world." Then he addressed John and said, "Go and find me the worst thing in the world."

The two court jesters left and then quickly returned. They each carried a package for the King. Simon bowed before the King and said, "Sire, I have found the best thing in the world." The King opened the package and discovered a human tongue.

The other court jester, John, said, "Your Majesty, I have brought you the worst thing in the world, as you asked." The King opened John's package and discovered a human tongue there, as well.

The moral of this story is that what we say can be used as the best thing in the world, or the worst thing in the world. With the tongue—our voice, our spoken words—we can encourage, motivate, and support others. Using the tongue—one's voice—in this and similar ways has a positive impact on the organization, or people, and increases the likelihood of organizational success.

On the other hand, the spoken word can degrade, demean and say negative things about others. As in *The Flatter Chatter Adventure*, we can also use the tongue or the spoken word to *flatter* others dishonestly as a way to apple-polish those in *higher places*. None of these uses of the tongue impact an organization positively. In fact, people in organizations who use the tongue in this fashion have a negative impact on organizational productivity and significantly lessen the probability of organizational success.

In a nutshell, we use the tongue—our spoken word, our voice—in both positive and negative ways. We must learn how to use the tongue—our voice—in a positive way, and eliminate negative usage and related consequences. We must stop and think before speaking so we never have to regret our words.

The following section helps us to understand why words, the building blocks of our messages, are so important.

THINK BEFORE YOU SPEAK

It's very important to *think* before you speak. Most sentences that we speak are made up of many words and within those words resides an emotional potency. In addition, each word that you use can have colossal impact. A word from a leader's mouth may, at first glance, seem inconsequential. But never think of words as inconsequential. Instead, think of them as very powerful. Words are used to communicate our thoughts and ideas, our feelings, our hearts. Words influence others and build relationships. And words can tear down relationships whether in business or personal lives.

Language has the immense power to create change whether it's good or bad. Marcus Aurelius, the Roman Emperor from 161 to 180 A.D., considered to be one of the most Stoic of the philosophers, said this: "Perform every act in life as though it were your last." I'd take this a step further and say: "Speak every word you say in life as though it were your last." Words can be as powerful as acts.

Choose the words that you use very carefully because they have the potential of accomplishing nearly anything or destroying nearly anything.[10]

Not many people stop and think before speaking. They don't think of the consequences of what they're going to say. Do you do this? Do you know how to *bridle* your tongue? Most of us have had negative things said to us, or written about us, at some point in time. Perhaps the words were so harsh, we've never forgotten them. And if they were kind words, perhaps they were so encouraging; we've never forgotten them either. Perhaps those kind and encouraging words boosted our self-confidence and helped us to soar. On the other hand, perhaps those negative comments tore down our self-esteem and crushed our spirit. People do forgive others for their unkind words, but it is hard to forget what was said.

Although positive, encouraging words can be comforting, careless or harmful, negative words can crush us and pierce our minds and hearts.[11] They hurt. They tear up our lives. Everything

---

[10] James 3:5, (*The Message*): …A word out of your mouth may seem of no account, but it can accomplish nearly anything—or destroy it!

[11] Proverbs 12:18, (*New International Version*): The words of the reckless pierce like swords, but the tongue of the wise brings healing.

contributes to building or tearing down our egos, our self-esteem. Just one negative comment can ruin a person's day. A few negative comments could even ruin the person's life. For these reasons, it's important to weigh our words wisely, even words to yourself. Do not chide yourself, berate yourself or belittle yourself. Don't tear yourself down for your own words about yourself can have a great, lasting impact on you.

The way you speak reflects the person you are and impacts everything around you. It can greatly contribute to your success or "non-success" both in business and your personal life.

SUCCEED OR FAIL WITH WORDS

How important are words to business leaders? As I've been discussing throughout this chapter, words are very important. Many would argue that leaders should think about words as being so powerful that they are the main reason a leader will succeed or fail. Sure, a leader who doesn't choose his words carefully may succeed to some degree, but the truly great leaders are great orators, as well. Think about one of the greats, President John F. Kennedy, inaugurated on January 20, 1960. He is known for his famous line: "And so, my fellow Americans: Ask not what your country can do for you, ask what you can do for your country."

Following in the footsteps of great orators, leaders should choose their words very carefully. Biblical thought is consistent with this idea by indicating that all of us will be held accountable for what we say even when we just casually or carelessly *mouth off* about something.[12]

Consider the words very carefully in following conversation between two employees discussing an empty coffee pot.

---

[12] Matthew 12:36-37, (*New International Version*): 36 But I tell you that everyone will have to give account on the day of judgment for every empty word they have spoken. 37 For by your words you will be acquitted, and by your words you will be condemned.

"I did not drink the last cup of coffee. There was coffee in the coffee pot when I used it last!"

"You know it's a company policy that the last person who uses the coffee pot when it is empty is supposed to make a new pot of coffee."

"Well, you're accusing me of something I didn't do!"

"Hey, I saw you at the coffee pot just a few minutes ago and then I looked and the pot was empty."

"Well, it wasn't me!"

"Who was it then?"

This conversation can go on and on. Neither person is *bridling their tongue*. Now this conversation won't *make or break* the company's profits or success, but it's an example of how *speaking without thinking first* can disrupt a person's day, or even life. And oftentimes, the arguments in the workplace focus on much more serious things than an empty coffee pot.

The point is: Words affect people. Words have power. Words can create, build, or tear down.

As a writer, I love words. I love the feel of them, the look of them, the sound of them, and the way they can paint a picture. I love the way they can influence a person in a meeting or in personal conversations. They can create moods and feelings. This being said, I also realize the power of words. Any time a person speaks or writes something, they have a responsibility to create the *best* in their words and writings.

WHEN THE TONGUE IS THE WORST

We learned from *The Tale of the Two Jesters* that the tongue—the voice—can be the *best thing in the world* and it can also be the *worst thing in the world*. It can be the worst thing for a businessperson when the tongue is used for flattery, backbiting, slander, too much talk, talk without listening, or gossiping. The following sections discuss each of these instances.

FLATTERY

Flattery was mentioned earlier in the chapter. Now let's discuss this topic in more detail. *Flattery* is extreme, undue, and disingenuous praise usually given to someone to promote one's own selfish good. Genuine flattery is complimenting someone because you're being sincere and is the opposite of what we're discussing here. Interestingly enough, we can even flatter ourselves into thinking that we're *something* that we're really not or what we're doing is not really wrong.[13]

Flattery is another form of not keeping a rein on one's tongue, of one's voice. When you don't keep a rein on it, you're not *bridling* the tongue. Just as spouting off angrily is nonproductive, so can be speaking *too much flattery*. The point is that people should at all times be conscious of what they're saying and think before they say anything. It's one thing to compliment someone. As I've mentioned already, there is nothing wrong with that and it can display emotional support and friendship. When it becomes wrong is when the praise is given to manipulate another.

Sure, it's common for employees to flatter their bosses during a business meeting. Everyone knows apple-polishers. We've met them in school and in the workplace. And it's common for employees to try to apple-polish their boss. An apple-polisher is not exactly an honest person. Though the apple-polisher may incorporate bits of truth in his or her flattery, it's still *false* and the intentions of the apple-polisher are suspect. I don't know about you, but I've had difficulty getting along with people who were apple-polishers. It's difficult to trust them. They *flatter* whoever is in charge and you never know if it's the way they really feel. These people do not instill trust in others.

Remember, flattery is mostly used to gain favor with another. To *con* that person into liking them. Interestingly enough, those

---

[13] Psalm 36:2, (*New International Version*): In their own eyes they flatter themselves too much to detect or hate their sin.

who show disapproval or criticism of another's actions often gain more favor than those who flatter.[14] The lesson here is that dishonesty shown in flattery is not as impactful in gaining favor as honesty shown in constructive criticism.

Matthew's challenge in *Flatter Chatter* was not to be influenced by such flattery, but to encourage employees to deemphasize flattery and focus more on objectivity and constructive suggestions for the company. Only those with naïve, egotistical minds succumb to flattery.

The employees could have *bridled their tongues* more and contributed much more to the meeting by offering original ideas.

Wise leaders need to examine flattery at all times to fully appreciate the negative impact that would occur if both they and their employees adopted flattery as a commonplace practice. Simply put, it's easy to get a *big head* when you hear all the flattery. Pretty soon, you're going to start believing those things that an apple-polisher tells you. You're going to become more egotistical. Don't be fooled. In this case, things like *ego* come to mind. If someone loves hearing all the *flattery* about himself, then soon that person might believe the flattery *stories* and start thinking a little too much of himself.[15]

Remember, words are a tricky thing and a powerful thing.

BACKBITING

Backbiting is speaking unfavorably about the character or reputation of someone who is not present. It's *talking behind their backs*. Whether the person is there or not, the Bible teaches that those who wish to live a moral life and to enjoy the

---

[14]   Proverbs 28:23, (*New International Version*): Whoever rebukes a person will in the end gain favor rather than one who has a flattering tongue.

[15]   Romans 16:18, (*New International Version*): For such people are not serving our Lord Christ, but their own appetites. By smooth talk and flattery they deceive the minds of naive people.

success that such a life brings do not slur others, hint or make accusations about others that will likely insult them or damage their reputation.[16] Always remember that benefits accrue to those leaders in organizations who do not speak unfavorably about others.[17]

Think about it. Are you guilty of badmouthing your neighbor, a family member, or even your friend? People do it without thinking about the consequences. We live in a negative world and it's all too easy to become negative about others in a habitual way and never even give it a second thought. Only comments which lift up, encourage, inspire, and are gracious and supportive should be expressed to, and about, others.[18]

SLANDER

Slander is another use of the tongue or voice that will make it the *worst thing*. Slander is making up or spreading something false regarding another person with the intention of ruining the reputation of that person. No business leader should go about slandering other people with whom he or she works, and they should not allow others to slander, as well. Damage to another's reputation caused by slander could endanger the career and/or

---

[16] Psalms 15: 1-3, (*New International Version*): 1 Lord, who may dwell in your sacred tent? Who may live on your holy mountain? 2 The one whose walk is blameless, who does what is righteous, who speaks the truth from their heart; 3 whose tongue utters no slander, who does no wrong to a neighbor, and casts no slur on others...

[17] Psalms 32:12-13, (*New International Version*): 12 Whoever of you loves life and desires to see many good days, 13 keep your tongue from evil and your lips from telling lies.

[18] Ephesians 4:29 (*New International Version*): Do not let any unwholesome talk come out of your mouths, but only what is helpful for building others up according to their needs, that it may benefit those who listen.

life of the slandered person. It could ruin that person's life and is totally unacceptable.[19]

Anyone—especially a leader—who is in business and slanders another is a fool.[20]

TOO MUCH TALK

Socrates is credited with a quote aimed at cautioning us about talking too much: "Nature has given us two ears, two eyes, and but one tongue—to the end that we should hear and see more than we speak."

Sometimes, you get the impression that people believe that they can appear smarter and smarter by talking more and more. On the contrary, the more and more you talk, the more and more foolish you appear.[21] To be prudent, do not simply increase how many words you say.[22] Instead, use only the number of words that suit your situation. Be a leader of fewer words. That can make you a wise leader. But speaking too many words can sometimes make you a foolish leader.

TALK WITHOUT LISTENING

If you're *mouthing off* in a conversation without listening to what another person is saying, this can be the worst thing in the world. You're not taking responsibility for your actions—for what you're saying. Conversation is the fuel that makes organizations function.

---

[19] Leviticus 19:16, (*New International Version*): Do not go about spreading slander among your people. Do not do anything that endangers your neighbor's life. I am the LORD.

[20] Proverbs 10:18, (*New International Version*): Whoever conceals hatred with lying lips and spreads slander is a fool.

[21] Ecclesiastes 5:3, (*New International Version*): A dream comes when there are many cares, and many words mark the speech of a fool.

[22] Proverbs 10:19, (*New International Version*): Sin is not ended by multiplying words, but the prudent hold their tongues.

The healthier the conversation, the better the organizational functioning will be.

What is a healthy conversation? By definition, conversations are exchanges about thoughts and opinions between or among people. To illustrate a simple conversation pattern, a first person might speak, then a second person listens and responds, and then the first person listens and responds again based upon what the second person says. A healthy conversation is a conversation in which a balance of speaking and listening is a catalyst for those in the conversation to communicate successfully. As a result of speaking and listening in a balanced manner, thoughts are modified and refined.

Oftentimes, people talk so much it seems that they simply like to hear themselves talk. They never stop to let the other person respond. Have you ever had a conversation on a phone with someone who talked nonstop, never coming up for air? I've been in this situation. I've even laid the phone down and taken a drink of water, only to pick up the phone and find the person still talking. That person didn't even know I had laid the phone down. Needless to say, I didn't relish talking to this person because the conversation was always one-way.

Artist Frederick Franck said, "Merely looking at the world around us is immensely different from *seeing it*."

In the same way, I also believe that merely talking *at someone* is immensely different than conversing *with someone*.

Talking is fine, but talking without truly listening to what another is saying is imprudent and rude.[23] (I devote an entire chapter to *Listening* later in the book). Listening is so important to building successful communication in organizations that wise

---

[23] Proverbs 18:13, (*The Message*): Answering before listening is both stupid and rude.

leaders should always encourage others to pay attention to what is being said.[24]

GOSSIP

Gossip is definitely one of the *worst things* from the tongue. Think of gossip as idle talk or rumor, mostly about the intimate or private matters of another, a conversation focusing on personal or intimate issues. Gossip is another example of using the spoken word—the tongue—in a way that creates discord, disharmony and negativity in the workplace and in one's life. When people gossip, they do not *bridle* their tongue. Just like *flatter chatter* is a dishonest way of building someone's ego and pride, gossip is a way of harming one's reputation.

When you don't pay attention to what you say, there can be numerous consequences—both good and bad. There is an old Jewish story about this, which is dramatized in the "Forgiveness" episode of the *Spiritual Literacy* DVD.

In many towns, there are people known as the town gossips. In "Forgiveness," a man known as the town gossip told stories about others that hurt them. When his Rabbi talked to him about the pain he had caused in his town, the man was surprised. He had no idea he had hurt anyone and was very upset about it.

He asked the Rabbi what he could do to make things right and repair the damage. The Rabbi told him to take some pillows out to a field, cut them open, and shake out all the feathers. The man thanked the Rabbi and hurried to get a feather pillow and run out to the fields. Later, he returned to the Rabbi and said that the wind has blown the feathers all over the field. The Rabbi told

---

[24] Proverbs 7:24, (*New International Version*): Now then, my sons, listen to me; pay attention to what I say.

him that was good and that now, he had to go back out to the field and collect all the feathers.

The feathers represented this man's gossip. When the man gossiped, his words were scattered to all parts of the town. It was his responsibility to go out to the fields and collect all the feathers. Likewise, he had to clean up the damage he had caused in the town as a result of all his gossip.

Wise leaders are very aware of *gossips*, those people who *spread* gossip. Unfortunately, gossips can have a ravaging impact on organizations. They tend to betray confidences,[25] destroy friendships in organizations[26], and promote continuing conflict.[27] Wise leaders take steps to eliminate both gossip and gossips from organizations.

IS WHAT YOU SAY GOSSIP?

I believe there are three questions that you can ask yourself to determine if what you're saying is gossip: *Is it true? Is it necessary? Is it kind?* I call these *The Three Golden Questions*. If a statement is true, then that's one thing. But, is it necessary to even state it? And, is it kind? It may be a fact that John is overweight, obese and unhealthy. So, yes, it's a true statement. But is it necessary to state it? And is it kind? No. And no.

If Mary is a co-worker who secretly smokes cigarettes, but claims she doesn't, and another co-worker says, "I know Mary is a smoker," then that is a true statement. But, is it necessary to tell

---

[25] Proverbs 11:13, (*New International Version*): A gossip betrays a confidence, but a trustworthy person keeps a secret.

[26] Proverbs 16:28, (*New International Version*): A perverse person stirs up conflict, and a gossip separates close friends.

[27] Proverbs 26:20, (*New International Version*): Without wood a fire goes out; without a gossip a quarrel dies down.

someone about it? And is it a kind statement? You can tear down one's reputation very quickly by spreading gossip.

If you think about it, no matter where you are, no matter where you work or where you go, there seem to be people who love to gossip. They are those who seem to enjoy *tattle-telling* on others and dishing the *dirt* on others. And the juicier, the better. When it's in the workplace, it can greatly harm the reputation of a co-worker or a boss.

PRACTICAL WAYS TO BATTLE GOSSIP

I can't conceive of a single organization of any type that isn't plagued by some level of gossip. Wise leaders continually focus on controlling gossip in organizations. The following are a few practical steps that you might take to control gossip in your own organizations:

1. *In staff meetings, focus from time to time on gossip and its negative effects on people and organizations.* Conduct special meetings on employee morale and talk about how gossip can tear down a person's self-esteem and actually ruin a person's career and life. Stress that you do not want this in your organization. Point out that gossip is unprofessional and unacceptable behavior in the workplace.

2. *When communicating with other organization members at any level, make sure that you stress communicating and making decisions based upon facts.* Your "What are the facts?" approach to organizational life should discourage gossiping since gossiping is not necessarily based upon fact.

3. *Make sure that others know what you think of a gossiper.* Describe a gossiper who enjoys talking about others and who loves to point out others' faults. People who do this are really trying to build up their own egos. They are generally insecure people, and criticize others as a way to

make themselves feel more important. These people can't be trusted. They might even take positive information and twist it to make it negative. When employees know what you, as their boss and leader, think of a gossiper, it should discourage them from gossiping at work or in the organization. Especially if they are brownnosers or "flatterers." They won't want to say anything to you that you will find distasteful because they will be afraid you won't like them.

4. *Don't be afraid to pray about ways to handle gossip.* You might already have prayers that you say, but if you don't, then a simple, short prayer might be: "God, please help me today to encourage my staff members to speak truthfully about others, and to only talk about the good, kind things in others that will support and encourage them. Make the best of me, today and tomorrow. Help me to refrain from gossip myself so I can be my best with my staff and my business."

5. *And always remember the Three Golden Questions*: Is it true? Is it necessary? Is it kind?

WHEN TONGUE IS THE BEST THING

We all know what encouraging others means even though we often forget to put it into practice. According to *Dictionary.com*, encourage means to inspire with courage, spirit, or confidence. Encouraging others in business or in any leadership situation is a critical part of spurring people on to do their best.[28] Leaders

---

[28] Acts 20:1, (*The Message*): With things back to normal, Paul called the disciples together and encouraged them to keep up the good work in Ephesus.

should not only encourage their top performers, but gently encourage those who are not doing so well to excel.[29]

You encourage people not only to do their best, but to remain as part of the team and be committed to a mission. If people are not encouraged, they will tend to lose commitment to a mission and desert the mission—perhaps leave the company.[30]

What I've learned in business is that encouragement or the "positive spoken word" can bring wonderful results. I'm not talking about *flatter chatter*, but about true encouraging, uplifting words that can motivate an employee to do his best. I've always believed that if you expect the best of someone, that person will strive to meet those expectations. If you expect the worst, then too often, that employee will give you exactly what you expect, the worst.

ENCOURAGING JARED

To see how encouragement can impact people, consider the following account of an experience involving a young man named Jared. Jared had just graduated from college and was just beginning his career as a freelance website designer. My friend, George, needed a website built for his international agriculture company. It wasn't an easy job as there were many pages which consisted of multiple languages including Chinese, Japanese, French, Spanish, and more.

I knew Jared was talented and had great potential, so I recommended him to my friend George. I explained that Jared was just beginning and would need to be nurtured and encouraged

---

[29] 1 Thessalonians 5:13, (*The Message*): ...Get along among yourselves, each of you doing your part. Our counsel is that you warn the freeloaders to get a move on. Gently encourage the stragglers, and reach out for the exhausted, pulling them to their feet...

[30] 2 Samuel 19:7, (*New International Version*): Now go out and encourage your men. I swear by the LORD that if you don't go out, not a man will be left with you by nightfall...

through the process. I also knew that George was an excellent motivator of others. He had the knack of bringing out the best in people.

After a few consultations, George hired Jared to design his international website. Jared made a few stabs at it, but kept missing the mark. Not used to designing pages for multiple languages, it presented a learning curve for him. Now, in my past I've seen employers ridicule and demean employees if they didn't perform optimally, but I knew George wouldn't do that. Instead, each time Jared submitted a few designs for George to review, George pointed out all the excellent parts of the design and then structured his comments and suggestions for improvements in a way that offered genuine encouragement and support.

George could have said: "Jared, this is awful. Can't you do any better than this? I'm not paying you to do lame work."

Instead, George said, "Jared, you're very talented and what you've started is excellent. However, it would help if the logo was larger and the font bolder, which would make it easier to read. Could you make another stab at it? I'm very confident that you are going to design an excellent website for me."

As a result, Jared felt validated and confident that he was doing a good job. He knew he needed direction and mentoring, so he was grateful for the help that George offered. Jared also exercised a maturity and confidence in the way he managed the job. Instead of getting angry at any corrections or suggestions that George provided, he accepted them and worked hard to meet his employer's expectations.

Jared could have said: "I've worked so hard on the website. I don't see what I can do more to make it any better. You just need to see it my way."

Instead, Jared said, "I understand what you mean. Hey, I appreciate you giving me constructive suggestions to make the site better. I'll do my best."

In the end, both George and Jared *bridled their tongues* throughout the work process. They both *thought* before they spoke, and the result was a beautiful website for George and an excellent reference for Jared, which landed him more freelance jobs.

Both Jared and his employer, George, thought carefully before responding to the other throughout their work project and because of this, they both won in the end.

YOU AND YOUR CHASE

Stay focused on your chase, always. And one way is by *bridling your tongue*. There are many interesting points made in this chapter about the Biblical theme of *bridling your tongue* and controlling what you say. Remember, the ultimate purpose of this book is to help you become wiser by *chasing wisdom* as you apply Biblical insights in your business life, and bridling the tongue is part of it.

This chapter has advised that you pay close attention to your tongue because it can make either desirable or undesirable things happen in your organization. In your business. In your life. You can help to maximize the desirable and minimize the undesirable simply by *thinking* before you speak and watching what you say.

Because the tongue, one's voice, can cause either desirable or undesirable events to occur, it can be thought of as both the best and worst *tool* available to you in the business world. The words you say will have a colossal impact on others and may be the primary determinant in you being either a successful or unsuccessful leader.

In summary, when you use the tongue for flattering, backbiting, slandering, talking too much, talking without listening, or gossiping, the tongue becomes your *worst* tool. Why do these uses make the tongue your *worst* tool? Because, in its own way, each time you use it in a negative way, it severely damages personal relationships in organizations. When personal relationships are damaged, organizations become dysfunctional and do not nearly achieve what they are capable of achieving.

On the other hand, the tongue becomes your *best* tool when you encourage others. To encourage others, you inspire them to be brave and have confidence in what they do. Helping people to achieve their best is always a useful way to encourage. Remember to encourage ongoing high performers as well as lower-level performers. Everyone needs encouragement. When wise leaders encourage organization members, they help organizations achieve more than anyone ever thought possible.

Here are a few additional tips you can use to *chase wisdom* and become wiser by bridling your tongue:

1. *Listen carefully to the words that people around you say.* Do their words reflect a "best tool" use of the tongue or a "worst tool" use? Try to encourage those around you to use the tongue, the "voice," in a "best tool" fashion rather than a "worst tool" fashion.

2. *Reflect on what you say to others.* Is it true? Is it necessary? Is it kind? Are you using what you say in the best possible way? Are you using insincere *flattery* to get what you want? Even leaders and bosses can sometimes use insincere flattery to get employees to behave a certain way. Focus on improving what you say and how you say it. Be kind to what you say to others and to yourself. Focus on *improving* yourself.

3. *Ask others who they believe are the most encouraging members of the organization.* You, as the leader and/or business owner, of course, cannot be nominated. Go to those individuals who are named. Ask them how they encourage others. Use their ideas as suggestions to promote ways others can encourage one another as well. Even discuss these ways in staff meetings to build camaraderie and harmony among the employees.

4. *Be patient.* Making progress in the area of *bridling your tongue* takes time and effort. Watching what you say and encouraging others to do the same is a skill that needs to be practiced over and over again in order to develop properly. Maybe you are in the habit of speaking before thinking and haven't thought too much about *bridling your tongue.* As you stop and think before speaking and practice this over and over, it will become a habit.

5. *Keep company with people who carefully control what they say.* It's all too easy to pick up the habits of those with whom we work and/or socialize. If someone loves to gossip and you're around them a lot at work or in social circles, it will be easy for you to pick up that habit. On the other hand, if someone excels at *bridling their tongue* and you're around them a lot, it will be easy for you to pick up that habit. So, as a business leader, be careful about the company you keep, especially at work.

Become the master at *bridling your tongue* and watch how this skill positively affects you in business and ultimately, in all areas of your life. Feel free to reflect back on this chapter for insights about how *bridling your tongue* can help you to better manage anger and anger backlash in organizations, the topic of the next chapter.

ANGER AND ANGER BACKLASH

Don't be quick to fly off the handle. Anger boomerangs.
You can spot a fool by the lumps on his head.

Ecclesiastes 7:9 (*The Message*)

The purpose of this chapter is to help you to become wiser by helping you to better understand the intricacies of anger. I'm going to discuss what anger is and how to better manage it. You may think you know all about anger. *But, do you? Do you know how to define anger? Is anger an emotional response to something? Should you ever be angry? Are the effects of anger always negative?*

This chapter helps you to answer questions like these and to gain insights about how you should react to anger—both yours and someone else's in your everyday leadership adventures.

Learn how the *wise* handle anger in the workplace by reflecting on Matthew's *Adventure of Performance Review Anger*.

ADVENTURE OF PERFORMANCE
REVIEW ANGER

It was 7:00 p.m. and I had just settled in to watch the Orlando Magic play the Miami Heat in basketball. I even had snacks ready to go, chips, popcorn, and Diet Coke. The Magic and the Heat have developed such an intense rivalry that their games are pure delight for a basketball fan. I was excited. This was one of my favorite ways to relax and enjoy a moment away from my duties as a professor and author.

Of course, just as the game was getting started, my cell phone rang. Caller ID told me it was Matthew. I hit *pause* on my TV remote.

Then, I answered the phone—not with a hello—but, "Hey, Matthew, how're you doing?"

He said, "I'm great, but do you have time to talk for a couple of minutes?"

I responded, "Sure, what's up?" I took a sip of my Diet Coke and thought, *I can get back to the game any time.*

He presented the following scenario: "This is the week that I evaluate the performance of each of my employees. Today I evaluated Miguel, one of my *star* designers. This guy really knows his stuff. He mostly produces outstanding website designs and is superior at developing good personal relationships with customers. One important area where Miguel could improve his performance is the area of developing positive working relationships with his peers. Most see him as having a bit of a superiority complex."

"Mmm, that's not good," I offered.

"No, it isn't," Matthew said. "I started the evaluation interview by highlighting all of his strengths. His technical abilities are beyond question and he very much enjoyed being complimented.

"As much as I didn't want to, I knew I also had to talk to Miguel about developing better relationships with his peers. He avoided my constructive criticism and even accused his co-workers of being jealous of his abilities. The more I defended my position, the angrier he became. Surprisingly, I became angrier and angrier as he became angrier and angrier. The whole thing escalated out of control and the session ended with us being very angry at one another and not accomplishing much.

"At this moment I'm pretty frustrated. I'm trying to understand how this happened. Right now, one of my *star* employees and I are angry at one another. The whole thing seems like a fiasco."

INITIAL REFLECTIONS ON PERFORMANCE REVIEW ANGER

Scenarios like the one about anger over performance reviews are very common in the workplace. One explanation for how this anger materializes is that the individual being evaluated takes issue with the manager's opinion and becomes defensive. The manager then becomes irritated because the employee is not accepting constructive criticism. These feelings build throughout the conversation and anger eventually gains a foothold with both people.

As Matthew and I discussed, one way that you eliminate anger gaining a foothold in a performance review and other organizational situations is by staying alert and being aware. If you do this, then you will sense when anger is building and you can focus on stopping its advance. A wise leader always tries to incorporate a measure of calmness into situations wherein anger seems to be gaining a foothold. Wise leaders focus on logic and data when trying to diffuse or eliminate anger. Continued sharp criticism is fertile ground for anger and will make sure that anger grows high and strong.[31]

Even if anger gains a foothold, the aforementioned advice still holds. Gentle words, perhaps starting with an apology, will help diffuse the anger. Focusing on data and logic as opposed to sharp criticism will help keep the anger at bay. Perhaps the individuals feeling the anger should sit down to work out a plan for working together in the future. Don't expect to work out such a plan in fifteen minutes. Such a plan could take several hours

---

[31]   Proverbs 15:1, (*The Message*): A gentle response defuses anger, but a sharp tongue kindles a temper-fire.

to develop and may entail several sessions over multiple days in order to allow adequate time for thought and reflection for all parties. Developing a plan will help all involved parties to mature as businesspeople. They will grow significantly in the area of anger management.

Don't fool yourself, though. Developing such a plan will not solve all of your anger problems in a typical organization. You will become wiser in handling anger in your organization as you gain a richer and more thorough understanding of anger. For example, you need to know what anger is in order to identify it along with the backlash that commonly accompanies it. These and other anger-related topics are discussed in the following sections.

WHAT IS ANGER?

Think of *anger* as a strong feeling of loathing or displeasure. It's an emotion. Anger is actually caused by thoughts that individuals have. Thoughts like *he is taking advantage of my situation*, or *she is being sarcastic to me*, or *she is punishing me unnecessarily*.

Anger is an emotion based upon an individual's perception of being wronged or offended in some manner. Everyone has challenging moments in business and life when they might get angry, and for some, this happens every day. It can happen when someone doesn't get the raise they want, or when someone pokes fun at an idea.

Feeling anger is usually accompanied by a strong desire to respond to the anger. By becoming defensive. One becomes angry, and then acts on that anger. This action commonly reflects resentment, annoyance, frustration, or rage. This action can include loudness, hitting, destruction, put-downs, verbal abuse, yelling, sarcasm, and even crying. These behaviors are outward expressions of anger, but the real issue of anger begins in the mind.

As a general rule, wise leaders do not act out of anger when managing a company and the employees. A wise leader will not overreact to an employee's anger.

One specific example in the Bible about not acting out of anger relates to discipline and anger. The Bible advises that wise leaders should not act of out anger to discipline employees.[32] Disciplining when angry can cause a leader to be *extreme* in disciplining and not disciplining in a measured way.

All human beings experience anger. But when anger affects your quality of life and your business, it helps to study how to better control this feeling before it manages you. Some anger in life is warranted and should be used to put things right. But there is, however, no need for rudeness. There is no need for or value in bullying.[33]

Simply finding out what is causing anger and then addressing the cause(s) helps to get rid of the anger and keeps it from building up.

Wise business leaders handle anger in productive ways. Handling anger, both your own and that of others, is an extremely challenging task. Perhaps Aristotle described this challenge best when he said that it's easy to become angry, but *it's not* easy to become angry with the *right* person at the *right* time, and with the *right* purpose in the *right* way.

By knowing what anger truly is, you've taken the first step in being able to handle anger wisely on your path to *chasing wisdom*. However, there are many other insights that you need to continuously manage anger wisely.

THE DANGER OF ANGER: BACKLASH

A backlash is a hostile reaction to some issue or event. The last section pinpointed examples of behavior caused by anger,

---

32 Jeremiah 10:23-24, (*New International Version*): 23 LORD, I know that people's lives are not their own; it is not for them to direct their steps. 24 Discipline me, LORD, but only in due measure—not in your anger or you will reduce me to nothing.

33 Proverbs 22:8, (*The Message*): Whoever sows sin reaps weeds, and bullying anger sputters into nothing.

like hitting, destruction, put-downs, verbal abuse, yelling, and sarcasm. Now think about this for a second. When one is the brunt of anger-related behavior like verbal abuse or hitting, what commonly happens as a result? You guessed it—the person who is the *brunt* strikes back in some way.

This striking back is called *anger backlash*, a hostile reaction to being the brunt of someone's anger. For the most part, people who act angrily can expect to face anger backlash. Wise leaders know that the odds of such a backlash occurring escalate as angry behavior escalates. Based upon Biblical advice, the wise know that anger backlash is a byproduct of anger and that one should not waste time trying to eliminate its occurrence.[34]

The bottom line is if you act on anger, be ready to face its backlash. The opening verse for this chapter from "Ecclesiastes" makes this point almost humorously by saying that you can tell an angry person by the knots on his head—the result of anger backlash. To support this notion, compare being angry to picking up a handful of broken glass and throwing it at someone—both people get harmed.

Many times, a person has no idea what the backlash of his anger has been. In the drawing at the beginning of this chapter, it's easy to imagine the scenario. Perhaps his customer was supposed to call. Perhaps a prospective new employer was supposed to call. But, no one did. So, he became angry and started taking his anger out on the phone, beating it into a million pieces. The backlash of his anger? He missed his phone call when that person finally did call. He didn't hurt anyone but himself.

All of us have been angry at one time or another in our lives. It's a human emotion—a passion of the mind—that is ordinary. We've all felt our hearts racing as the anger fills us. We all express our anger in many different ways. We yell. We push. We argue.

---

[34] Proverbs 19:19, (*The Message*): Let angry people endure the backlash of their own anger; if you try to make it better, you'll only make it worse.

We resist. We bury it. We hide it. We deny it. And sometimes we even engage in fighting.

But we want to be *extraordinary*, don't we? Not ordinary. When we operate from a place of wisdom, we will have better insight into anger and anger backlash and focus on keeping anger from having a negative impact in our business and in our lives. Since we probably cannot avoid being angry from time to time, perhaps the best strategy for the wise is to use the Lord as a role model and simply strive to *be slow* to anger.[35]

ANGER BACKLASH: A GOLF ILLUSTRATION

Brian, Matthew, and I were golfing together on a Sunday afternoon at Eagle Dunes Golf Club in Sorrento, Florida. The day was sunny, clear, and mild—a perfect day for golf. Being the amateurs that we are, some shots were good and some were not so good.

We had just finished playing the seventeenth hole and were about to begin the 18th. This hole was a long par five. We were all very much looking forward to playing the 18th hole because it has a very challenging design. There is a street on the left of the fairway that's out of bounds. There are huge long bunkers on the right side of the fairway that add extreme difficulties. It's quite a feat to hit a ball into the narrow fairway from the tee.

Per family tradition, whoever wins hole 18 has *bragging rights* as the *Best Golfer* for the ride back home. As usual, we all wanted to win the hole.

When it was my turn to swing, I placed my ball on a tee and got in position to hit. My swing started back and then came forward. Once struck, the ball went straight down the middle of the fairway. Then, suddenly, it started to hook quickly to the left and landed out of bounds by the street.

---

[35] Psalm 145:8, (*The Message*): God is all mercy and grace—not quick to anger, is rich in love.

I'm embarrassed to admit it—although I didn't show it—inside, I was very angry at myself for the shot. *I know, very silly!* This was a *usual* family competition and I knew it would be recounted again and again until the next time we played. All part of it, during the car ride home, I'd have to weather the loving razzing of all the usual jokes. I drove my golf cart away in disgust and told myself over and over again on the way to my ball what an idiot I was.

I was so upset that the rest of the hole was an absolute disaster. I couldn't concentrate on my next swings and couldn't achieve focus on determining accurate yardage estimates for my shots.

You know what? That's exactly what anger backlash is all about; the anger only ricochets back to hurt you. If not handled properly, anger normally brings about unwanted results in the future. When leaders lose their tempers, a backlash can lessen their abilities to perform well in the future. Better control of my anger after a bad shot on the golf course—instead of dwelling on it—might have enabled me to improve my shots on the rest of the hole—perhaps even come back to win the hole. I wasn't being very wise that day.

Wise leaders follow God's lead and don't hold onto their anger.[36] They try to eliminate it in order to raise their chances of enhancing their futures and avoiding anger backlash.

ANGER IN THE WORKPLACE

Today, bullies who are angry at the world are everywhere. They show up in the schools, in the workplace, and in the home. It also happens on the roads as road rage has increased in the past years and ends up killing and harming individuals. It also happens in politics where politicians are intolerant of one another. And what

---

[36] Psalm 103:9, (*American Standard Version*): He will not always chide; neither will he keep his anger forever.

about the Internet? You'll see anger being displayed on Facebook and Twitter as people express their anger over the smallest things.

A good book that discusses anger in today's world is *The Civility Solution: What to Do When People Are Rude*, by Pier M. Forni, who is also the director of *The Civility Project Initiative* at Johns Hopkins University in Baltimore.

Anger exists. It's in our homes, our schools, and our workplaces. We all know it and sometimes, after a long day at work, we take it home with us. Sometimes, it can lead to tragic consequences. According to *Reuters,* that's what happened on August 24, 2012 in New York City, when Jeffrey Johnson, a 58-year-old man who was a fashion designer and who reportedly had been laid off from Hazen Imports near the Empire State Building, returned with a gun and killed a former co-worker on the street. He was later killed by gunshot by police. Eight bystanders were wounded, possibly all of them by the policemen's gunshots, but none of their injuries were life-threatening, according to the police.[37]

Not everyone who gets angry at the office will act out violently like this man did in New York. But, there are connections, as John Rifkin, a licensed clinical psychologist and author of *The Healing Power of Anger* explained to www.unionleader.com. "It's pretty normal to have feelings of anger," said Rifkin, "And anger is seen as bad by a lot of people because if you get angry in a way that is out of your control and is spilling over into destructive behaviors, it's going to cause problems. But the reality is that lots of people are dealing with angry feelings a lot of the time and the question is how do you use that energy effectively."[38]

People in the workplace can naturally get upset with a co-worker or a manager/leader/boss. And often, people feel that

---

[37] "Two dead, eight wounded in gunfire near NY's Empire State Building," by Lily Kuo and Chris Francescani, New York, August 24, 2012, www.reuters.com.

[38] Chicago Tribune, "Coping with workplace anger," www.unionleader. com, September 2, 2012.

they must vent their anger. I imagine many people fantasize about taking out their aggression on their bosses, or even having harsh words with them. Perhaps some even work out in the gym as a way to vent the anger, which is a constructive way to channel the anger! Exercise can empower you!

The poor economy, housing, lack of jobs—all contribute to frustration that naturally causes anger to build throughout the world. The business world is not as stable as it was back in the day of our parents and grandparents. It seems that more and more we read or hear on the news about disgruntled employees in the workplace.

There is no shortage of angry people in the world. The Bible cautions us continually against giving in to anger when we are upset by other people's words or actions.[39] Despite this warning, anger seems on the upswing.

CONTROL YOUR ANGER BEFORE IT CONTROLS YOU

When a person gets angry, the anger can become a factor that if not controlled, can make a negative impact on the organization in which the person operates—or even on family and friends. Wise leaders constantly focus on controlling their anger so their anger doesn't control them. Being slow to anger allows leaders the opportunity to limit action based upon emotion and gives them the opportunity to gain a richer understanding of situations they face.[40]

---

[39] James 1:19-20, (*New International Version*): 19 My dear brothers and sisters, take note of this: Everyone should be quick to listen, slow to speak and slow to become angry, 20 because human anger does not produce the righteousness that God desires.

[40] Proverbs 14:29, (*The Message*): Slowness to anger makes for deep understanding; a quick-tempered person stockpiles stupidity.

As an example of an individual allowing anger to control him, you may remember a situation involving Steven Slater. In 2010, Slater made headline news all over the television, radio, newspaper, and Internet when he lost his temper and let anger control him.

A career flight attendant, Steven Slater finally lost it one day. He had been a flight attendant for twenty years. One day, a passenger ridiculed him on a flight. According to the *Washington Post* and other news outlets, the Jet Blue flight attendant got angry and proceeded to scream at the passenger over the intercom.

Slater opened the emergency chute and exited the plane on foot down the tarmac. Slater was later arrested for reckless endangerment and criminal mischief, among other charges.

CNN News reported that the Jet Blue Flight 1052 was arriving at JFK International Airport from Pittsburgh, Pennsylvania. According to CNN, as the plane hit ground and taxied toward the terminal so the passengers could de-board, an in-flight passenger stood up to retrieve his bag before the pilot had given the all clear.

Steven Slater, the flight attendant, told the passenger to sit back down. CNN reported that exactly what happened wasn't known, but it was clear that either Slater was hit by a bag that had fallen out of the overhead bin or the passenger hit him with his fist.

The passenger allegedly cursed at Slater. Then, Slater turned on the intercom and announced to all the guests on the plane that he was quitting and started cursing at everyone. Allegedly, Slater opened the emergency chute, took some beer bottles from the galley and then exited the plane. He was later arrested at home for his behavior.

Perhaps if Slater had better prepared himself to manage his anger—if he had controlled his anger—he could have avoided this whole incident. It really is important that you do not let anger control you. When you face an uncomfortable situation, consciously choose whether or not you will become angry. Although we all get angry from time to time, only the wise understand its implications and strive to control it accordingly.

CHANNELING ANGER TO ACHIEVE SUCCESS: GEORGE, THE BOXER

Usually, and in the context of this chapter, we have been discussing anger as a bad quality. Anger, however, can be very useful. It can stimulate your dedication to work harder to achieve success. However, it is not easy to use anger as a positive force and far too few try to use it as such.

George was a professional boxer in his twenties. He had been a professional boxer for ten years and as he began to age, he decided he would train others to become physically fit by using boxing techniques. It wasn't easy. He had a difficult time finding anyone to support his idea emotionally. His family was negative and always told him he couldn't succeed. His friends told him that not many people would be interested in boxing—that the people who wanted to be physically fit were more interested in group aerobic classes or fusion classes that focused on a variety of training methods. Everyone told George he was wasting his time. His father even told him he should get a nice stable job in a bank—that he was living a fantasy life by wanting to create a boxing and personal training business.

George became angry. In fact, he became quite furious that others would downgrade his *dreams* to nothing but mere fantasy. But, he didn't lash out at his family and friends, which is what he wanted to do. He wanted to say, "How can you all be so *bleepity-bleep* negative?" He wanted to scream at them to leave him alone. He wanted to, in turn, tell them all to just go away—that they would never amount to much in their lives at all because none of them had the guts to go for their dreams. But, he didn't. He bit his tongue and decided to channel his anger into something productive.

Was it right to get angry? Did it help George in any way? The way he managed his anger made all the difference. He took his anger and said, "I'm going to succeed. I'm not going to let these naysayers get the best of me. I'm going to surround myself with positive people—people who believe in me and trust me. And I will build a business model that works."

Anger is an emotion that comes with a lot of energy. You can take that anger energy and use it to construct something good in your life or tear something down with it. George decided to use all that anger energy to build something good. He decided to be patient and work toward his dreams.

As a result, he created a personal training and boxing business called *Ultimate Boxing & Sports Fitness* (not its real name) that is now thriving. In just two years, it has become one of the premiere companies in the Southeast that trains men and women in boxing and physical fitness. If he had listened to the naysayers, he would have given up and gotten a job at a bank—denying his true passion and calling in life. If he had used his anger to lash out at his friends and family, that could have caused an *anger backlash* that damaged or eliminated valuable personal relationships forever.

RIGHTEOUS INDIGNATION: JUSTIFIED ANGER

Up to this point, most of the discussion in this chapter has focused on wise leaders avoiding becoming angry because the results of anger and anger backlash seem to have only negative impact on people and organizations. To this point, anger has been discussed as a factor that is mostly damaging in organizations because it typically promotes hurtful action against other people like gossip, hitting, or maligning in some other way.

You need to be aware, however, that there is special type of anger in the Bible that is justifiable and encouraged.[41] As in the boxer's story. This justified anger is called *righteous indignation*. In this sense, *righteous* means being consistent with moral law. *Indignation* means anger. Putting the two words together, righteous indignation is anger that supports moral law.

To me, the classic example of righteous indignation involves Jesus and a situation commonly referred to as *cleansing the temple*.[42]

According to the *Book of John*, Jesus visited a temple in Jerusalem to celebrate Passover, a Jewish religious festival. People were selling sheep and other animals at the temple along with moneychangers, a type of broker who exchanged money of one country for that of another country.

Upon seeing this, Jesus became extremely angry. He devised a whip to drive the animals and the salespeople, along with the moneychangers, out of the temple. This is an example of *righteous indignation*. Jesus was angered by, and reacted to, what he saw as the people disrespecting the temple, which was a serious violation of morality.

As a business example of righteous indignation, let's assume that a CEO of a Fortune 500 company has assigned to a committee the task of recommending to him a new VP of Marketing. The CEO very carefully outlined the type of person

---

[41] Ephesians 4:26-27, (*The Message*): Go ahead and be angry. You do well to be angry—but don't use your anger as fuel for revenge. And don't stay angry. Don't go to bed angry. Don't give the Devil that kind of foothold in your life.

[42] John 2:13-16, (*New International Version*): 13 When it was almost time for the Jewish Passover, Jesus went up to Jerusalem. 14 In the temple courts he found people selling cattle, sheep and doves, and others sitting at tables exchanging money. 15 So he made a whip out of cords, and drove all from the temple courts, both sheep and cattle; he scattered the coins of the money changers and overturned their tables. 16 To those who sold doves he said, "Get these out of here! Stop turning my Father's house into a market!"

needed to best fit the job and outlined various headhunters that the committee might engage. The CEO asked the committee to recommend a pool of five candidates to him for the position within three months.

As time passed, the CEO asked the chair of the committee to discuss candidates in the pool. The CEO was astonished to find out that there were no women in the pool. In discussing this issue with the committee, the CEO came to the conclusion that there were indeed talented women trying to win the position, but that the committee was somewhat and subtly biased against women.

Since the committee's functioning was fundamentally unfair for women applicants, and since this unfairness was a violation of moral code, the CEO had every right and, in fact an obligation, to be righteously indignant. His indignation could result in replacing the committee, requiring a certain proportion of female applicants in the pool, or formally reprimanding the committee for the way it functioned.

Admittedly, this action may cause anger backlash temporarily from the committee, but the morality of the situation requires that the CEO display his indignation and handle the backlash as it occurs. The CEO needs to view handling the backlash as a short-term cost that must be incurred in order to build a moral and respectful functioning organization for the long run.

Simply put, the CEO would be using anger the way Jesus did in the temple. In the CEO's company, his hiring committee disrespected women and their right to apply for an advanced position. Using his anger in a constructive way, he will teach his committee respect for all people, regardless of gender.

The Bible suggests that anger shouldn't go on and on and should be followed by comfort. Perhaps this limited display of anger and comfort afterwards is useful in helping the wise leader to minimize any anger backlash that might materialize.[43]

TIPS ON CONTROLLING YOUR ANGER

Due to the potential negative impact on organizations, wise leaders work continuously on controlling their anger. Controlling anger means managing it. The following are tips based upon Biblical thought that you can use to help you in this effort.

Do not associate with individuals in the organization who commonly get angry.[44] Making friends with individuals or associating with people who commonly display anger can be very dangerous.

After a while, it's quite possible that you take on the same characteristics of these people. Although it is wise for you to work on controlling your anger, it is unwise for you to expose yourself to forces like friends or associates whose actions are models pulling you in the direction of commonly displaying anger.

Know when your anger is growing and turn from it before it severely damages you.[45] All of us feel angry from time to time. If you feel anger, be careful. As your anger grows in a situation, the anger could become more and more volatile. Turn from your anger—cut it off—before it gets too extreme. The more extreme your anger, the more fierce and cruel your response might be, and the more violent you might be to the people around you. So, do not let your anger become extreme!

---

[43]　Isaiah 12:1, (*New International Version*): In that day you will say: "I will praise you, Lord. Although you were angry with me, your anger has turned away and you have comforted me."

[44]　Proverbs 22:24-25, (*The Message*): Don't hang out with angry people; don't keep company with hotheads. Bad temper is contagious – don't get infected.

[45]　Genesis 49:7, (*New International Version*): Cursed by their anger, so fierce, and their fury, so cruel!

Build patience as an antidote to anger. Patience is defined as the ability to accept difficulty without becoming angry. When you think about this definition, patience is a natural antidote for anger. What better way to have authority over anger than to have an antidote? Biblical advice seems consistent with this antidote concept by instructing that it's better to be patient and self-controlled than focused on conflict, aggression, and overwhelming and retaliating against others.[46]

YOU AND YOUR CHASE

When *chasing wisdom*, it is important to grow in your understanding of one of the most commonly discussed themes in the Bible—anger. Understanding anger is important because anger in the workplace is commonly encountered in organizations of all sizes and types. Think of *anger* as strong feelings of loathing or displeasure.

Sometimes, these feelings will be yours and you will have to decide how to best manage them, while at other times, these feelings will be someone else's. Either way, you'll still have to decide how to handle them as a wise leader.

In all cases, be ready for *anger backlash* as a reaction to anger. This backlash is a hostile reaction to anger. If you cannot control anger, be alert for the backlash and be prepared to handle it.

Do not give in to your feelings of anger. You must not let your anger control you—you must control it. The more mature a person is, the more he or she should be able to control their anger.

Think about your anger when you feel it, try to decide what is causing it, and take steps to try to reduce it. Why? Because reducing the anger will help to eliminate the negative impact that anger commonly has on organizational success.

---

[46] Proverbs 16:32, (*New International Version*): Better a patient person than a warrior, one with self-control than one who takes a city.

If you find it difficult to reduce your anger, take steps to try to channel it in positive ways. Don't attack others, for example, when you do not win an important account. Use your anger to motivate yourself to never again lose an account like that. Use your anger to motivate you to succeed, as in the earlier story of the boxer.

Sometimes you should become righteously indignant, which is a special type of anger. In this case, you should become angry when moral correctness needs to be upheld. For example, if you feel that people are being treated unfairly or someone is cheating to gain an advantage to win a promotion, become righteously indignant and use that anger to defend others. To generalize, righteous indignation is warranted in business whenever Biblical principles are violated.

You will indeed experience anger throughout your life— your own anger or someone else's. That's only natural. But you don't have to let anger control you, your business, or your life. The following are some practical strategies that you might use to help manage your anger in a wiser, more mature manner as you *chase wisdom*.

1. *Think before you speak.* One of the worst things we can do when we're angry is to act rashly and say something for which we will be sorry later. Anger tends to cloud the mind. This cloudiness tends to cause us to act impulsively. We say things that we shouldn't, we regret saying them later. Always.

    It's always good to count to ten before you say anything. If we just *react*, we also increase our chance of screaming and yelling—of using violence of some sort to make our point. Just say nothing until anger dissipates and you feel ready to tackle an issue more objectively. It's okay to say, "Can I think about this for a while? Can we discuss this later?" It's important to not *fly off the handle* and let your anger/temper get the best of you.

2. *Identify why you're angry.* Sometimes, we get angry, but we're not sure why. When you get angry, think about it for a few moments in a quiet place. What made you angry? Did you feel violated in some way? Did someone usurp your authority? Did someone you love or care about speak harshly to you? Did someone disrespect you?

   Take the time to contemplate and identify what makes you angry. Only by knowing what makes you angry can you take the right steps to deal with anger or avoid getting angry again in the future. You have to understand why anger exists before you can take useful steps to handle it.

3. *Discuss your anger.* Don't be afraid to tell someone how he or she made you angry. This will help them to understand you and your needs better. Some people will care that they made you angry and others will not. Don't deny or bury your anger. Recognize that this is a signal that tells you something's wrong and needs to be cleared up.

4. *Take responsibility for your anger.* Overall, if you have reacted to something in anger, take responsibility for your actions by acknowledging what you did to offend the other person. If you have lost your temper, apologize for losing your temper. Even if it is painful to admit, let the person know that you understand it was your fault, and that you want to make it right. Find out what you need to do to restore your relationship damaged by anger. What's next? Do it!

5. *Pray.* Remember that God has promised to give us wisdom—all we have to do is ask. Ask God to help you understand anger and how to deal with it. Any insight that God gives you about solving anger-related problems will be invaluable. Pay attention to what God gives you. This

whole process of learning how to manage anger doesn't happen in a split second. Be patient. It takes practice.

Keep in mind that heredity has no impact on your anger. You are not born with a quick-temper, so you can't blame it on your parents. There is no reason that you cannot improve the way(s) that you handle anger. Focus on it. Pray about it. Persevere and you will indeed improve.

PRIDE

Each one should test his own actions. Then he can take pride in himself, without comparing himself to somebody else.

Galatians 6:4 (NIV)

I think that many people misunderstand what pride is. The purpose of this chapter is to help you to become wiser by helping you to better understand pride. Throughout, there will be insights about what pride is and how to best handle it.

Do you know how to define pride? Can you discuss the two types of pride? Should wise leaders have pride? How can bad pride impact an organization negatively? How can good pride impact an organization positively?

I want to help answer questions like these, so you can gain deeper insights about how you can deal wisely with pride in business situations. To begin learning about how the wise handle pride in the workplace, reflect on Matthew's following *Adventure of Mr. Prideful* and then continue by seeing how chapter concepts relate to it.

ADVENTURE OF MR. PRIDEFUL

Early in the history of Websolvers, at Matthew's request, I commonly conducted various sorts of organizational development workshops for him and his employees. Topics like "How to Lead" and "How to Manage Strategically" were commonplace.

On this particular day, I was facilitating an office luncheon discussion over pizza. Essentially, the discussion was a brainstorming session on how to recruit new clients for the company. There were six of us at the session, Matthew, four of his account executives responsible for enlisting new clients, and myself.

The session started out very well. All were involved in the discussion and the ideas that were surfacing seemed to hold promise. Eventually though, the discussion took a turn toward *dysfunctional*. One particular account executive began to dominate the conversation with *how he does it*. It was clear that this executive saw his ideas as the best and he began arguing the case for why his ideas were better than everyone else's. He sounded like *Mr. Prideful*, very proud of his ideas, and knowingly or unknowingly, presented himself as the *best* account executive. As a result, others stopped listening to his comments and our discussion evolved into a lecture by this executive. He began *preaching* his sermon to everyone at the meeting.

Despite my best efforts at trying to include everyone, new ideas from others came to a grinding halt.

As the lunch hour came to a close, Matthew thanked all who attended the meeting for their input and asked if I had a few extra minutes for conversation. I said that I did and followed Matthew into his office as the meeting ended.

The first few seconds in Matthew's office were silent. We stared at one another. Neither one of us said a word, then I proceeded to give my initial reflections on the meeting and *Mr. Prideful*.

INITIAL REFLECTIONS ON MR. PRIDEFUL

Sooner or later, it seems that all leaders will face a meeting like the one Matthew faced. The meeting started fine but evolved into more of an ego-oriented lecture that was not very productive.

It's not bad to have pride in your work. In fact, it can be a very good thing. You should feel good about using your God-given talents to do a job well.

On the flip side, pride can be dysfunctional. When you see yourself as superior to others and present yourself as *better than everyone else,* people become offended, try to avoid you, and are reluctant to build meaningful relationships with you. Such pride contains a sort of *self-worship* for what one is, what one has accomplished, and what one will accomplish. In addition, those possessing this type of pride seem to expect this sort of *worship* from others.

The account executive in the above scenario that dominated the conversation seemed to have an arrogant, exaggerated view of the level of his talents and accomplishments and wanted others to feel that as well. You saw the results.

Consistent with Biblical thought, having such a view was disliked by others at the meeting and had the effect of turning them off.[47] If a business leader exudes pride in this way, followers will simply find subtle ways to avoid committing to both the leader and the leader's agenda.

You are well on your way to learning about pride and gaining pride-related insights about right and wrong in handling business problems. You are well on your way to becoming wiser in handling pride-related issues. The remainder of the chapter focuses on additional pride-related discussion that will help you grow even further in this regard.

---

[47] Proverbs 8:13, (*New International Version*): To fear the Lord is to hate evil; I hate pride and arrogance, evil behavior and perverse speech.

WHAT IS THIS THING CALLED PRIDE?

Initially, think of *pride* simply as feeling proud of persons, places, or things. To adequately understand pride, however, you need to delve much more into its meaning. Much confusion exists over the meaning of pride. Sometimes, the Bible seems to describe pride as a vice—*bad pride*. At other times, the Bible suggests that pride is more like a virtue—*good pride*.

The following sections describe both good and bad pride in an effort to give you more sophisticated insights about right and wrong in handling pride-related situations. Each of these types of pride represents very different circumstances and issues. As the names imply, wise leaders see good pride as a factor that should be encouraged in organizations, and bad pride as a factor that should be discouraged in organizations. Read on to learn more about good pride in order to deal with it wisely in business situations.

GOOD PRIDE

The *King James Dictionary* gives us insight about the healthy or right way to be proud—good pride. According to this dictionary, *good pride* is a significant feeling of elation caused by a sense of esteem, based upon an understanding of true worth, about self and others. This definition says that it is good pride when a person feels proud of himself and others out of a true, not fictional, sense of value. Good pride recognizes that God has given us gifts for achieving in this world and, as a result, attributes God as the reason that we're able to achieve. The phrase *understanding of true worth* in the above definition refers to not only knowing the inherent value of what you have achieved, but knowing God's role in enabling us to achieve.

You know you have good pride when....

...You are proud of yourself because of how you're using God-given gifts. Here, you recognize that God has given you certain talents

and you've achieved because you've used them well to meet challenges. You are using the talents that God has given to you. In addition, you do not create a false sense of self-importance by comparing your achievements to those of others.[48] After all, since others have probably received different gifts from God, comparing what you've achieved to what they've achieved would be like comparing apples and oranges.

In the Bible, Paul gives us such a good pride example when he discusses pride in his ministry.[49]

… You are proud of the contribution to the growth of others that you're making. When you are proud of what you are doing because it is valuable, you have good pride.

Paul indicates that he was a contributor to the growth of the apostles and took pride in this ministry.

Think of good pride more as satisfaction you gain by helping others grow in a positive way. Wise leaders point out such growth that others are experiencing and encourage them to continue growing. For example, when wise leaders help others to become more competent, the leaders point out the growth and encourage others to continue growing in competence.

… You are proud of good works of others. In this situation, you are proud of others because of the good they are doing, have done, or will do. The Bible refers to this "good pride" when it refers to parents being the pride of their children.[50] Paul refers to this type

---

[48] Galatians 6:4, (*New International Version*): Each one should test their own actions. Then they can take pride in themselves alone, without comparing themselves to someone else...

[49] Romans 11:13, (*New International Version*): I am talking to you Gentiles. Inasmuch as I am the apostle to the Gentiles, I take pride in my ministry...

[50] Proverbs 17:6, (*New International Version*): Children's children are a crown to the aged, and parents are the pride of their children.

of pride when telling the Corinthians that he's proud of whom they have become.[51]

Refer back to the drawing at the beginning of the chapter. Being proud of the good works of others is easily illustrated in a work group setting. Here, for example, good pride could entail a group member being proud because of the way group members care for one another as people, handle conflict without personal attacks, and never gossip about one another. Because wise leaders realize that such behavior contributes immensely to the group staying focused and productive, they encourage such good pride in organizations.

Wise leaders recognize the value of good pride in organizations and try to possess it themselves and encourage it in others. People exhibiting good pride tend to have characteristics that promote organizational success. Such people tend to be satisfied with their individual performance and don't get involved with tearing down others in order to look like achievers. They don't boast about their accomplishments because they recognize God's role in their successes. In addition, people with good pride tend to have high levels of self-respect and encourage others to do well, and celebrate the accomplishments of others.

Wise business leaders understand good pride. People with good pride are definitely ones that you want working with and for you. People who take such pride in their work are contributors to organizational success.

This is good pride. Employees who are actively plugged into it will help to increase profit, reduce loss, and open new opportunities for growth. A wise business leader knows this and will help groom and encourage his or her employees so that they exhibit good pride at their work.

---

[51] 2 Corinthians 7:4, (*New International Version*): I have spoken to you with great frankness; I take great pride in you. I am greatly encouraged; in all our troubles my joy knows no bounds.

People show good pride by achieving something good, getting credit for it, but then use success to lift others up, as well. As a wise leader, using your achievements to inspire others to do the same. Use your strength to coach others who struggle with having good pride.

BUILD GOOD PRIDE INTO YOUR CULTURE

Wise leaders focus on building a company culture that promotes and rewards good pride. Why? They know how powerful good pride is in helping to build organizational success. Wise leaders can build good pride into a culture by taking action like establishing a mission statement that focuses on developing it and being a role model demonstrating how to possess and use it. As Mike Slater said on his blog on *The Mike Slater Radio Show*, "Pride plays a part in determining how well I achieve my purpose, my destiny. Pride has very little to do with determining my intrinsic value as a person."[52]

YOU AND YOUR CHASE

Visualize your organization or any organization with good pride as a major component of its culture. I believe that any organization with such a culture will inevitably benefit from the positive working relationships and individual focus on achievement that good pride causes. Wise leaders continually focus on building good pride into the cultures of their organizations.

It's easy to say that you should build good pride into company culture. The hard part is actually doing it. Fortunately, management research gives us some useful tips on building organization culture.[53] Based upon this research, you can help to

---

[52] The Mike Slater Show Blog, www.http://mikeslaterradio.com

[53] Certo, Samuel C. and S. Trevis Certo, *Modern Management: Concepts and Skills* (Prentice Hall: New York) 2012, pp. 462 – 464.

make good pride a part of your organization's culture by taking steps like:

Developing and Circulating a Values Statement. A *value* is a belief of a person or group in which they have emotional investment. To build good pride into your organization and business culture, you must show people how much you value it. It is good to establish a *values statement* for your company, which is a formally drafted document that summarizes the primary values supported within an organization. In this case, the values statement would define "good pride" and indicate to all that it is highly valued by management.

Rewarding People for Possessing Good Pride. Rewarding people for acting in a way that reflects good pride will encourage them to have good pride. For example, when you reward those who show cooperation in helping others to succeed as well as themselves—a reflection of good pride—they will tend to repeat that behavior. Such activities can be formally built into the performance appraisal process to make sure people know how important you think such behavior actually is.

Circulating Good Pride Stories. From time to time, leaders hear stories about how people act in ways that reflect good pride—perhaps critical incidents of how people cooperated to enable everyone to reach a critical goal. Repeat these stories in an organization as you talk to others. Such repetition will help to ensure that others see how important you think good pride is and encourage them to act in a way that reflects good pride.

GOOD PRIDE: MATTHEW'S BOYHOOD LESSON

As soon as Matthew was able, about ten or eleven years old, he was assigned to mowing our lawn as one of his jobs. One Saturday morning, bright and early, I asked Matthew to mow the lawn. At that time, we were living in Terre Haute, Indiana. Needless to say, Matthew was not excited about doing this job. To his credit, however, he respectfully got up from watching TV and went to the garage to get the lawnmower.

I heard the lawnmower start and through the window could see Matthew beginning his job. Comfortable that all was okay with Matthew, I went out to clean up the garage. After about twenty-five minutes, I heard the lawnmower stop. I then heard Matthew walking the mower up the driveway with the idea of putting the mower away.

When Matthew reached the garage, I asked him if he was finished. "Yes!" he replied. Matthew and I both knew that mowing our lawn normally took about forty minutes.

I asked him to walk along with me while I inspected what he had done. Sheepishly, Matthew trudged behind me, shuffling his feet slowly, seeming to know what was about to happen.

Upon inspection, I pointed out several problems with Matthew's job. Spots of grass were not cut up to the tree trunks, strips along the sidewalk were not cut properly, and one fairly large section in the backyard was not cut at all. After our inspection, Matthew and I both agreed that the job was not properly completed.

"No big deal, right?" he asked.

"No! This is a very big deal," I responded, "Whatever job you do in life, you have to do it the right way even if it's cutting the grass. Always perform a job to the best of your ability. Don't look for a quick way out. Get used to knowing that jobs worth doing take time and you need to do them the right way. Commit yourself to doing your work the right way."

Take pride in doing your work. Taking pride in your work means that you apply all of the talent you have in doing a job to the best of your ability. No matter what it is. No matter if it's just mowing the lawn. It will make the difference in everything you do in life.

I tried to convince Matthew that God has given each of us special talents and we all need to be committed to using those talents.

Matthew got the lawnmower and spent the next forty minutes re-mowing the lawn and doing it the proper way.

PRIDE IS A TRICKY WORD

Pride is a tricky word. To be wise, you should never think about the abilities and talents that you have as being totally from you. Instead, remember that God has given you your own unique abilities and you should always recognize that what you've accomplished is not *really* because of you, but because of the talents that God has given you. Bottom line is that you should always use, and encourage others to use, talents to the best of their ability, recognizing that people only have those talents because God has gifted them. When people have too high an opinion of themselves and their talents, they become too impressed with their own abilities, dignity, and importance. They forget God's role in their lives.

BAD PRIDE

Think of *bad pride* as an inflated, unrealistically high opinion of oneself. Why does the Bible have so much to say about this issue? Because, ultimately, a person with bad pride is saying, "I don't need God. I can do it on my own."[54] Bad pride is based on the belief that you know more than you actually do or are more talented than you actually are.

---

[54] Romans 12:3, (*New International Version*): For by the grace given me I say to every one of you: Do not think of yourself more highly than you ought, but rather think of yourself with sober judgment, in accordance with the measure of faith God has distributed to each of you.

Pride of this nature comes from the world and is not encouraged by Biblical principles.[55]

Often, this unrealistically high opinion of oneself is achieved by devaluing others. Those who have bad pride tend to be focused on themselves. It's all about them. Because bad pride tends to distort reality, those who hold it are charged with self-deceit.[56]

Bad pride results in a kind of attachment to oneself and aversion to others. God dislikes bad pride.[57]

Review the verse at the beginning of this chapter. This verse tells us how we should act towards each other—the exact opposite of bad pride.

We should not worry about the actions of others, but focus more on what we do than on what they do. We should not build our own importance by tearing down what others do. We should have pride in what we do without having to compare ourselves to others.

In the chapter-opening verse, Paul is actually supporting the notion of good pride—feeling good about what you do without reference to others. We should not degrade other people in order to feel good about ourselves. We should listen and take advice from others in order to get ideas about how we can do what we do better.[58]

---

[55] 1 John 2:16, (*New International Version*): For everything in the world— the lust of the flesh, the lust of the eyes, and the pride of life—comes not from the Father but from the world.

[56] Obadiah 1:3, (*New International Version*): The pride of your heart has deceived you, you who live in the clefts of the rocks and make your home on the heights, you who say to yourself, "Who can bring me down to the ground?"

[57] Isaiah 13:11, (*New International Version*): I will punish the world for its evil, the wicked for their sins. I will put an end to the arrogance of the haughty and will humble the pride of the ruthless.

[58] Proverbs 13:10, (*New International Version*): Where there is strife, there is pride, but wisdom is found in those who take advice.

Notice that this verse does not condemn feeling good about our successes and accomplishments *if* we achieve these feelings in the *right* way—which is not by comparing ourselves to others. Bad pride becomes bad when we start comparing our strengths with others' weaknesses.

Some people become conceited or vain and put other people down just to make themselves look better. Sometimes, it's what one says to another. Sometimes, it's simply how one looks at another.[59] A *look* can say a thousand words.

Have you ever been the focus of someone else's conceit or vanity in the workplace? I bet that your answer is yes. Be careful not to be the one putting down others. Remember that only fools lash out with pride at others. Conversely, the words of the wise protect other people—their feelings and reputations.[60]

WHY AVOID BAD PRIDE?

Bad pride is being over-confident or arrogant. One could argue that the executive in Matthew's company meeting had bad pride. He was seen as bragging, boasting, and being defensive. In particular, boasting is not good in organizations or life situations of any type.[61] Boasting turns people off and diminishes their need to be involved in any way with what a boaster says. The Bible

[59] Isaiah 10:12, (*New International Version*): When the Lord has finished all his work against Mount Zion and Jerusalem, he will say, "I will punish the king of Assyria for the willful pride of his heart and the haughty look in his eyes."

[60] Proverbs 14:3, (*New International Version*): A fool's mouth lashes out with pride, but the lips of the wise protect them.

[61] 1 Corinthians 5:6, (*New International Version*): Your boasting is not good. Don't you know that a little yeast leavens the whole batch of dough?

has a clear position on boasting–do not praise yourself. Let your praise come from the mouths of others.[62]

Sometimes, a person boasts because he is overly confident. The boasters have no room for others in their lives. They are narcissistic. They are concerned only with elevating their own importance in the eyes of others. They are not interested in having a relationship with God.[63]

Sometimes, however, a person boasts simply due to insecurity. Here, boasting is a simply a smokescreen intended to help gain respect from others. If an individual is truly confident in whom they are, he or she would not have to brag.

Bad pride, in itself, is bad for organizations just like it is for individuals. Through bad pride, individuals feel superior to others. Such feelings can only lead to unnecessary conflict in organizations and harm interpersonal relationships to the level of negatively impacting the quality of people working well together. Organizations are not successful when people do not work well together and find it hard to succeed when they are characterized by people having bad pride.

The Bible indicates that pride can cause a leader's downfall.[64] Be astute, aware. The pride focused on here is bad pride and not good pride. Leaders who are arrogant and demonstrate strong feelings of self-importance, narcissism, or superiority cannot expect people to be committed followers. Instead, such leaders will only experience followers abandoning them, dooming the

---

[62] Proverbs 27:2, (*New International Version*): Let someone else praise you, and not your own mouth; an outsider, and not your own lips.

[63] Psalm 10:4, (*New International Version*): In his pride the wicked man does not seek him; in all his thoughts there is no room for God.

[64] 2 Chronicles 26:16, (*New International Version*): But after Uzziah became powerful, his pride led to his downfall. He was unfaithful to the LORD his God, and entered the temple of the LORD to burn incense on the altar of incense.

leader to failure. Wise leaders avoid having bad pride and having followers with bad pride like the plague.

Leaders with bad pride tend to ignore or deny their negative impact on people. Why? Such leaders have such high opinions of themselves that they find it difficult to believe that they can have a negative impact on the organization. They are blinded by their own narcissism. All may seem well in the short run to such leaders, but in the long run they suffer the humiliation, degradation, and embarrassment of failure.[65]

BAD PRIDE IN REAL LIFE

Betty was a partner in her family's direct-mail business. Whenever the family had a board meeting—a business meeting—Betty was determined to convince everyone that she was right. No matter what the situation was. Her brother, Bob, was in charge of advertising and marketing. Betty was in charge of accounting.

During one meeting, Bob showed the family board members his new ads and advertising copy. Betty took the ads and changed them, declaring that she was better at determining what was the best ad and how it should be written. Her brother had been doing this for twenty years and was a skilled marketer, but Betty always fought with him when it came to writing copy for their ads. She thought she knew best.

In reality, Bob knew best. He pointed out to her that he didn't try to do her accounting job and she shouldn't try to do his marketing and copywriting work. The family had many battles over things like this and mainly, it was due to ego and pride. In the end, the family had to vote on whose ad they should use and the majority voted for Bob's ad. He was the most talented, the most experienced, and he knew what he was doing. Betty, on the

---

[65] Proverbs 11:2, (*New International Version*): When pride comes, then comes disgrace, but with humility comes wisdom.

other hand, was operating clearly from a prideful place. This is an example of bad pride.

WHY ENCOURAGE GOOD PRIDE?

As discussed earlier, good pride is a significant feeling of elation caused by a sense of esteem, based upon an understanding of true worth, about self and others. It's feeling good about yourself. Pure and simple. When you feel well and are doing the best you can, you are displaying good pride.

This section discusses encouraging good pride because unlike bad pride, good pride has the most positive effects on organizations and contributes to moving them more toward success than failure.

The positive effects that good pride can have on an organization include:

1. *Good Pride Makes People Committed to Organizational Success.* Individuals with good pride are committed to organizational success because they feel they're a part of something—department, organization, club, etc.—that is accomplishing something valuable. Those with good pride are pleased with what they, as well as others around them, have accomplished. Wise leaders feel pleased to belong to their organizations and focus on surrounding themselves with others who feel the same way.

   Overall, pride in belonging to an organization makes people more committed to making an organization successful than when no pride in belonging exists. *Why the commitment?* Because people with good pride find organizational life pleasing and commit to having organizations succeed so that such pleasure can continue.

2. *Good Pride Helps Eliminate Dysfunctional Conflict and Makes the Organization a Comfortable Place to Work.* People with good pride feel good about themselves without

having to lessen the importance of people around them. This lessening the importance of others can involve activities like emphasizing the weaknesses of others in the organization while de-emphasizing their strengths. Such actions in organizations typically result in dysfunctional conflict and, in general, make an organization a very uncomfortable place to work. Wise leaders know that having people with good pride in organizations will help avoid such conflict, make the organization a comfortable and pleasing place to work, and help to raise the odds of an organization being successful.

3. *Good Pride Develops Confidence and Strength in Organizations.* Essentially, good pride eliminates the feeling in organizations that you need approval from others in order to feel good about yourself. Those with good pride are confident and strong in whom they are. Good pride gives you the comfort of knowing that you know you did the best you could with the gifts and opportunities God gave you at that moment.

The strength and confidence that result from good pride make those with good pride extremely valuable to the organization. Wise leaders know that such people are not afraid to confront difficult challenges and persist until the challenges are met.

4. *Good Pride Spurs Workers to be Proud of what Others in the Organization Accomplish.* People with good pride are proud of the accomplishments of others. They are not self-centered and don't overreact to what those around them are doing, and take steps to help others in their efforts to be successful. Such pride is invaluable to organizations. Think about it. How would you like to be a leader who has followers who genuinely want those around them to succeed and will do all they can to help them succeed?

What a gift for a leader! Wise leaders know that having followers who want to help others to accomplish is an invaluable key in helping to make organizations successful.

GOOD PRIDE IN REAL LIFE

Tom and Jon own a small videography and production company. With only seven employees, each staff member has to contribute all of his or her talents to make the company successful. What I've noticed in this organization is that all seven employees, including the two owners, are very proud of their business. They take inordinate pride in their work. No job is too small. Each one contributes to cleaning the office, organizing files, and providing customer service on the phones. As a result, this small videography company stays very busy and is extremely profitable. This is an example of good pride.

YOU AND YOUR CHASE

To grow in wisdom, you must grow in your understanding of *pride*–one of the most commonly discussed themes in the Bible. Understanding pride is important for you because pride exists in all sizes and types of organizations and has significant impact on how successful organizations can be. Think of *pride* as existing in two very different forms—*good pride* and *bad pride*.

Think of bad pride as an unrealistically high opinion of oneself. As a wise leader, understand that because bad pride mostly retards organizational success, you need to make sure that you do not possess it and that you discourage its existence any place in the organization.

Bad pride evidences itself through behaviors like boasting, conceit, self-deception, and comparing oneself to others. All such behaviors serve to diminish positive working relationships in an organization and in personal lives, and impede your efforts to be successful. Make serious and constant efforts to eliminate bad pride from your organization.

Think of good pride as a feeling that makes you pleased about something in which you place effort or affection. It's about your hard work. Keep in mind that because good pride mostly improves organizational success, you need to build it within yourself and focus on building it within others. Help others to feel special about belonging to your organization. Help others take satisfaction in not only what they accomplish, but what those around them accomplish.

You've read Matthew's *Mr. Prideful Adventure* and the thoughts related to it. *What did you think?*

Yes, you will indeed experience pride—*good and bad*—in various business situations, as well as in your personal lives. This is normal. And it's all part of *chasing wisdom* in business and life. The following are some practical strategies that you might use to help make good pride more prominent in your organization than bad pride:

1. *Compliment and Support Others:* Compliment other people and honor their achievements. Refuse to engage in minimizing what others accomplish.. Make an effort to encourage and compliment those around you. Congratulate them on their achievements. This complimenting will encourage others to do the same. In the process, you'll become respected and this, in turn, will help build your self-confidence.

2. *Help others feel secure in the workplace.* Insecurity in the workplace often gives rise to bad pride. Will I have a job tomorrow? Will my friend get the promotion instead of me? Will I get the raise that I need? Workers who ask such questions are insecure. Wise leaders know that if such insecurities are eliminated from the workplace, people will not resort to tactics like bad-mouthing others in order to become secure—keep a job or gain a promotion or raise.

Eliminating such tactics makes work environments more satisfying and as a result, more productive.

3. *Don't be argumentative.* Your ideas aren't always the best. Carefully consider the ideas of others. Valuing your own ideas more than those of others and always tearing down the ideas of others are signs of bad pride. Wise leaders know that if they continually argue with others in organizations, they eventually develop the reputation of having to be right. You do not have to always be right. Let go of your ego. Your pride. This type of a reputation will turn people off and eventually block new and creative ideas from being offered by others. Why offer new ideas if all the boss does is argue with them and show why the ideas aren't of any value? They won't.

4. *Be patient.* Wise leaders tolerate delay without getting angry. When a leader becomes angry because of delayed progress on a project or delays in the rate of making changes in a department, for example, the leader is commonly seen as being haughty, condescendingly proud. Haughtiness is a typical result of bad pride and tends to alienate people. In being haughty, the leader seems to be saying that he or she could make the expected progress quite easily and therefore is better than workers who could not. *Listen More Than You Talk.* Wise leaders want to listen more than they want to talk. If leaders talk more than listen, bad pride may be causing the behavior. A workplace characterized by leaders talking more than listening becomes quite monotonous for workers. Workers in this situation tend to perceive such leaders as seeing themselves as more important to the organization than the workers. This unrealistically high view of self-importance is at the very foundation of bad pride. Organizations with leaders who

don't listen more than they talk tend to flounder and never really reach their maximum potential.

5. *Pray for Help in Gaining Good Pride and Eliminating Bad Pride.* This chapter emphasizes that wise leaders eliminate bad pride in themselves as well as workers. It also emphasizes that wise leaders encourage good pride in themselves as well as workers. Remember that God can help you to accomplish any difficult task that you face. Ask for his help in trying to gain *good pride* and eliminating *bad pride.*

Following these suggestions will help make your organization healthier and more productive.

Accomplishing these tasks by yourself at times might become overwhelming. Even asking for help from those around you to accomplish these tasks at times might seem futile. In such situations, don't be afraid to pray for help in accomplishing these difficult tasks.

What people find difficult or impossible to accomplish, God finds easy to accomplish.[66] *Doesn't it seem foolish not to ask God for help?*

---

[66] Psalm 146:3, (*New International Version*): Do not put your trust in princes, in human beings, who cannot save.

JUSTICE

Don't pervert justice. Don't show favoritism to either the
poor or the great. Judge on the basis of what is right.

Leviticus 19:15 (*The Message*)

Justice is not simply for the courtroom. It's not simply a
judge banging his gavel on his desk and saying, "Order in the
courtroom!" No, it's something that's at work in every waking
moment of our lives.

The purpose of this chapter is simple and straightforward—to
help you become wiser by helping you to better understand the
role of justice in wise leadership, whether in business or personal
relationships. This chapter discusses further insights about what
justice is and how to carry it out. *Do you know how to define
justice? Do you know the relationship between justice and mercy? Do
you know the meaning of organizational justice? Do you know how
justice and concern relate to one another?*

Hopefully, as you read this chapter, you'll gain knowledge
about how wise leaders carry out justice in organizations. This
will help you in your own organization and life.

Learning how the wise handle justice in the workplace begins
by reflecting on Brian's *Adventure of the Gone Dark Manager* and
continues by analyzing how the chapter concepts relate to it.

ADVENTURE OF THE GONE DARK MANAGER

It was 9:00 a.m. and I was in a meeting with the Provost at Rollins College. The college was contemplating the establishment of a new school within the college and the Provost was in the process of conducting interviews to gather opinions about the worthwhileness of the proposed change. It was my turn to be interviewed by the Provost.

Of course, before the interview started, I was very careful to put my cell phone on vibrate mode. At just ten minutes into the interview, I could feel my phone vibrating in my pocket. I ignored the call. The phone immediately started vibrating again, then yet again after being ignored. I knew this was a signal from Brian that something important was up.

I called Brian immediately after the interview. He had not heard from the manager of the Eden's in downtown Orlando for three days. Essentially, the manager had *gone dark*. AWOL. All Brian had heard from the manager that morning was that he was coming in to work.

In commenting on the situation, Brian was well pleased with the manager's performance to that point. However, this episode of unexplained absence for three days was a serious breach of company policy. Not to mention trust. Undue strain on the company due to shifting employees to cover for the absent manager took its toll. It was clear that the team at the Orlando location was more than a bit demoralized because of the manager's strange disappearance.

In talking through the situation, Brian concluded that whatever he did concerning this manager, Brian wanted to be fair to everyone. He had to be fair to all involved, the manager, the restaurant team, employees—who had to be transferred into the store to cover for the vacancy— and above all, the customers. Without customers, you don't have a business.

Brian allowed the manager to work that day when the manager resurfaced after the three days of absence, but informed him that they would talk about his situation when the workday ended. Brian didn't want to lose a good manager, but this *going dark* episode was serious. He had to be careful about the signal that his actions would send to the manger, the store, and the rest of the company.

INITIAL REFLECTIONS ON THE GONE DARK MANAGER

Like Brian, I'm sure that you would be very concerned about how to act in response to a manager *gone dark.*

Such a manager's poor attendance results in decreased productivity and profit. Employees with good attendance feel resentful toward those with unexcused absences, and for good reason. They are the ones who have to work harder when someone isn't there in order to pick up the slack.

In situations like this, you need to be fair to all involved. You have to determine what is fair for all organization members and customers as well. Behavior by such a *gone dark* manager needs to be addressed very carefully. Through such action, a *gone dark* manager has not been fair to others in the company. Those whom the manager abandons are penalized in many ways as a result of her or her absence. They generally have to work longer and harder.

You have to do something about this AWOL manager. The question is, *What?*

Focusing on being *just* in situations like the gone dark manager's situation is extremely important. The Bible teaches that being just or *fair* with those in our lives is extremely important.[67] Focus on being fair to others because you have a moral duty to do so. When you see being just to others as a duty rather than an option you will take being just much more seriously. If you will have no room for injustice in your life, you will be a wiser leader.

---

[67] Proverbs 21:3, (*The Message*): Clean living before God and justice with our neighbors mean far more to God than religious performance.

Be just in small things as well as large things. Be just in situations like the gone dark manager. Be just in handling situations like the Exxon Valdez dumping millions of barrels of oil along the Alaskan coastline—deciding if and how Exxon should pay the residents punitive damages for destroying their way of life.

Read on for further insights regarding how the wise handle justice in business.

WHAT IS JUSTICE?

Wise business leaders are *just*. In general, think about *justice* as maintaining what is fair, what is equitable in life, what is done without cheating. Can you be fair if you show partiality? No. Can you be fair if you're concerned with self-interest? No. Can you be just if you're concerned about the race of people? No. Can you be fair if you're prideful and egotistical? No.

In essence, a leader who shows partiality, is concerned about self-interest, or is concerned with race perverts justice through decisions he or she makes. As the chapter-opening verse indicates, you should not pervert justice. Justice is based upon what is fair. Justice is protecting the rights of others and punishing for wrongdoings.

For the world of business, think about justice as maintaining what is fair in organizations, *organizational justice*. This chapter discusses insights about fairness and justice in business—fairness with employees, fairness with customers, and fairness with all stakeholders.

The concept of justice makes sense to those who follow Biblical teachings, but it's is difficult to understand for those who do not.[68] Those who do not follow Biblical teachings are prone to believe that you should do whatever is necessary, fair or unfair,

---

[68] Proverbs 28:5, (*The Message*): Justice makes no sense to the evil-minded; those who seek God know it inside and out.

in order to maximize success. These individuals believe that you shouldn't worry about favoritism – you can and should use it to enhance your success. Believe me, this is a very shortsighted view of not being fair.

Being just should be one of the fundamental duties of a leader.[69] Why? Justice tends to develop employees who are satisfied and productive. To help ensure organizational justice, wise leaders take action like informing employees of the rules and regulations that govern their organizational lives. Employees must clearly understand the do's and don'ts they must follow.

Once this understanding is established, wise leaders hold organization members accountable for following these regulations. The wise know the do's and don'ts, know *when* the do's and don'ts are not followed, know what is fair in holding people accountable for infractions, and take steps to implement this accountability.

Wise leaders know that determining what is fair in a certain situation may be extremely difficult. Sometimes, the rules and regulations might be difficult to understand or could have various interpretations.

Wise leaders like judges sometimes have difficulty determining what is fair in certain situations.[70] Facing such difficulty in determining what is just, wise leaders seek the opinions of others before making a final decision.

---

[69] Proverbs 29:4, (*New International Version*): By justice a king gives a country stability, but those who are greedy for bribes tears it down.

[70] Deuteronomy 17:8-9, (*The Message*): When matters of justice come up that are too much for you—hard cases regarding homicides, legal disputes, fights—take them up to the central place of worship that God, your God, has designated. Bring them to the Levitical priests and the judge who is in office at the time. Consult them and they will hand down the decision for you.

ORGANIZATIONAL JUSTICE: THE DETAILS

As defined earlier, *organizational justice* is fairness in organizations. The same as with other aspects of life, people normally see organizations as *just* if life *within* them seems fair, meaning free from factors like favoritism, prejudice, or dishonesty. People normally see organizations as *unjust* if they see life *within* as typified by such factors, meaning morally wrong as judged by their sense of ethics, equity, or law.

Wise leaders try to be fair in organizations in three primary ways. First, they try to be fair in the way they *allocate resources* in organizations. In this area, wise leaders try to reward people fairly by considering the amount of responsibilities that employees have, the amount of work employees do, the degree of effort employees show, and the amount of experience that employees possess. Most agree that it is fair for employees who have greater responsibilities, produce more output, display more effort, and have greater experience to be paid higher wages.

Second, wise leaders try to be fair in *the way they interact* with employees. In this area, wise leaders try to interact with people fairly by emphasizing behavior like honestly and openly considering employees opinions, quelling any personal biases, being truthful, and providing timely feedback about important organizational issues. Generally, those leaders who honestly and openly consider employee opinions, quell personal biases, are truthful, and provide timely feedback are considered fairer than leaders who do not.

Third, wise leaders try to be fair in *making decisions*. In this area, wise leaders try to establish procedures that gather accurate information upon which to make decisions, allow and encourage employees to appeal or challenge decisions made, and give all people in the organization affected by a decision under consideration an opportunity to share their insights about what decision should be made. Generally, the more accurate the information upon which a decision is made, the more allowance for employees to challenge a decision, and the more people affected by a decision have an opportunity to influence the decision, the fairer people judge the decision to be.

There is a lot of controversy over what is just and unjust these days. Social media has introduced some new and interesting problems regarding employees' rights and a company's rights. According to the *New York Times*, in 2010 there was a leading-edge case involving employee use of social media. A company was accused of firing an employee for criticizing her boss on Facebook. According to the National Labor Relations Board, this was illegal.

This was the first case in which the Labor Board argued that an employee's criticisms of their bosses or companies on a social networking site is a private activity—and that employers would be violating the law by firing or punishing workers for such statements. The complaint was filed against American Medical Response of Connecticut for firing an emergency medical technician. The company issued a statement that she violated a policy that prohibited employees from depicting the company in *any way* on Facebook or other social media sites where they post pictures of themselves.

The Board's acting general counsel said that employees have a right to discuss their working conditions and supervisors. Pure and simple.

American Medical Response of Connecticut rebutted the Labor Board's claim by indicating that the fired employee was discharged because of several serious complaints about her behavior and not her Facebook activities.

In late January 2011, only a few months after the complaint was filed, American Medical Response agreed to settle out of court. The settlement involved promises by the company to revise its social media policy and to grant employee requests involving union representation. Evidently, the girl in question posted her comments on Facebook because she was denied union representation and thus, the reason for her derogatory comments.

The question here is, *Was the company justified in terminating an employee because of a comment made on Facebook?* The law can be complex regarding some of these issues and each one requires careful examination. It takes an inordinate amount of wisdom to lead your staff and you must build your understanding of justice in order to build your wisdom.

And what rights do employers and employees have concerning what information is shared through social media? The key seems to be making sure expectations are fully communicated and kept updated as social media changes. What may seem *just* today might change tomorrow as social media becomes more and more intertwined in our lives both professionally and personally.

Why do wise leaders focus so much on establishing organizational justice in their businesses? First, the Bible teaches that being just in organizations is what principled people do. Principled people are those who are honorable, upright, and moral.

Given that the wise struggle to be honorable people, it follows that the wise also struggle with the job of establishing justice in organizations, as well as in all other facets of life. The Bible is very clear about God wanting us to attend to matters of justice in organizations and all other places.[71]

In addition to the Biblical rationale, wise leaders tend to focus on creating organizational justice because its existence commonly leads to organizational benefits like decreased employee absenteeism, increased employee job performance, increased job satisfaction, and higher employee motivation levels. All of these benefits increase the probability of organizational viability and success.

---

[71] Jeremiah 22:3, (*New International Version*): This is what the Lord says: Do what is just and right. Rescue from the hand of the oppressor the one who has been robbed. Do no wrong or violence to the foreigner, the fatherless or the widow, and do not shed innocent blood in this place.

People are significantly impacted by the justice—or lack thereof—of actions taken, and decisions made in organizations. Most people see themselves as deserving to be treated fairly and justly in organizations. Employees need to see that organizations are treating them justly in areas like fair pay, opportunities for promotion, and hiring practices. When they perceive themselves as being treated unfairly and unjustly, their commitment to the organization and its leadership tends to dwindle. If employees perceive there is justice in an organization, then there is more likely to be an increase in organizational success.

ORGANIZATIONAL JUSTICE: BRIAN'S HIGH SCHOOL LESSON

During Brian's junior year in high school he tried out for and made it onto the school's golf team. He practiced very diligently, took a few lessons at his own expense, and even made some of his own golf clubs in order to improve his game.

One afternoon after school, the golf team had a qualifying round to determine which four players from the golf team of ten would qualify to play in an upcoming match against another school. Brian was very excited about competing in the qualifying round and couldn't wait for the qualifying match to begin.

Typical of Florida weather, on the day of the qualifying round the afternoon sky began to cloud over and a thunderstorm seemed to be rolling in. I was unable to attend the qualifying match but was distracted by the clouds rolling in as I tried to prepare for a lecture that I had to give the following day. *Would the team be able to finish its qualifying round before the storm?*

I arrived home about 5:00 p.m. only to find out that the thunderstorm that did indeed materialize, had been spotty and had not hit the area of the city where we lived, or where the qualifying match was played. I was excited that the qualifying match was not postponed.

It started to rain about 5:30 p.m. and Brian had not arrived home yet. Then, 6:00 p.m. came and went, and Brian was still not home. At 6:30 p.m. Brian was still not home and the rain had been falling hard for over an hour. Clearly, something was wrong.

Finally, Brian walked into the house about 6:45 p.m. He was soaking wet and very, very upset. His car had broken down and he had been walking over an hour in the rain. Frazzled looking and wet, Brian slumped down in a chair all defeated-like and began to tell me about the match without even thinking about drying off or changing his clothes.

Brian was not upset about his car, but he was upset because he had not qualified to represent his school in the upcoming match. He wasn't so much upset because he didn't qualify, but because of *how* he didn't qualify. In Brian's mind, the coach unfairly interpreted several rules that culminated in raising his final score.

Also in his mind, Brian was sure that the coach made his judgments in order to allow one of his *favorite* players to qualify over Brian. I had never seen Brian as upset as when he was talking about what had happened.

At that point, my attempts at discussion to help Brian become less upset were futile. In his mind, he had just experienced extreme organizational injustice. Sure he was disappointed that he didn't qualify for the match. It wasn't so much that he didn't qualify, but that he was a victim of an injustice.

I took some consolation in hoping that this experience might teach Brian to be vigilant about being fair as a leader in an organization where he would someday work.

Wise leaders always strive to be just, and make decisions about *who should play in the game* by emphasizing impartiality. In being partial or unjust, a leader would inevitably alienate followers, damage the success of the organization, and cause personal stress and grief for those to whom he had been unjust. To ensure being seen as just in decision making, you should always stress explaining to others how you make decisions and why the decisions that you make are fair.

Although continued discussion did not completely relieve Brian of the negative feelings he had toward the coach, he seemed to take some comfort in reflecting more thoroughly on what had just happened to him. I felt that Brian had resolved to be *just* with others in life. Although painful, this experience helped Brian to learn the ways of wise leaders. If so, the pain was well worth the gain.

MERCY: NOT GETTING WHAT'S DESERVED

Mercy is not getting what you justly deserve. Mercy is not simply feeling sorry for someone or simply looking the other way—pretending something didn't happen. Actually, mercy is quite the opposite. Infractions have been made and are recognized, but people who commit them are given a chance to express remorse in order to be renewed in good standing.

Justice gives people exactly what they deserve based upon what they've done. In a sense, mercy is a pardon. Real wisdom, God's wisdom, is characterized by mercy—being reasonable and overflowing with grace and blessings.[72]

Most of us want to see ourselves as being the epitome of justice and grace. We want to be very objective in determining what, *if any*, behavior deserves punishment. And we're probably all a little lenient when it comes to determining our punishment. Most of us would like to be the recipient of mercy and grace when we've made a mistake rather than the recipient of justice. We know that

---

[72] James 3:17, (*The Message*): Real wisdom, God's wisdom, begins with a holy life and is characterized by getting along with others. It is gentle and reasonable, overflowing with mercy and blessings, not hot one day and cold the next, not two-faced...

we've made a mistake and we know that we deserve some type of discipline or punishment because we made the mistake.

Biblical prayers clearly show that people appreciate justice and what it rightly brings, but look forward to, and ask for, mercy for wrongdoings.[73] [74]

Wise leaders are compassionate leaders. They are kindhearted in their feelings about others. In addition, they show empathy toward others and at times do not punish others for offenses committed. Be clear, however. Wise leaders do indeed discipline others. They are not afraid to show compassion as well. They understand that kind mercy wins out over harsh punishment every time—even though the punishment may be just.[75]

From time to time you need to be willing to forgive employees and not give them exactly what they deserve.

Reflecting back on the *gone dark* manager, Brian's remedy to the situation involved mercy. He suspended the manager for a time but didn't fire him, the just punishment for the infraction committed.

---

[73] Habakkuk 3:1-2, (*The Message*): A prayer of the prophet Habakkuk, with orchestra: God, I've heard what our ancestors say about you, and I'm stopped in my tracks, down on my knees. Do among us what you did among them. Work among us as you worked among them. And as you bring judgment, as you surely must, remember mercy.

[74] Luke 18:13, (*New International Version*): But the tax collector stood at a distance. He would not even look up to heaven, but beat his breast and said, God, have mercy on me, a sinner.

[75] James 2:12-13, (*New International Version*): 12 Speak and act as those who are going to be judged by the law that gives freedom,13 because judgment without mercy will be shown to anyone who has not been merciful. Mercy triumphs over judgment.

How would Brian or any other manager know when mercy is appropriate? The Bible gives us some good insights to help us make this decision.[76] Mercy can be warranted when someone admits their mistakes and commits to not making them again.

In Brian's case, because the manager admitted wrongdoing and committed to not making the mistake again, Brian judged that a suspension was all that was necessary.

Brian could anticipate a couple of interesting results at Eden's because he showed mercy. First, because Brian showed mercy, he was more likely to receive mercy from others when he made mistakes.[77]

People tend to appreciate receiving mercy and are likely to show mercy to those who have shown them mercy. This forgiveness within organizations tends to eliminate conflict and thereby helps to make organizations more satisfying and productive workplaces.

Because Brian showed mercy to the *gone dark* manager he should expect that the *gone dark* manager would show mercy to others at Eden's. Such action taken by the *gone dark* manager will help to build Eden's into a forgiving organization—not discipline free, but forgiving and just. Brian should not only expect that this should happen, but feel free to display displeasure if this doesn't happen. The Bible illustrates such displeasure.[78]

Why should Brian show strong displeasure if those to whom he extended mercy don't extend it to others? The answer

---

[76] Proverbs 28:13, (*New International Version*): Whoever conceals their sins does not prosper, but the one who confesses and renounces them finds mercy.

[77] Matthew 5:7, (*New International Version*): Blessed are the merciful, for they will be shown mercy.

[78] Matthew 18:32–33, (*New International Version*): 32 Then the master called the servant in. You wicked servant, he said, I canceled all that debt of yours because you begged me to. 33 Shouldn't you have had mercy on your fellow servant just as I had on you?

is simple. Mercy and justice tend to be very valuable building blocks of a productive workplace culture. Brian cannot build the entire culture himself. He must be sure that others at Eden's see the value of mercy within the culture and take serious steps to establish it.

CONCERN: JUSTICE'S PREREQUISITE

Wise leaders strive to be just in all that they do. Such leaders, however, in order to truly be just, must possess a genuine concern for the wellbeing of other people. What is concern? *Concern* is a careful regard for the interests and welfare of others.

This genuine caring for the interests and welfare of others is what focuses wise leaders on being fair in their dealings with others.

The Bible often discusses this concern as love for your neighbor.[79] God has been clear to both men and women in how we should think about and treat those around us. Wise leaders genuinely care for others. In addition, wise leaders are not self-centered. They care for others and do not see their own importance as driving how they act.

Having a genuine care for those around you also means that there are certain things that you shouldn't do.[80] For example, you shouldn't carry out grudges. You shouldn't seek revenge—try to inflict injury or pain on someone because of what they've done

---

[79] Micah 6:8, (*The Message*): But he's already made it plain how to live, what to do, what GOD is looking for in men and women. It's quite simple: Do what is fair and just to your neighbor, be compassionate and loyal in your love, And don't take yourself too seriously—take God seriously.

[80] Leviticus 19:18, (*New International Version*): Do not seek revenge or bear a grudge against anyone among your people, but love your neighbor as yourself. I am the LORD.

in the past. Concerning grudges and revenge, you shouldn't hold ill will against anyone resulting from past insult or grievance. It's impossible to be just with someone if you're focused on getting back at someone for what they did to you in the past. Revenge is not the answer.

JUSTICE REQUIRES...

Wise leaders must meet certain demands if they aspire to be just. These demands include:

Being honest in all business dealings. This honesty extends to dealings with all organizational stakeholders. Groups like employees, stockholders, and customers. The Bible focuses on honesty with customers and teaches us that deceit aimed at customers is offensive to God.

One guideline discussed in the Bible regarding this honesty with customers relates to dishonest scales or cheating customers by not giving them the amounts or kind of product that they think they're buying.[81] Describe honestly the amounts and characteristics of products that you sell your customers, and charge them fairly for what they buy. You cannot have concern for customers or treat them honestly by deceiving them about products they buy from you.

Even when leaders are completely honest in this regard, however, they should expect to have their honesty with customers questioned from time to time. One recent example of customer honesty being questioned in an organization involves Taco Bell, a taco fast food restaurant. In January 2011, Taco Bell was sued over using meat in their products that allegedly was just 35 percent beef. A class-action lawsuit was filed against the fast food

---

[81] Proverbs 11:1, (*New International Version*): The LORD detests dishonest scales, but accurate weights find favor with him.

chain, claiming that its taco beef filler wasn't really beef according to federal standards.

The suit was comprehensive and stated that there was a problem with the company's advertising – certain claims about the *seasoned ground beef* or *seasoned beef* in its food products were allegedly false.

According to the suit filed by the Alabama law firm Beasley, Allen, Crow, Methvin, Portis & Miles, the chain had been using a meat mixture that contained inordinate proportions of binders and extenders like cracker crumbs or oatmeal. If this were true, the company products would not have met certain requirements established by the U.S. Department of Agriculture and could not be labeled as containing *beef.* The purpose of the suit was for the court to mandate that Taco Bell be honest and forthright in its advertising.

According to Fox News in 2011, Taco Bell said that its advertising was not misleading and that it would *vigorously fight the suit.* Taco Bell planned to take legal action for the false statements about their food.

According to an online article in the *Huffington Post* in April 2011, the class-action lawsuit was withdrawn. The fast-food chain upheld its stance by firmly stating that the allegations were absolutely wrong. No money was exchanged and according to the article, Taco Bell would not change any of its foods or advertising campaigns. Essentially, Taco Bell was exonerated from any dishonesty.

There certainly could be companies that deceive the public concerning what is or isn't in their products. Hopefully, there aren't that many. Hopefully there are none. Too often, however, leaders seem to compromise their ethics and morals in order to make more profits. A true, wise and just leader does not do this.

Listening carefully to complaints.[82] Wise leaders do not always know everything that happens in their respective business organizations—especially if it's a large conglomerate consisting of thousands of people. Sometimes, leaders do not know how policies are truly impacting employees, and sometimes leaders do not know how other leaders are treating employees in other parts of the organization. And, sometimes, leaders do not know how employees are treating one another.

In December 2011, *Security Newswire* and *The New York Times* reported that Warren Glover, an National Basketball Association (NBA) security director for ten years, had been fired in July. The firing appeared a bit strange since Glover's overall job performance record seemed quite acceptable.

As a result of the firing, Glover filed a lawsuit alleging that senior NBA security officials created a work environment in which he was *belittled and treated differently from other employees.* Glover also alleged that he was denied promotions because of his voiced workplace criticisms. Glover had told his bosses that women workers were being sexually harassed and discriminated against at work. His comments about women in the workplace were ignored..

Glover claimed that as a result of his being outspoken, he was fired for his actions—all for standing up for the women. He filed a lawsuit against the league for lost wages and damages. As of September 2013, there had been no news of the results.

Cases like this are good examples of how problems can exist in a corporation and how sometimes, complaints can get overlooked. Whether the aforementioned is true, or not, and in this case we'll assume it *could be* true and also, it may not be true, anyone with

---

[82] Job 31:13-14, (*New International Version*): 13 If I have denied justice to any of my servants, whether male or female, when they had a grievance against me, 14 what will I do when God confronts me? What will I answer when called to account?

common sense should know that a wise leader would have taken Mr. Glover's complaints seriously instead of ignoring them.

When employees bring complaints to a leader, it's wise for the leader to listen carefully to the complaints. Through this listening, wise leaders may be able to uncover and eliminate unfairness in the organization that they didn't know about previously.

Wise leaders are careful not to promote more frivolous tattle-telling, trying to get someone else in trouble by telling incomplete or fictitious stories about the person. Instead, wise leaders promote serious feedback about serious issues, not to be vindictive with others, but to promote the serious motive of promoting justice in organizations.

Maintaining a constant emphasis on justice.[83] The wise emphasize justice continually. To them, justice is not a part-time endeavor. Justice is not emphasized only when problems arise. Wise leaders build organizations to promote constantly justice with all stakeholders, including the citizenry of the communities in which they exist.

Wise leaders execute judgments continually in order to promote fairness in all business operations. They understand that their emphasis on justice must include constantly sticking up for people in organizations who may not have a strong voice.[84]

JUSTICE: THE WHAT AND WHY

Time and time again you will make a business decision that others do not think is fair. A decision which they think is unjust. Always consider that others may not understand the data that you used or the reasons that you had for making your decision.

---

[83] Jeremiah 21:12, (*New International Version*): This is what the Lord says to you, house of David: "Administer justice every morning..."

[84] Proverbs 31:8-9, (*New International Version*): 8 Speak up for those who cannot speak for themselves, for the rights of all who are destitute. 9 Speak up and judge fairly; defend the rights of the poor and needy.

They simply do not fully know why you took the action that you did and your motives for doing it.

Wise leaders strive to have followers completely understand not only what they do and why they do it, but also how they act—always doing what is just. Wise leaders take charge of what others see in them. Wise leaders communicate to followers about what they do and why they do it. They take every opportunity to explain what they do and why they do what they do. To wise leaders, it's difficult to find an action they take that is too insignificant to explain this *what* and *why*.

By following this *what* and *why* principle, a leader like Brian must explain to other employees *what* he did about the *gone dark* manager and *why* he did it. Taking such action would help Brian to stress that he is a fair manager and that all employees can rely on his fairness in the future.

Wise leaders know that work-related actions impact the lives of employees both at work and home. Employees continue to think about what their business leaders do even after the workday ends. If they see their leaders as taking unfair action, the odds are they will be tormented by thoughts of injustice whether at the workplace or at home. Under such circumstances, the employees will lose their commitment and desire to work and simply go through the motions like zombies to look like they are working and to stay out of trouble. And no one wants zombies at work, do they?

As a result, wise leaders take all steps possible to make sure that they are perceived as just and fair. It takes explaining their actions to employees to make sure they know why leaders do things. Wise leaders explain, and then explain *again and again* until they are confident that employees know why they do things. Such action by wise leaders helps to ensure that the work environment is satisfying and that the employees' commitment and efforts in building a successful organization are unwavering.

Being fair is a foundation principle in *God's Word*. Wise leaders think about how they would like to be treated fairly and then treat others accordingly. As examples, wise leaders pay employees fairly because they would like to be paid fairly, they restore damage they cause to others because they'd like for damage that they suffer to be restored by those who cause it, and they are honest with others because they'd like for others to be honest with them.

Wise leaders work at establishing a just business environment because it follows from a foundation Biblical principle: *Be just*. As with following other Biblical principles, wise leaders believe that being just is of great advantage in building a successful business and life.

YOU AND YOUR CHASE

This book is all about you becoming wiser in business and life. In this chapter, becoming wiser has involved growing in your understanding of *justice*. It's one of the goals in your chase.

As you think about justice, keep in mind that it's one of the most prominent themes in the Bible, as in life. To grow in wisdom, grow in your understanding of justice, in fairness. It's critically important that you learn all that you can about justice. And it may take a great deal of maturity to finally understand it adequately.

Think about being just first, because you will be following *God's Word*, and second, because you will be positively impacting how your company operates and the success it achieves. Remember that positively impacting your company can be the effect of following *God's Word*—the cause.

Keep in mind that wise leaders do not follow *God's Word* because they want to impact their organizations. They follow *God's Word* because it's the right thing to do. When they do what's right, good things simply happen—often things they can't even predict.

Strive to be *just* by being fair and equitable. In order to enable yourself to be fair, make sure that you don't show any partiality for certain employees. Make sure you rid yourself of any self-interest in actions you take, and liberate yourself from any bias.

Think about doing what is fair in your business life as *organizational justice*. Being just as a leader should not be an occasional effort. Instead, think of being *just* in business as a fundamental duty that you emphasize continually. Emphasize justice continually because it's consistent with *God's Word* and impacts organizational success favorably.

Remember that you need to be fair with all business stakeholders—employees, customers, suppliers, etc. To be *just*, to be fair, you must not display characteristics like favoritism, prejudice, or dishonesty. To be fair in organizations, take action like paying people justly—considering factors like their effort given, the amount of work accomplished, and experience possessed.

Think about the way that you interact with employees as a way of enhancing your fairness in organizations. Your interactions should be characterized by honesty, consideration of the opinions of others, freedom from personal bias, and containing feedback about how and why you took actions.

Also, be just in your organization by making decisions fairly. Make decisions fairly by emphasizing factors like basing decisions on accurate information gathered, encouraging employees to appeal or challenge decisions, and giving people affected by a decision a chance to convince you about how the decision should be made.

Remember that the effort you put into maintaining organizational justice is worthwhile not only because organizational justice is morally correct according to Biblical principles, but because organizational justice also spawns organizations that are likely to succeed. Why? Because organizational justice tends to nurture trends like decreasing employee absenteeism, increasing employee job performance, and increasing job satisfaction as well as the level of employee motivation.

As a wise leader, you should exercise both justice and mercy. Don't think that you must be just and exact punishment for each and every infraction employees make. Take the time to listen about *why* infractions were made. If there are extenuating circumstances, for example, don't be hesitant to withhold punishment for the infraction. Think of mercy as a process wherein all agree that infractions were made, but because of remorse by those who commit infractions, for example, employees are renewed to good standing.

Wise leaders are compassionate. As with you, your employees will appreciate mercy. You will find that mercy wins over punishment when you decide to use it. Mercy should not replace justice. You should be merciful when someone admits their mistakes and commits to not making them again. Show mercy and expect others in the organization to do the same when warranted.

If you hope to be *just* in organizations, make sure that you truly have concern for people, that you have high regard for their interests and welfare. To show this regard, make sure that you don't exhibit behavior toward employees like carrying grudges or seeking revenge. Basically, love your employees as you love yourself. I'm not referring to *romantic love* when I say love your employees as you love yourself. I'm referring to a detached, respectful love. A love for others. For mankind.

The following are some practical suggestions to help you maintain *just* dealings in your business life.

1. *Let all know that you disagree with making profits through unjust means.* As a leader, you're responsible for ensuring that your business makes profits through fair practices. Deceit and bribery, for example, should be clearly labeled as tactics that should not be used within your business. The Bible says that it's better to make a little profit through *moral* means than high profits through *unjust*

means.[85] Wise leaders let others know what's acceptable and unacceptable in an organization.

2. *Do not take advantage of people by giving them lower wages simply because they're needy.*[86] Do not take advantage of workers unjustly by paying them lower wages or delaying payment to them simply because you know they're in a financial or personal bind and will accept it. That's not fair. Never take advantage of employees in such ways.

3. *From time to time, review company policies with employees to gain feedback about what policies might be fair or unfair.* Company policies, in essence, establish the rules by which employees must live. Asking employees for opinions about such rules should give you valuable insights about which policies to improve, assuming that some improvement may be necessary. Employees will probably have some feelings about the fairness of certain policies that you hadn't thought about previously. Such conversations with employees will help you to maintain organizational justice and thereby, help employees to remain committed to the organization.

As you venture into your own world as a leader and strive to be *just* with others, remember that being *just* means being *fair* to all regardless of race, gender, skin color, socioeconomic status, or religion. It's just one little step on your road to *chasing wisdom*, but it is everything.

---

[85] Proverbs 16:8, (*New International Version*): Better a little with righteousness than much gain with injustice.

[86] Deuteronomy 24:14, (*New International Version*): Do not take advantage of a hired worker who is poor and needy, whether that worker is a fellow Israelite or a foreigner residing in one of your towns.

DISCIPLINE

For lack of discipline they will die, led astray by their own great folly.

Proverbs 5:23 (NIV)

Take as truth that wise leaders can significantly increase the likelihood of their business success by thoroughly understanding the intricacies of *discipline* and applying this knowledge to help solve complex business problems. Don't doubt it. Discipline is such an important Biblical theme that I would be remiss if I didn't include it in this book.

If one is going to *chase wisdom in business*, one should commit to *understanding* discipline. This will help wise leaders gain clearer insight about right and wrong in handling business problems.

Think about discipline, reflect on its meaning, read Biblical passages about it, and think about how to link these passages to the way you do business. Achieving a thorough understanding of discipline is not as easy as it sounds because the word is used a number of different ways in the Bible as well as in business discussions and in your personal life.

When most people hear the term discipline, they think of some sort of penalty or punishment that they must inflict on another in order to get that someone to act properly. Certainly, getting others to act in a certain way may include penalties when people act improperly. However, penalties are only part of the discipline story. Discipline also normally includes other activities like training and even giving out rewards.

The purpose of this chapter is to help you to become wiser by enhancing your understanding of discipline. In this chapter you will learn what discipline is and how to use it in order to promote the overall good of the business. *Can you define discipline? Do you understand what self-discipline means? Do you know how to mix rewards and punishment in order to discipline properly? Do you know specific steps that you should take in order to discipline successfully?*

This chapter will help you analyze and answer these and other discipline-related questions to help you gain deeper insights about discipline. To begin, read Brian's *Adventure of the Poor Preppers* that follows and determine how concepts and other stories throughout the chapter relate to it.

THE ADVENTURE OF THE POOR PREPPERS

As you know by now, Eden's is a fast-food and casual restaurant specializing in healthy foods like salads and salad wraps. Customers enter the store and walk down a line, choosing which ingredients they would like in their salads or wraps. All ingredients are fresh and on display, and easy for the customers to see. Ingredients include makings like spring mix or romaine lettuce, carrots, cheeses, olives, chickpeas, broccoli, walnuts, sunflower seeds, and protein including meats.

Eden's employees arrive early each morning to prep all salad and salad wrap ingredients necessary for the day's sales. All ingredients must be chopped and trimmed just right for easy inclusion in the customer's salad or wrap of choice. Proper prepping is critical not only to maintain the quality of product from day to day, but also to properly control costs.

One of Brian's frustrations that he faced in the past was that employees were not prepping ingredients properly. One day, the meat was sliced too thinly and lettuce leaves were not chopped into small enough bite-sized pieces. The next day he would find that the broccoli was chopped too finely or the tomatoes were too chunky. This may seem like a small thing, but these details can greatly affect food costs.

Brian's frustration grew until he realized that he had to discipline his employees regarding food prepping. It was a journey that he didn't want to take. He concluded that it was a necessary journey.

INITIAL REFLECTIONS: THE POOR PREPPERS

Brian's employees were not prepping food properly at Eden's. In essence, Brian needed to discipline them, and change their behavior to ensure that they did indeed prep properly.

Perhaps it's a case where one employee was told how to prep properly but ignored what he was taught and helped to lead others astray.[87] One employee not prepping food properly can actually become a role model for how *not* to prep food. In this situation, other workers who see the poor prepping might have assumed that it is acceptable at Eden's and prepped in the same fashion.

There could be many other reasons why the employees aren't prepping properly. Maybe poor training is the reason. Maybe it's a type of employee resistance or retaliation. Maybe it's that the employees simply aren't capable of doing the job.

Prepping seems like such a simple thing to carry out properly. Slice a piece of meat, cut up some vegetables. *Can it really be so hard?* Regardless of the difficulty involved in the task, these employees were probably just being careless in their food-prep— cutting pieces of meat too thickly or too thinly, cutting the vegetables sloppily so that they were not good sizes to put in a salad.

---

[87] Proverbs 10:17, (*New International Version*): Whoever heeds discipline shows the way to life, but whoever ignores correction leads others astray.

Who wants to go into a restaurant that doesn't meet one's expectations? You want to know that the food will be consistent from visit to visit—that you'll always get a nice serving of meat and that the vegetables will be fresh…just right. It's such a little thing, but it's such a great example of how attention to detail is so important in virtually any job. And it affects the bottom line, which affects profits, paychecks, and ultimately, employee satisfaction.

In a nutshell, Brian had employees who were not prepping food correctly. In response, many might argue that the employees should be punished for their poor behavior. That's the remedy. People might say: "Punishment will get the employees to prep food properly." But is that truly the way to handle the situation? *Is that the wisest way? Is it a complete way?* Wise leaders know that discipline is so much more than punishment.

Simply put, think of punishment as a penalty that one incurs and justly deserves as a result of doing wrong. Like going to prison for theft or murder. Like being fined because your parking meter time has run out or being ticketed for speeding.

In this case, Brian could impose a penalty on employees who aren't properly prepping food. The penalty could be a number of different actions like reducing pay for the extra time needed to go back and prep the food correctly, a harsh reprimand, or even dismissal of one employee to set an example to the others that they must shape up and *get with the program*. Of course, this might be kind of extreme for being sloppy with food prep.

The traditional logic behind punishing his employees in this situation is that after being punished, Brian's employees will prep food properly in order to avoid further punishment and all will be fine. The punishment is intended to correct the manner in which the employee is acting, and to encourage them to prep food the correct way.

The word *punishment* might sound harsh or not politically correct in today's society, but there are times when wise leaders should consider punishment or penalty as a vehicle to change the behavior of others. People sometimes do things that justify a leader penalizing them.[88] Keep in mind that the wisest of leaders punish judiciously to make sure that punishments are fair and thereby avoid incurring a negative backlash from their employees.

Although punishment might be undesirable at the time for employees, wise leaders understand that punishment can produce skills that will make employees' lives more rewarding in the future.[89]

However, remember that discipline is a much broader concept than "punishment" per se. Remember that wise leaders know that such penalty or punishment is not discipline in its entirety. Let's examine discipline a bit more closely.

WHAT IS DISCIPLINE?

Most people might think of discipline as in spanking your child or making him or her go to *time out*. This is a very simplified explanation, but it's true that it might be our first association with discipline because as a child, most of us have been put in *time out*. Most of us were spanked for something we weren't supposed to do. But discipline is more than that.

Think of *discipline* as direct action aimed at establishing, correcting or improving the behavior of another. Discipline can include punishment but doesn't end with punishment. Penalties of various sorts in response to *inappropriate* or unwanted behavior as well as various rewards in response to *appropriate* or desired behavior are both necessary components of disciplining.

---

[88] Jeremiah 4:18, (*New International Version*): Your own conduct and actions have brought this on you. This is your punishment. How bitter it is! How it pierces to the heart!

[89] Hebrews 12:11, (*New International Version*): No discipline seems pleasant at the time, but painful. Later on, however, it produces a harvest of righteousness and peace for those who have been trained by it.

Concerning Brian's situation, discipline should probably include both penalties that employees incur when prepping improperly and rewards when prepping properly. Both rewards and punishment in combination will best ensure that discipline is effective—employees will prep properly over the long run.

DISCIPLINE IN THE NFL

Rewards can be very powerful in encouraging people to act in a desirable fashion. Wise leaders always make sure that their rewards encourage such behavior. As the following material illustrates, sometimes in organizations, foolish leaders use rewards to encourage undesirable behavior.

I love sports and often read articles online or in the newspaper about the National Football League—the NFL. It particularly interests me when I read about examples of wise and unwise actions by NFL leaders like managers and coaches. I find such examples so very powerful in illustrating what business leaders should and shouldn't do. People seem to relate very easily to such examples and quickly learn from them.

An article posted on the www.profootballweekly.com site in March 2012 is an example of using rewards to bring out the worst in a team. Following is the story, which I will paraphrase from what I learned on this site.

As a result of creating *bounty rewards*, the New Orleans Saints faced disciplinary action for breaking the NFL's *bounty* rule. What this involved were several defensive players on the Saints and one assistant coach, who ran a *bounty* program that violated NFL rules during the 2009, 2010, and 2011 seasons. This program issued bonuses to players who caused harm or inflicted injury on opposing players that would necessitate the opposing players being taken out of a game.

Supposedly, players donated to a fund and received cash payments from that fund, at least in part, based on their success in inflicting injuries on opposing team members. The payments were given for plays that included interceptions and fumble recoveries, as well as *cart-offs*, a term used for when an opposing player has been carried off the field.

According to the article, the NFL said the total of the collection of cash for bounty bonuses topped out in 2009 and may have reached $50,000 or more. According to news sources, the *bounty* program paid $1,500 for a cart-off with payments doubling or tripling during the postseason.

At the time, the NFL Commissioner, Roger Goodell, said this was a very serious violation committed by the Saints and indicated that discipline for the infraction could include fines, suspensions, and even forfeiture of draft choices.

Since then, commissioner Goodell's discipline of the Saints included a $500,000 team fine, suspension of head coach Sean Payton for the 2012 NFL season without pay, suspension of general manager Mickey Loomis without pay for the first eight regular-season games, and an indefinite suspension of Saints defensive coordinator Gregg Williams.

All I can add is *What were they thinking? How could a reputable team do such a thing? How could one of the assistant managers have not only allowed this, but encouraged it?*

According to the article, the Saints owner, Tom Benson, cooperated with the investigation, and evidence established that he had not been knowledgeable of the program. *But what about the assistant manager who condoned it?* It shows a lack of moral code or ethics, and overall foolish leadership.

Naturally, when found out and written about in the media, the a number in the Saints' organization apologized and commented on how sorry they were. Unfortunately for the NFL and the Saints, such apologies are often received with skepticism after one *gets caught*.

"The payments here are particularly troubling because they involved not just payments for 'performance,' but also for injuring opposing players," NFL Commission Goodell said. "The bounty rule promotes two key elements of NFL football: player safety and competitive integrity."

There is nothing wise about a *bounty* program that encourages team members to hurt others—nothing moral, nothing ethical. This is a clear example of foolish leadership using rewards to promote immoral or unethical behavior in organizations.

DISCIPLINE IN THE MILITARY

We've all seen movies about a rag-tag group of soldiers who are molded into a seeming unconquerable fighting unit. How does that happen in the movies? The soldiers internalize a controlled, orderly way of working together. How did they acquire this? Through discipline by a strong leader.

The illustration at the beginning of the chapter illustrates military discipline. Soldiers are marching together, precisely synchronized. This is a learned behavior. It is the result of a well-designed and executed discipline process involving a combination of training, rewards, and penalties initiated and maintained by a wise leader.

We have all been protected in America by our military, our men and women in Afghanistan and other places where war is an ongoing issue. We trust these soldiers to defend our country and our freedoms. We trust that they are disciplined and will carry out their missions as needed. Let me add here that I am eternally grateful for these soldiers. They epitomize what discipline is all about on a grander scale than just our personal and business lives.

Discipline reflects and contributes to the success of military action in any number of ways. The importance of discipline to the success of military units is widely known and has been highly touted throughout the centuries.[90] Soldiers are disciplined

---

[90] Joel 2:7, (*The Message*): The invaders charge. They climb barricades. Nothing stops them. Each soldier does what he's told, so disciplined,

in every aspect of their lives: physically, mentally, emotionally, and spiritually.

Wise leaders know that the importance of discipline to the success of business organizations is just as high as its importance to the success of military organizations.

HOW WISE LEADERS VIEW DISCIPLINE

Just like wise leaders in the military, wise business leaders are very aware of the important role of discipline in building strong organizations and businesses. Disciplining others is a critical part of being a wise leader and is a prerequisite for building successful organizations.

Wise leaders are profoundly aware that they themselves need to be disciplined in order to be successful. They value being disciplined and gratefully accept it from others. Leaders cannot ask their followers to accept being disciplined if they don't set the example. As a wise leader, you must always set the example of *what to do*, even if it results in you accepting being disciplined yourself.

How can leaders expect others to value discipline if they themselves do not value discipline imposed upon them? Wise leaders talk to others about how they themselves are disciplined and share how the discipline has helped them. They act on it.

Reflecting Biblical thought, wise leaders see discipline as a special favor or benefit that will enable them to become better in their jobs.[91] To become better leaders, better people. They view someone stepping in to discipline others as a good thing. True,

---

so determined. They don't get in each other's way. Each one knows his job and does it.

[91] Job 5:17-19, (*The Message*): So, what a blessing when God steps in and corrects you! Mind you, don't despise the discipline of Almighty God! True, he wounds, but he also dresses the wound; the same hand that hurts you, heals you. From one disaster after another he delivers you; no matter what the calamity, the evil can't touch you.

when leaders are disciplined themselves, just like anyone else, they can feel the sting of discipline and related penalties of their actions, just as the coach and several players did when they were involved in the Saints' *bounty* program. And if they're wise, they'll learn from it and never do it again.

Wise leaders acquiesce to being disciplined by others without grumbling. They *take it like an adult.* They know that without correction, they may become ineffective leaders in the long run.[92]

THE IMPORTANCE OF DISCIPLINE

Many credible sources provide support for the thought that discipline is very important in building organizational success. There is hope for greater success when we discipline properly and show others the right way to do things.[93] As in the story of the food preppers, it was important that the employees learn the correct way to prepare food, and it was important for Brian, as their leader, to show them the way.

Can you think of an organization for which discipline is not an important determinant of success? I can't. Discipline is a critical ingredient of all types of organizations and is just as important to the success of business organizations as it is to nonprofit organizations.

Discipline helps leaders in organizations of all types and sizes to accomplish important tasks like reaching organizational goals, maintaining fair standards, and identifying ambiguous rules or procedures.

---

[92] Proverbs 10:17, (*New International Version*): Whoever heeds discipline shows the way to life, but whoever ignores correction leads others astray.

[93] Proverbs 19:18, (*New International Version*): Discipline your children, for in that there is hope; do not be a willing party to their death.

Organization members must be orderly in carrying out their job duties if their organizations are to be successful. They must know their jobs, not get in one another's way in carrying them out, and be determined to accomplish them. Disciplined employees follow policies and rules and thereby enhance the probability that an organization will succeed.

In thinking back to *The Adventure of the Poor Preppers*, employees at Eden's were not consistent and didn't correctly prep food day after day. As a result, for Brian to help these employees become more reliable in their work, he had to take steps aimed at ensuring that the way the employees prepped food on a day-to-day basis was correct.

If employees like those at Eden's do not prep food properly, it can lead to many internal problems. Controlling costs can become a real challenge for a manager, for one thing. When employees are not consistent in the way they prep food, it can become almost impossible to forecast accurately related labor costs. Such inconsistency can also make it quite difficult for a restaurant manager to forecast food costs for making salads and salad wraps for a week, two weeks, or even a month.

Inconsistency in food preparation can also cause problems with Eden's customers. A customer might visit Eden's one day and rave about a particular salad, but when the customer returns the next week the consistency of the salad is different and not as desirable.

Product inconsistency can be a major impediment to building a base of repeat customers. As people become more and more frustrated with not knowing exactly what salad or wrap they will actually get for their money, they will become less likely to return to buy that salad or wrap again. Conversely, when customers like a product and get that exact same product over time, the probability of a customer being a repeat customer increases and the probability of success of the organization is enhanced.

Wise leaders are very attentive to disciplining others as a vehicle for building successful organizations. If a leader does not discipline followers, this will most assuredly result in many problems in the organization.

DISCIPLINE AND THE LAW OF EFFECT

Wise leaders always remember that the purpose of discipline is to encourage desired behavior by others and to discourage unwanted behavior. As the Biblical verse at the beginning of the chapter implies, without a leader establishing desired or wanted behavior from employees, the employees will certainly fail and, as a result, their organizations will shrivel up and die.

Behavior modification is a tool that wise leaders can use to discipline others. I'm not talking about using shock therapy, which was used eons ago to change people's behavior, or using pharmaceutical drugs to get people to act in a desired fashion. I'm talking about generally accepted behavioral science, psychology.

Behavior modification is a process that focuses on encouraging appropriate behavior, behavior that leads to accomplishing organizational goals, and discouraging inappropriate behavior, behavior that lessens the probability that the organization will achieve it goals, by controlling the *consequences* of behavior. It is a scientifically developed technique that gives leaders insight about how to meet this challenge of disciplining employees.Behavior modification is primarily based on the principle that behavior that results in a reward tends to be repeated, while behavior that results in a penalty tends to cease. This notion springs logically from the *Law of Effect*, an outcome of research of Edward L. Thorndike first published in the early 1900s. Thorndike's research uncovered the principle that any behavior which results in a desirable *effect* or reward, is more likely to occur again, than behavior that results in an undesirable *effect*, or a punishment or penalty of some sort.

Think of the pattern of behavior that an employee performs as the result of rewards and punishments that he or she has encountered for performing various behaviors over time. Using God's Word for clearer insight, wise leaders observe the behavior of employees and reward or punish that behavior according to what it deserves.[94] This is the *Law of Effect*.

The basic tenet here is that behavior that you reward tends to be repeated while behavior that you punish tends to stop. Simply stated, if you put a child in *timeout* after performing undesirable behavior, then this punishment will encourage the child to stop the undesirable behavior. And, if you give a child a hug after performing desirable behavior, the desirable behavior will tend to be repeated.

Although behavior modification programs typically involve the use of both rewards and penalties, it is rewards that are generally emphasized more because they tend to have less negative backlash than punishments over the long run. Take care to use penalties to decrease the likelihood that unwanted behavior appears again. But also use rewards to raise the probability that when unwanted behavior stops, and wanted behavior occurs and is rewarded, the *wanted* behavior will likely continue and the likelihood of the *unwanted* behavior occurring again diminishes.

I realize that this is probably not the first time that you've heard about the impact of rewards and punishments on behavior. You might be saying that this is too simple of a concept to be included in this book. Keep in mind that it's the simplest things that are most often overlooked.

In my experience, most leaders know of the potential impact of rewards and punishments. They know their potential impact on behavior in organizations, but few actually take the time to

---

[94] Jeremiah 17:10, (*New International Version*): I the LORD search the heart and examine the mind, to reward each person according to their conduct, according to what their deeds deserve.

adequately reflect on how to systematically use them in the best way possible.

Take my advice. Take the time to reflect on this.

Brian had to do this at Eden's Fresh Company and most of you will, too. Clarify in your mind specific behavior in others needed to make the organization strong. Clarify how to systematically reward and penalize your staff in order to appropriately encourage the right behaviors in others. If you do so, you are taking a giant step forward in helping your organization to thrive. You will be pleased that you invested the time.

This discussion of rewards and punishments gives you a powerful but broad overview of how to discipline others in business settings. The following section builds upon this broad overview by providing more detailed information on how you should discipline others.

STEPS TO DISCIPLINE

When employees are not performing up to standard, corrective action must be taken in order to get their behavior up to standard. There are many sound reasons for this. Substandard behavior can, and often does, result in unwanted issues like low worker productivity, poor quality of products offered for sale, or even customer alienation.

One less discussed but critical reason for getting behavior up to standard is that employees who are not up to standard often become role models for performing in substandard ways. Employees, at least partially, learn what is acceptable by watching what other employees do. The bottom line is that employees can come to erroneously believe that substandard behavior is acceptable simply by watching others perform it without being challenged.

Think about discipline as a process whereby you get employees up to standard. Don't shy away from disciplining others simply because you know that the discipline process might be painful or uncomfortable for you or them. Take consolation in knowing that in the long run your discipline will help others to become more comfortable in their existence because they will be able to make more worthwhile contributions to the success of the organization.[95] Make this point to others when disciplining them.

To discipline others successfully, stay focused. Remind yourself to take the following series of steps to encouraging your employees to act in an acceptable way. It's not mandatory that you take *all* of the steps discussed below or even in the sequence listed, but following all of them in the sequence presented will probably enhance your success in disciplining.

Step 1: *Clearly identify behavior that needs to be changed.* If you want employees to act in an acceptable way, you need to explain precisely what they are doing wrong. Such an explanation can and should incorporate any and all methods for enhancing your communication success and might include, for example, oral conversation, written explanations, videos, and demonstrations. Carefully communicating your explanation will minimize any confusion that may exist regarding what the employee needs to correct.

Try to be as specific as possible during your explanation. Do not use broad statements like: "You are not a good team player," or "You are not committed to helping the organization be successful," or "You are uncooperative."

Instead, be specific with statements like: "You have arrived late for work three times in the last week, travel expense reports that you have been submitting are not itemized properly," or thinking back to Brian's challenge

---

[95] Hebrews 12:11, (*New International Version*): No discipline seems pleasant at the time, but painful. Later on, however, it produces a harvest of righteousness and peace for those who have been trained by it.

at Eden's, "You are not chopping lettuce into acceptable sizes."

As a leader you have an obligation to discipline followers—to discipline them if they get out of line. Remember that you are in charge.[96] A good first step to take to correct another's behavior, to discipline, is to clearly explain to a follower what he or she is doing wrong.

Step 2: *Explain the standards that employees are violating with their behavior.* Now that you've explained to employees what they are doing incorrectly, make sure that they know the established standards that pinpoint their incorrectness.

Is it possible that employees are not behaving in an acceptable fashion simply because they do not understand the rules they are to follow or the standards they must meet? Of course! This step will eliminate any possibility that employees are not performing adequately because of misunderstanding or confusion about what constitutes proper behavior.

Step 3: *Monitor resistance to discipline.* After the first two steps are complete, be aware of any resistance to well-meaning discipline from any employee. If you sense that such resistance is substantial or will escalate significantly, try to eliminate it as soon as possible. Wise leaders do not want this resistance to grow during later steps of the process. If resistance grows, followers will only become more stubborn as the discipline process continues. If the resistance continues to grow, it could eventually cause an employee to fail and become beyond any help that a leader may offer.[97]

---

[96] Titus 2:15, (*The Message*): Tell them all this. Build up their courage, and discipline them if they get out of line. You're in charge. Don't let anyone put you down.

[97] Proverbs 29:1, (*The Message*): For people who hate discipline and only get more stubborn, there'll come a day when life tumbles in and they break, but by then it'll be too late to help them.

Although most of the time it can be quite difficult for a leader to sense if there is resistance to discipline, sometimes, it's obvious, as in the following story of the employee who worked at a morgue:

Brent worked at a particular morgue on the west side of Chicago and was facing discipline for some of his behavior. Brent had recently threatened to leave work and indeed left, but returned with a gun after it was explained to him that he could be fired due to his tendencies to create unhealthy and unsanitary working conditions at the facility.

There's no doubt that this employee strongly resisted disciplinary action. In this situation, the resistance was clear and strong and the Sheriff had to be called to defuse the situation.

In most situations, however, the leader will have to be on the alert in order to sense more subtle resistance and defuse it adequately. Signs to look for regarding subtle and not-so-subtle resistance in your employees include anger at being disciplined, defacing company property, and refusing to work. Not every employee needs a Sheriff on the scene in discipline matters.

Step 4: *Show employees how what they're doing is not consistent with rules or standards.* Here, drive for absolute clarity about what rules or standards exist and how employees are violating them.

As an example, you might tell the employee that company policy states that no one can arrive late for work, but that the employee in question has arrived late three times in the last week. Thinking back to Brian's prepping challenge at Eden's, he could have told an employee that although company standards indicated that lettuce must be cut in strips one-inch wide and three-inches long for easy inclusion in salads and wraps, employees were cutting strips that were at least two inches wide.

Step 5: *Explain the reason why employee behavior must change.* Employees need to know that rules and standards exist for a good reason and that violating them can be harmful to the company. Seeing why the standards exist and how violating them harms the company should help to make employees more amenable to changing their behavior. Leaders need to emphasize *why* followers need to change.

Continuing with the example of Brian's challenge at Eden's, he might have told employees that maintaining the standard size of lettuce strips would help him to better forecast costs, purchase lettuce in a timely fashion, and even make rolling lettuce into salad wraps easier. Hopefully, when employees at Eden's Fresh Company saw the importance of prepping standards, they would become more focused on meeting them.

Step 6: *Make sure that employees understand exactly what you expect to see in the future.* As a leader, you should be crystal clear in your expectations. Precision is important. What kind of behavior do you expect in your employees in the future? You need to be precise. A lack of precision at this stage will simply confuse your employees, and this greatly jeopardizes the success of discipline efforts.

I could write many examples of precise statements regarding expectations in this phase of discipline. Two useful ones are: "I expect you to arrive for work on time starting tomorrow," or "I expect to see all lettuce prepped into strips that are no bigger than one inch wide and three inches long."

Think about actually writing out precise expectations in a handbook or as guidelines. Taking the time to write out your statements and even rehearse discussing them could be worthwhile.

Step 7: *Explain the personal consequences of changing or not changing.*

At this point in the discipline process, employees sometimes quietly and privately decide if they are going to modify their behavior. Leaders should explain to employees the consequences that they will face as a result of changing and *not* changing their behavior. Employees should know what to expect if they do not adhere to standards related to their jobs as well as what to expect if they do.

Remember that standards related to jobs exist to enhance company success and that by *not* adhering to them, employees actually can harm a company. As a result, the purpose of discipline is to have employees behave in a way that is consistent with established standards. Employees who do not adhere to standards are generally seen as inadequate and are commonly transferred to other departments and lower paying jobs, or even dismissed entirely.

Based upon prior discussion of behavior modification and the *Law of Effect*, consequences of behavior should include both rewards and punishments. Reflecting Biblical thought, as a general rule, employees should expect to incur a penalty of some sort if they ignore a leader's instruction about what to change and how to change it. On the other hand, they should expect a reward if they follow through on what the leader thinks is appropriate.[98]

Step 8: *Be encouraging.* Being involved in disciplinary action of any sort can be extremely trying for employees. Wise leaders understand this difficulty for employees and will always be as encouraging as possible in helping employees to meet disciplinary challenges.

Reflecting Biblical thought, wise leaders focus on encouraging employees as a way to build them up and inspire them to deal with the challenges of discipline.[99]

Wise leaders encourage employees in many different ways. One way is to make sure that employees know that

---

[98] Proverbs 13:13, (*New International Version*): Whoever scorns instruction will pay for it, but whoever respects a command is rewarded.

[99] 1 Thessalonians 5:11, (*New International Version*): Therefore encourage one another and build each other up, just as in fact you are doing.

discipline is based upon care for them and not upon using authority to punish them.[100] Employees are encouraged as a result because they see leaders being *human*, with genuine feelings, and not as vindictive and *punishing* as a way to demonstrate superiority.

Leaders can also encourage employees to better deal with disciplinary action by explaining that they primarily view discipline as a vehicle for transforming their abilities into valuable skills. In this case, the employees are encouraged because they see leaders not as wanting to *dominate* them, but as people who want to help them maximize their potential.

Another thought—leaders can encourage employees to deal with disciplinary issues by stressing to employees that they are confident the employees can make necessary changes. In addition, leaders let employees know that they feel confident that such changes will contribute to the success of the organization and that the employees will become a valuable and critical part in the organization's future. Here employees are encouraged to deal with discipline because the leader shows respect for them, sees a bright future for the organization, and see the employees as a part of that future.

Expressing a genuine and sincere concern for employees and their futures is yet another way that leaders can encourage employees to deal with discipline.[101] Wise leaders show compassion or genuine concern for others in their decisions and this makes all the difference in the world. Too often, leaders think that compassion is weak, but it's just the opposite. A wise leader is always compassionate. When employees sense that a leader is

---

[100] Proverbs 13:24, (*New International Version*): Whoever spares the rod hates their children, but the one who loves their children is careful to discipline them.

[101] John 13:34, (*New International Version*): A new command I give you: Love one another. As I have loved you, so you must love one another.

compassionate, they are more prone to respect and deal with the leader's discipline.

The last example of how leaders can encourage employees to deal with disciplinary issues involves leaders helping employees. Leaders can tell employees honestly, and with conviction, that they should feel free to ask for any help that might assist them in making any needed changes in the way they work. Employees are encouraged by this message because they feel that they are working as partners with leaders in making changes that leaders want.

Overall, by encouraging employees to handle disciplinary challenges, leaders can help employees to become more confident, excited, and passionate about correcting their behavior in the workplace. It's a win-win situation for everyone.

Wise leaders encourage employees regarding disciplinary issues in order to help maximize any positive change that the discipline might yield.

Step 9: *Monitor employing rewards and penalties.* Following steps 1 through 8, as discussed above, will provide a solid foundation for correcting employee behavior.

Wise leaders reinforce this foundation by either encouraging desired behavior by others by rewarding it, or discouraging unwanted behavior by others by penalizing it. The Bible encourages us to offer reward as a way of encouraging behavior.[102] The Bible also supports the use of penalties as a way of discouraging behavior that ignores instruction or direction.[103]

Penalties, however, should be used judiciously. If penalties are too harsh or severe, a leader can crush the

---

[102] 2 Chronicles 15:7, (*New International Version*): But as for you, be strong and do not give up, for your work will be rewarded.

[103] Leviticus 26:18, (*New International Version*): If after all this you will not listen to me, I will punish you for your sins seven times over.

spirit of the employee.[104] And that can eventually crush the spirit of the organization or company.

DISCIPLINE: FACING CONFLICT

Most of us can understand how people who are being disciplined can develop negative feelings toward the one doing the disciplining. A student can get angry at a teacher for making him stay in detention after school. A child can get mad because he is repeatedly in *time out*. An employee can get frustrated when his boss continually calls him into the office to have a talk about his behavior.

Most people do not ever look at the other person's viewpoint. He or she doesn't put himself in the other person's shoes and realize that disciplining someone can make a leader feel very uncomfortable, as well. A parent doesn't generally enjoy disciplining his child. A teacher might not enjoy disciplining his student, and a business leader might not enjoy reprimanding or disciplining his employee. Perhaps the main reason for this discomfort is that discipline often results in conflict between the leader and the employee, and the leader feels awkward about managing conflict.

Disciplining employees is seldom an activity that leaders look forward to because it provides them an opportunity to be in conflict with that employee. I don't know anyone who really enjoys conflict. Because of this, many people will avoid it. But this can be a big mistake. For these leaders who don't like conflict, it's easier to let things slide than it is to face discipline issues and deal with them.

Thinking back to *The Adventure of the Poor Preppers*, the result of Brian avoiding disciplining his employees for poor food preparation could result in less-than-stellar customer service. A

---

[104] Colossians 3:21, (*The Message*): Parents, don't come down too hard on your children or you'll crush their spirits.

leader like Brian should take charge immediately of the situation on his food-prepping line. Such leaders should not be concerned with conflict between themselves and employees. Instead, they should initiate discipline tactics that will remedy the situation quickly before it gets out of hand and negatively impacts business success.

Sometimes, a boss or supervisor might notice that one of his employees is not performing up to standards. And often, the boss or supervisor will do nothing about it. Sometimes, he or she might make offhanded comments referring to that employee, which will generally go over the employee's head. Naturally, after the problem has gone on for a long time, the boss or supervisor might lose his or her temper and be forced to face the conflict. I have heard stories about bosses throwing temper tantrums in front of their staff members, and often this is the reason why.

A leader like Brian cannot let a problem like poor food prepping go on, or it would likely disrupt the whole organization over time. Such leaders need to take charge of the situation and confront the employees about the problem now! Fortunately, Brian did.

Wise leaders are always ready to discipline others to build successful organizations. This is fundamental to *chasing wisdom in business and life*.

WHAT IS SELF-DISCIPLINE?

Up to this point, this chapter has focused on a leader disciplining others. This part of the chapter shifts to the topic of self-discipline. Think of *self-discipline* as controlling one's own behavior in order to reach goals more effectively. When leaders monitor and regulate their own behavior, they are utilizing self-discipline.

Through self-discipline, wise leaders evaluate their own behavior and determine and implement strategies and tactics aimed at improving their own behavior in order to enhance organizational success. They understand that self-discipline is a tool for improving themselves as well as their employees.

Biblical principles intimate that a person without self-control is incomplete and unprotected, somewhat like a house missing doors and windows.[105] Leaders must control themselves—their appetites and passions—by utilizing self-discipline. They must not act against reason, morality, or conscience. That's why they should keep their thoughts, desires, inclinations, and resentments in good order.

If you want to improve your own self-discipline, then spend time reflecting on how you might improve. Take a look at yourself. Perhaps your weakness exists in gossiping too much about others or becoming too angry, too quickly. Perhaps your weakness exists in the area of not trusting others, or not being fair or just in certain situations.

After determining areas of leadership weakness, you can spend time reflecting on ways to change. Do you need to focus on how to develop trust in others? Do you need to become more fair-minded? Do you need to develop methods for controlling anger?

Naturally, after determining what you need to change, you and other leaders can make necessary changes in behavior and monitor whether or not these changes are having the desired impact. If not, more reflection is needed to determine why not. It's vital to make whatever modifications are necessary to ensure that the desired impact will be achieved in the future.

Overall, self-discipline is a continual process of reflecting on what you're doing, determining how it can be improved, taking the steps necessary to facilitate the improvement, and then reflecting on these implemented steps. Self-discipline is hard work requiring constant focus, but if you're serious about becoming a wiser leader, then you'll do it.

---

[105] Proverbs 25:28, (*The Message*): A person without self-control is like a house with its doors and windows knocked out.

THE FRUITS OF SELF-DISCIPLINE

In a recent conversation with my son, Matthew, he was adamant in saying that the most successful run he had ever had in athletics was on a twelve-year-old all-star baseball team. He still remembers that he was had 13 hits in 26 at bats during that season which gave him a batting average of .500. For any player at any level, that is a remarkable run.

I asked him why he thought he was able to have such an outstanding run. Essentially, he said he remembered being very self-disciplined and taking a lot of batting practice with teammates, but also working individually by hitting off of a tee that we had set up in the garage.

Hour after hour, day after day, Matthew would place the baseball on a hitting tee, then swing, hitting the ball into a blanket that we hung from the garage ceiling. Using this system, he could work on his own. Matthew remembered setting up a camera, taping his swing and watching his swing on TV looking for weaknesses and areas for possible improvement.

Before he knew it, Matthew discovered that he became hooked on trying to be the best hitter he could be. In reflection, it became clear that the focus and intensity that Matthew put into his efforts to be the best that he could be resulted in a very successful all-star campaign. He learned that you cannot always control the results of what you do, but you can control the amount of effort that you put into your work. And that involved being self-disciplined to become the very best.

This story about Matthew is an excellent one to show how self-discipline can reap personal rewards. And this same self-discipline can be used in the workplace to reap the fruits of strong leadership and to help you achieve amazing results.

YOU AND YOUR CHASE

Discipline is a significant contributor to the success of virtually any type of organization. As you're *chasing wisdom in business and life*, use discipline to establish, correct, or improve acceptable behavior of teammates and/or employees. Discipline others wisely because successful discipline is a prerequisite for building successful organizations.

Remember that discipline is a critical part of what you do as a leader because through discipline you show followers the right way to do things and encourage them to behave accordingly. Through discipline, you create order and consistency in the way people do their jobs. Of course, by establishing order and consistency you increase the likelihood that your organization will be successful. Remember that discipline is not an option, rather, for a leader, it is a requirement.

Remember to follow the logic of the *Law of Effect* when disciplining. That is, use both rewards and penalties in a systematic way in order to encourage acceptable behavior and discourage unacceptable behavior.

Start disciplining with a few focused steps. Clearly identify behavior that needs to be changed, explain standards that employees are presently violating, and try to determine if there is any resistance to your attempts to discipline. If you sense any such resistance, focus on attempting to eliminate it in order that it will not contaminate the success of your discipline.

Subsequent steps will further ensure that your discipline efforts are successful. Show employees how what they are doing is inconsistent with company rules or standards, and fully explain why the employees must change their behavior. Make sure the employees understand exactly what they're supposed to do.

As additional steps when you are disciplining employees, be encouraging by expressing your confidence in them. Monitor employees to ensure they are actually making the necessary changes according to guidelines. Use both penalties and rewards.

Keep two important points in mind when thinking about discipline. First, don't avoid disciplining others because you want to avoid or are afraid of conflict. Second, remember to discipline yourself in order to maximize your impact on the business and others.

You've read Brian's *The Adventure of the Poor Preppers* and other stories throughout this chapter for lessons in developing practical strategies for disciplining others. Below are a few additional, practical strategies that you can use to better manage your own discipline challenges:

1. *Honor those who accept correction.*[106] Be sure to recognize those individuals who respond positively to your discipline. Think about building a pool of such people in your organization by recruiting and supporting employees who want to learn and grow in their jobs. These generally appreciate discipline and the correction that naturally accompanies it.[107]

   You can honor those in various ways who accept correction. Certainly, such honoring can be accomplished by an increase in their wages. Such honoring can also take place by a leader simply thanking one in front of others for making the needed change that helped to improve organizational success. Verbal gratitude will help the employee to feel proud of changes made and increase the likelihood of the employee accepting suggestions for how to improve behavior in the future.

2. *Be confident in self-discipline.*[108] Have conviction in your ability to discipline yourself. Think of self-discipline as a

---

[106] Proverbs 13:18, (*New International Version*): He who ignores discipline comes to poverty and shame, but whoever heeds correction is honored.

[107] Proverbs 12:1, (*The Message*): If you love learning, you love the discipline that goes with it— how shortsighted to refuse correction!

[108] 2 Timothy 1:7, (*New International Version*): For the Spirit God gave us does not make us timid, but gives us power, love and self-discipline.

God-given gift. God gives us the gift of self-improvement to help us become better, more useful to others and to society as a whole. Use this gift.

A wise leader not only focuses on self-discipline, but openly discusses the challenges of the process with others, especially employees or followers. Through this discussion, the leader confirms the importance of self-discipline to others and becomes a role model for how to conscientiously pursue self-discipline. In essence, the leader is actually training others in disciplining themselves.

3. *Make sure that employees receive rewards because they do work the right way.*[109] The Bible tells us that God rewards people according to the degree to which they carry out His Word.

Wise leaders follow this biblical model by establishing policies, procedures, and rules of the organization and rewarding people according to the extent that they adhere to them and contribute to building organizational success.

Remember, you can gain clearer insight about right and wrong in solving difficult problems by studying what the Bible has to say about self-discipline and discipline of others in your organization. Being human, sometimes we feel like doing neither—disciplining others or disciplining ourselves.

As Rory Vaden stated in his book, *Take the Stairs: 7 Steps to Achieving True Success*, there are only two types of activities, things we feel like doing and things we don't. Admittedly, there are times when we don't like disciplining ourselves or disciplining others. He goes on to explain that if we can learn to make ourselves do the things we sometimes don't want to do, like disciplining ourselves and others, then we have literally created the power to produce very positive results in our lives. And that is a powerful thing.

---

[109] 2 Samuel 22:25, (*New International Version*): The LORD has rewarded me according to my righteousness, according to my cleanness in his sight.

FOOLS

The wise inherit honor, but *fools* get only shame.

Proverbs 3:35 (NIV)

What a concept. *Fools* is an interesting topic and would have to be the exact opposite of *wise*. As the above verse suggests, these two opposites usually experience very different outcomes for what they do—the wise are usually honored and fools are usually shamed. Sadly, there are many, many foolish people in our world and there are many smart people who do foolish things.

The wise know both fools and foolishness. The drawing above could encompass a variety of scenarios. It could easily be about a man who has just stolen money from his company and is trying to escape quickly, not realizing that it's a long way to jump and could hurt him in the process. It could also be about a man who is *passing on* important information to the enemy. Okay I admit, I'm letting my imagination run away with me. The drawing could be an honest man trying to escape a thief, but when I looked at it, I felt like he had a dishonest look on his face. For the purpose of this chapter, we'll go with that. He could easily be called a fool for whatever he's attempting to do.

This section of the book will focus on fools and foolishness, and how fools can derail your business. By acting like a fool, you're certainly not acting like a wise leader. You might even see yourself in the following adventure involving Brian in which he learned valuable lessons by comparing and contrasting wisdom and foolishness in business.

THE QUIETWIND ADVENTURE

When Brian was a senior in high school, he asked me an interesting question: "How do I start a business of my own?"

At that point, I had not heard anything about Brian wanting to start his own business, so this question caught me a bit off guard. Brian was into technology and he explained that he wanted to produce and sell a DVD based upon his senior class and the graduation ceremony at Lake Brantley High School in Longwood, Florida.

In sharing his ideas, it was obvious that Brian was very excited about the prospects of his new business. He was sure that he could sell his first entrepreneurial project to his high school and his classmates. He was also sure that this would just be the first of many projects that he could sell to many different high schools in the area.

Looking even further down the road, he was confident that someday he would be selling his graduation DVDs to high schools and graduating seniors throughout the country and even throughout world. Big goal for a young guy!

I asked Brian what his projections were for costs related to equipment he would need, people he would have to hire, and materials he would need to produce his DVDs. Brian had already begun gathering this data. That was a good sign. He even had profit projections for the sale of his first DVD to his high school and fellow students and he had already selected a company name—Quietwind.

Brian believed that his first project would be extremely profitable, returning about 300 percent on his investment. Knowing that 300 percent is an extremely high and almost never seen rate-of-return, I began to talk to him about evaluating product pricing. Understandably, Brian was more focused on how he could maximize his profits.

Our product pricing discussion was very thorough and focused on issues like fixed costs, variable costs, elastic and non-elastic demand curves, seasonality, and even pricing morality. The conversation emphasized the overall complexity of price setting.

Brian hadn't taken any of these issues into account. Slowly, he understood for the first time that setting a price too high could not only hinder the long-run viability and success of any business, but could also be morally wrong. In addition, he began to realize that he could be foolish for overpricing his product.

The look on Brian's face told me that he'd like more advice on how to move forward in a wise way in making decisions about the future of Quietwind. What advice would you have given to Brian? Read on to see how chapter concepts on fools and foolishness can give Brian more specific detail on how to move forward in making his decisions wisely.

INITIAL REFLECTIONS ON THE QUIETWIND ADVENTURE

Upon reflecting on Brian's situation, he had a good business idea, but seemingly unrealistically high expectations. The fact that he thought his first project could result in a 300 percent profit was likely unrealistic. To avoid foolishness in product pricing, wise leaders need to consider *both* consumer fairness and business realism in their quest for a fair profit.

I began to talk to Brian about all of the issues that wise leaders have to consider in setting a fair price of a product—for example, the pricing of competitive products, the uniqueness of a product in the marketplace, and demand for the product. As we talked, I could see that he was beginning to see how complex the process of product pricing could be. As a senior in high school he was beginning to understand how wise leaders handle the product pricing challenge. I could also see that he desperately wanted to avoid foolishness in setting the price of his DVD. I was very proud.

WHAT IS A FOOL?

The King James Dictionary defines a *fool* this way:

"In common language, a person who is somewhat deficient in intellect, but not an idiot or a person who acts absurdly; one who does not exercise his reason; one who pursues a course contrary to the dictates of wisdom."

The antidote to foolishness is wisdom.

WHAT FOOLS DO

Fools slander others.[110] They lie about people and generally base their lies on little truth. The stuff that they say about others isn't based on facts, and it is probably often based on perceptions. Or worse, it's based on their own *opinions*. Based upon their opinions, fools can make false statements about people and not stop making the statements even when contrary facts are presented.

One young man named Alfred who worked as a paralegal for a law firm had a bad habit of talking about others. He was jealous because he wasn't as good at his work as his co-workers.

So, he randomly made untrue statements about them, such as: "Mary gets in trouble all the time with the attorneys because her work is sub-par." In reality, this wasn't the case. Alfred was simply jealous of Mary.

Other co-workers knew that Alfred made up stories about others all the time, and Alfred ended up looking like a fool. There

---

[110] Proverbs 10:18, (*The Message*): Liars secretly hoard hatred; fools openly spread slander.

are many reasons why people slander others and end up looking like fools. Jealousy, hurt feelings, and envy are a few.

FOOLS MOCK GOD'S WORD

We are told in Proverbs about how a fool will mock at sin.[111] This use of the word *mock* is referring to making fun of sin, or scoffing at it—even laughing at sin.

When we sin we are actually mocking God's commands to act in a proper way.[112] Therefore, when we *mock* at sin, we are actually mocking God and His Word.

For example, a young man named Dwayne had gotten into a bad habit at his place of employment at a fast-food restaurant. He continually stole money from the cash register. The managers weren't aware of this, but Dwayne would often brag to some of his friends that he was making extra money on a weekly basis by taking money out of the cash register. Each week, the managers would be confused as to why there seemed to be a deficit by as much as two hundred dollars. Not only was Dwayne breaking the law, and sinning, or breaking God's Law, but he was also laughing about it to others. He was *mocking God*. Eventually, he tried to steal some of the customers' credit cards and was caught and put in jail. By going to jail, he reaped what he sowed.[113]

---

[111] Psalm 74:22, (*New International Version*): Rise up, O God, and defend your cause; remember how fools mock you all day long.

[112] Proverbs 14:9, (*New International Version*): Fools mock at making amends for sin, but goodwill is found among the upright.

[113] Galatians 6:7, (*New International Version*): Do not be deceived: God cannot be mocked. A man reaps what he sows.

FOOLS ARE COMPLACENT AND
BLAME OTHERS

The *Merriam-Webster Dictionary* describes complacency as: "Self-satisfaction when accompanied by unawareness of actual dangers or deficiencies." Complacent people can be quite difficult to work with because they don't often possess a clear or accurate view of the world around them. Overall, complacency destroys the complacent. [114]

The world has many complacent people in the workplace. It is impossible to avoid them. In dealing with such people, some of us will try to develop positive work relationships, but fail. The Bible has explained that complacent people are *fools*. And if you have ever dealt with a fool, you will agree with me when I say that you must use a special kind of intelligence and wisdom—a special kind of tactic or strategy—which we'll discuss later in this chapter.

FOOLS ACCUSE OTHERS AND
SEEK QUICK RETURNS

Have you ever noticed how fools accuse all but themselves for their personal problems? For example, when Dwayne was caught trying to steal customers' credit cards at the restaurant, he said, "Well, if the company paid me what I was worth, then I wouldn't have to steal in order to make enough money to live on."

Wise people blame themselves and take responsibility for their lives. The *fool* does not. Dwayne should have reduced his living expenses or gotten another part-time job to supplement his income. Instead, he blamed everyone else for his lack of money.

---

[114] Proverbs 1:32, (*New International Version*): For the waywardness of the simple will kill them, and the complacency of fools will destroy them.

In addition, fools seek quick returns, instant gratification, which is what Dwayne was doing when he stole money out of the cash register and tried to steal customers' credit cards. His foolish thoughts and behavior eventually got the better of him, and he was arrested and taken to jail.

Wise leaders work diligently to improve themselves; they get more education and advanced training, they look for better jobs. They are the opposite of Dwayne.

FOOLS ARE OVERLY CONFIDENT

Some people think it's good to have high self-esteem. And, sure, it is. And some believe they should be very confident in everything they do. And, sure, being confident is good. You need confidence to achieve your goals. However, when this confidence is out of balance, or more simply, when someone is *overly* confident, then you're faced with arrogance and self-importance, which are traits of fools.

It's quite unpleasant working with someone overly confident who is also arrogant. They are too sure of their own opinion or own view and that means that they won't listen to anyone else. The grass could be green, but if that overly confident person believes it is brown, then you probably won't be able to convince him otherwise.

By Brian seriously considering the product-pricing issues at Quietwind that we discussed, he exhibited the beginning seeds of chasing wisdom. If he had been one of the overly confident individuals who were also arrogant, things might have proceeded differently.

Unlike Brian, there are many fools who are overconfident and who won't listen to advice. Sometimes, an overly confident person might take on more than she can handle and be arrogant enough to think that she can do anything. Many overly confident and arrogant people can't see their own weaknesses, and plunge into trouble.

Many teachers and/or bosses believe they're always right. Sometimes, a student or employee might know more than the teacher or the boss. Perhaps that student has access to information the teacher isn't aware of. It would be wise for the teacher to listen to the student. He or she might learn something. Often, the teacher or boss is too arrogant and unwise to listen.[115]

Someone who is overconfident might be overly boastful and annoying as a result, and they might even put other people down by viewing themselves as superior.

If you're working alongside overconfident people, then be cautious. They could get your organization into trouble and this could indirectly affect your own career.

If these overconfident people are friends or family members, then it may be especially frustrating and annoying as you watch them make fools of themselves.

DON'T BE A WILLING FOOL

The *willing fool* is someone who will follow others without a thought as to whether it's a wise decision or not. Teenagers often do this. If a friend is smoking pot and looks cool, then the teenager might smoke pot, too, because his friend is doing it. In this way, the teenager becomes a *willing fool*.

This carries over into business, as well, once we're adults. There are many followers out there who do what someone else does because they think it's cool. They simply don't think for themselves and are easily guided astray. There's no way they'll ever succeed in life because they don't even know who they are. They're too busy following everyone else without giving a thought to their own morals and ethics. A wise business leader will often detect these *willing fools* in a workplace and work hard to eliminate their behavior.

---

[115] Proverbs 12:15, (*New International Version*): The way of fools seems right to them, but the wise listen to advice.

Bob, a manager I know, ran a successful telemarketing firm. But, from time to time, he had employees who preferred having fun on the job and making prank calls instead of the telemarketing calls to potential customers.

Bob noticed one of his employees, Steven, who seemed to be the ringleader for making prank calls. Steven had a great personality and was a lot of fun for the staff. But he wasn't really interested in doing a good job. He didn't take the job seriously and mainly, he wanted to just have fun. There were several employees who looked up to Steven and tried to be like him. They began to goof off at work and neglect their telemarketing calls. They became the *willing fools* when it came to workplace behavior.

Not only did Steven end up getting in trouble, but he also brought down several other employees with him—all because they were willing participants and didn't think for themselves.

The willing fool is typically easily persuaded, seduced, or guided into specific workplace behavior. Sometimes, the willing fool will participate in making an important business decision that acts against the interest of a business or agency he or she works for. Steven's friends at the telemarketing firm certainly did this. The friends wanted to be liked and popular the way Steven was. Walking in the path of the unwise is never advisable.[116] Steven's friends didn't care much about the work.

Most of us have been around someone who has smelled something and exclaimed in disgust how terrible the smell was. "This smells terrible!" Next, the person says, "Here, smell this." And did you proceed to smell it even though it allegedly smelled horrible?

Yoda, the wise Jedi master in the *Star Wars* movies, once said, "Who is the more foolish? The fool, or the fool who follows him?" I love this movie. To paraphrase Yoda's comment, "Who

---

[116] Proverbs: 4:14, (*New International Version*): Do not set foot on the path of the wicked or walk in the way of evildoers.

is more foolish, the fool who smells initially, or the fool who smells second?"

People often too readily fall into the role of willing fools.

FOOLS DON'T GET WISE CONVERSATION

Fools do not understand a conversation that's filled with wisdom. [117] Perhaps you've noticed this from time to time when conversing with business associates friends, or family members. Sometimes, they don't *get* the full meaning of the discussion. It can be amusing or frustrating, depending on the context.

I had a conversation with an associate at school and was reminded of a quote by Socrates: "As for me, all I know is that I know nothing." Socrates wasn't implying that he didn't know *anything* about life. He meant that he was aware that he still had a lot to learn. I mentioned this same thing to an associate at school when we were discussing students and their interests in learning along with certain guidelines and rules at a university where I taught. The associate, who was lacking in wisdom, looked at me and said, "What do you mean, you know nothing? You're a smart man. I follow your advice all of the time!" I knew that he couldn't grasp the thought behind the comment. It was over his head.

An example of fools not *getting* wise conversation is clearly shown in the short story *Ship of Fools*. Written by Ted Kaczynski, the story focuses on various people, representing oppressed groups in society. The characters complain about frivolous things on the ship they're on. Instead of worrying about the fact that they're heading toward the North Pole, which is dangerous, they complain about blankets for their beds, food, and treatment of their pet dog. The cabin boy seemed to be the only one who had any wisdom whatsoever. He warned them about the dangerous route they were on and begged them to take over the ship from the captains.

---

[117] Proverbs 24:7 (*The Message*): Wise conversation is way over the head of fools; in a serious discussion they haven't a clue.

But no one paid any attention to him because he was merely a *cabin boy*. He is labeled more or less as a troublemaker. The ship continued on its path to the North Pole and was crushed between two icebergs and everyone drowned.

The story is a good example of the foolishness of people who discredited someone's warning simply because he was a cabin boy, and not considered to be important. They didn't understand or *get* the wisdom behind the boy's words. I wonder how many times something like this has happened in our lives? When foolish people have neglected to pay attention to someone they deemed not important, and as a result, failed in business and in life?

FOOLS ARE NEVER CONTENT

Fools have not learned how to appreciate what they have. They have not learned how to be grateful for their lives. They always want more. And then when they get more, they're not satisfied because nothing will fill that void in their hearts.[118] You can't fill it with material goods or with academic achievements. It has to be filled with God. That's wisdom in its truest form. When people have God in their hearts and act in accordance with God's Word in business and in life, they will be contented. If not, they will never be content.

THE GOLDEN EGG

Perhaps some of you have heard the story about the man who had a hen that laid a golden egg daily. This man could not see the value of this golden egg. Being a fool, he wanted more. He thought that if the hen could lay a golden egg, then the insides of

---

[118] Ecclesiastes 4:8, (*New International Version*): There was a man all alone; he had neither son nor brother. There was no end to his toil, yet his eyes were not content with his wealth. "For whom am I toiling," he asked, "and why am I depriving myself of enjoyment?" This too is meaningless— a miserable business!

this hen must be filled with more gold than he could ever dream of. So, he killed the hen and looked *inside* to find treasure. He actually learned a good lesson, because as they story goes, when he found out that the hen didn't have any gold or treasure inside, he said, "While chasing after hopes of a treasure, I lost the profit I held in my hands!"

Not everyone learns his lesson. The man with the hen was foolish because he wasn't grateful for what he had. He thought he could have more *gold* or *treasures* by slaughtering the hen. The fable shows that people often grasp for more than they need, and thus lose what little they have. I've seen this in the workplace. A person might have a very good job, but he isn't satisfied because he wants a better job that pays more. He is never satisfied and that can be a detriment in the long run. He may lose the *gold* that he receives daily in his current job if he isn't careful.

Many people also do this in the stock market or in the casinos in Las Vegas. They might earn a million dollars one day in the stock market, and because they *don't get out* while the *getting is good*, they might lose all their money the next day, or the next. And everyone knows people, or has heard stories of people, who win big bucks in Las Vegas, but end up sitting there at the gambling table and playing until they lose it all again. These are examples of discontented people and foolish behavior.

It's important to remember, however, that there's nothing wrong with, and it's even admirable, to want to continually improve yourself. This golden egg scenario illustrates that it becomes foolish to excessively want to gain more and more.

FOOLS ARE NOT GROUNDED IN REALITY

One man I know named Albert was not grounded in reality. He was smart in many ways but foolish in others. The man had a great job as a CFO in healthcare, a six-figure salary, a good wife and two healthy children. He lived in a nice home and took expensive vacations with his family. He had everything most men could only dream of. But he was not contented. He was not satisfied with what he had. He wanted more and foolishly believed he deserved more. He lived in a world of illusion.[119]

Part of his problem was jealousy. His brother-in-law Michael earned $100,000 more in salary per year than Albert in his job as a CEO of a major hospital. Albert wanted to earn the same salary as his brother-in-law, Michael, in a similar position as CEO even though Michael was older, had a Master of Hospital Administration degree, and had more experience. Michael had worked hard for many years to earn his position and salary.

Certified as a CPA, Albert only had a bachelor's degree, but he thought this was sufficient to get a job as a CEO. Because Albert was not content, he started job hopping.

He accepted an interim position as a CEO at a *problem* hospital several states away and uprooted his family to relocate. He thought, *"Ah-ha! This is my chance to show my company that I'm smart enough to run the hospital. That I can be a CEO. I've earned this!"*

Consequently, the children were miserable in the new school and his wife was unhappy to be away from her siblings and parents.

Ultimately, Albert failed miserably at the job because he simply wasn't qualified to do the work of a CEO. His arrogance and ego had reassured him that he was *as good as* his brother-in-law, Michael, and that he deserved the kind of salary Michael was earning. In the end, Albert lost his job with the healthcare corporation and ended back up in his home state in an auditing position for another company, earning a lot less money. Albert hadn't learned to be grateful for all that he had been given.[120]

FOOLS DON'T LEARN

---

[119] Proverbs 14:18, (*The Message*): Foolish dreamers live in a world of illusion; wise realists plant their feet on the ground.

[120] 1 Thessalonians 5:18, (*New International Version*): Give thanks in all circumstances; for this is God's will for you in Christ Jesus.

Albert made some critical mistakes when he accepted an interim position as a CEO and then failed miserably. The sad thing is that he didn't learn from that mistake.

He is still trying to get that better job as a CEO and a higher salary without getting the education needed. If a man doesn't realize his mistake and take action to correct his behavior, then he will repeatedly make the same mistake over and over again, and he won't gain much wisdom in the process.

Winston Churchill said, "All men make mistakes, but only wise men learn from their mistakes." You can also learn by watching the foolish mistakes of others. If you repeat the action of a fool, you become an even bigger fool. Think of it this way. If you see someone jump off a roof and that person breaks a leg, then you decide you can jump and refrain from breaking a leg then you're the most foolish of all. And don't laugh. These kinds of things happen every day.

According to King Solomon, a fool is different than a wise person in one important way—*How he or she learns.*[121]

THE WISE LISTEN – NOT FOOLS

A wise person will listen without being defensive. He or she will accept responsibility without blame, and will change his or her actions at once.

If working with the wise in your family, within your group of friends, or at work, then you're fortunate and in this case, talking to them can be useful. They accept feedback as a tool to improve their lives. They listen to you and your input can truly make a difference. *Listening* is discussed in greater detail later in this book.

---

[121] Proverbs 1:5, (*New Living Translation*): Let the wise listen to these proverbs and become even wiser. Let those with understanding receive guidance.

If working with a fool, however, constructive feedback is a waste of time. A fool does not accept feedback and resists any change associated with it. A fool's ego takes over and being wrong is not an option. Some friends and family members tried to advise Albert that perhaps he should purse a Master's Degree in Hospital Administration if he had long term goals of being a CEO. But he thought he was smart enough to bypass that step. He thought his experience was greater than the degree. He always blamed the organization he worked for. It wasn't his problem, in other words. It was the organization's problem. And Albert blamed everyone at his corporation for not being promoted. So a conversation with him about getting a higher education or accepting his level of competency was wasted on him.

This is why some conversations never seem to go anywhere. The *fool* won't recognize that he needs to correct his or her behavior. Trying to talk to someone like this is a waste of time.

There are many successful people who do foolish things. By many accounts, Albert is a successful businessman, and he's smart. He still earns six figures and has a nice lifestyle. He just failed at one job because he was foolish, thinking he could manage a CEO's position when he wasn't qualified.

How do wise leaders deal with fools? Don't try to convince them that you're right and they're wrong. They'll never believe it. So, just remain quiet and let them brag and talk all they want. If that person is an employee, however, set boundaries and limits concerning their responsibilities and activities. And finally, give consequences if they don't respect your authority. Albert's consequences were that he lost the job as interim CEO, terminated from the mega corporation he worked for. There are always consequences for every action. Learning to work with fools effectively requires a great deal of wisdom.

FOOLS FOCUS ON UNIMPORTANT ISSUES

There is a popular French proverb that states, "A penny wise is often a pound foolish." The idea behind this cliché is to communicate how some people focus excessively on small things, insisting on success, but missing larger items that are more important. The saying that people *can't see the forest for the trees* is similar. People are so intent on focusing on a tree that they can't see the whole forest. The bigger picture. I've seen this happen to many businesspeople. They fret and worry over something that's inconsequential while overlooking bigger, more worrisome issues.

For example, one business owner, who ran a public relations firm and shall remain anonymous, insisted that all his employees keep their office desks clean and free of any rumpled paper, debris, or clutter. He was so intent on the cleanliness of the desks that he totally overlooked the importance of profitability, happy employees, and company success.

One of the employees, a young woman, Genevieve, had a problem with this. She was the company's star performer and had numerous clients and responsibilities. During the day, papers would pile up on her desk and, to the unknowing eye, look completely disheveled and messy. The thing is that Genevieve did an excellent job. She was creative, fast, and a dynamo when it came to creating publicity campaigns for her clients. She brought in a lot of business for the owner due to her outstanding work.

However, her boss could not get past this one detail—the messy desk. It sounds ridiculous, but this is a true story. At the end of the week, if her desk was messy when she left Friday afternoon, he would leave her nasty notes telling her that it was imperative that she maintain a neat desk. He even gave her warnings. She was so busy; she could barely get her work finished, let alone worry about having a clean desk. She ended up leaving the company due to his constant nagging and pressure. And she started her own company and took all her clients with her. The owner of the business that she left could not see the forest for the trees and he ended up losing his business shortly thereafter. The *forest* was the profitability that Genevieve earned for the company, and the *tree* was the messy desk.

This example sounds frivolous and elementary, but it is more commonplace in business than you might think. Perhaps you've known someone like him. The boss who can not get past his own obsession with clean desks and lets it interfere with his business. Ultimately, this one obsession took him down. Genevieve's boss wasn't a very wise businessman. He was a fool in the most classic sense.

If you're on the road to *chasing wisdom,* I recommend that you strive to be *pound wise and penny foolish* and take a look at the whole forest instead of the trees. And for heaven's sake, if you have an excellent employee who likes a messy desk, who cares?

There is a very specific reason that I advocate *pound wise and penny foolish* along with being wise. The reason is because each of us has a limited span of time and attention that we can invest into actions, relationships, decisions, research, and life. Thus, if we want to make the best decisions, it requires that we focus on the consequential and allow the rest to slip through the cracks. Those non-important things. This is the part where people who have a *perfectionist* tendency can run into difficulty. Like the story about the business owner I just described. He was a perfectionist who thought it was more important to have a clean desk and to *appear* professional than it was to actually let someone be creative and work in the best manner possible to achieve optimum results.

FOOLS FOCUS EXCESSIVELY ON PERFECTION

Some people are perfectionists and aren't wise enough to know when something is fine the way it is. Some writers continually rewrite and rewrite something, never content with their work. Some people go on extreme diets, thinking they are never skinny enough. They become foolish in their pursuits.

People do this in their everyday lives and in the workplace. Nothing is ever good enough, so they continually nitpick over inconsequential details. This is foolish and while these people may not be foolish in everything they do, they are foolish in their attempts to be perfect. It's useless to chase minute details because, aside from God, there is no perfection.[122]

Consider an artist as an example. There are those who never finish a painting because it is "never good enough." They worry and worry over some detail—perhaps the way a tree looks in the foreground. They paint it and repaint it and are never satisfied. The result is that the painting remains propped up in a corner unseen forever. Simply because the artist was a perfectionist and could not "let go" when it was done.

Businesspeople do this, too. Some don't know how to accept that what their staffs are doing is *enough*. They always want more out of them because they don't believe their output is good enough. Some leaders might have an outstanding group of employees, but never be satisfied with their work, always expecting them to do more.

Let's revisit Bob and the telemarketing company once again. Bob had another employee at his telemarketing firm named Gloria. This young lady was a dynamite salesperson and very diligent. Unlike those other *willing fools*, Gloria didn't let the guy who always goofed off, Steven, sway her into emulating him. She kept her eye on her sales goals and did very well.

One week, Gloria wasn't feeling the best and as a result, did not have the highest in sales that week. Bob looked over her sales reports and at first wanted to go to her and demand to know why her sales had slipped. After careful review of her overall performance, though, he decided to let it go. Gloria was a stellar employee and he knew that she had been suffering all week from a nasty cold. If he had obsessed over this and confronted Gloria,

---

[122] Psalm 119:96, (*New International Version*): To all perfection I see a limit, but Your commands are boundless.

demanding to know why she hadn't given him *more* in sales, all he would have done was tear down her self-esteem and make her feel bad.

Gratefully for all involved, he was wise in letting it go and simply encouraging her to *feel better*. True to form, once she began to feel better, her sales improved. Not all bosses or leaders are like that, though, and many will push for more when the employee has given all they have to give. Like the artist who thought her painting was never good enough and that she had to push to make it better and better, foolish bosses will push their employees in the same way.

With some businesspeople, a desire to make sure everything is done properly and correctly can very easily become an obsession with details that occupies so much of your time that none is left for the big things—as in the case with the boss and Genevieve. It's perhaps a form of being obsessive-compulsive.

Being overly obsessed with inconsequential details is the antithesis to being "a pound wise and a penny foolish." If you're wise, you know how to set priorities for your personal, professional, and financial life. You know how to discipline yourself and obey those priorities and let go of the small stuff. Wisdom is knowing when to "let go" and accept the situation the way it is instead of obsessing over it.

PARETO'S LAW

Another way of articulating this principle is through Pareto's Law, which states that 80 percent of the outputs result from 20 percent of the inputs. *This is also called the 80-20 principle.* What this principle is getting at is that we should focus on the things that generate the greatest results.

Since a decision to emphasize or focus on one thing is implicitly a decision to de-emphasize something else, it necessarily follows that the other half of the Pareto Principle is to let go of things that do not produce optimal results. If the boss had *let go* of his obsession for Genevieve to keep a clean desk, he would not have lost her and ultimately wouldn't have lost his business.

In practice, this frequently means that a focus on the big decisions and important things in life will mean letting some small things go. A person working for his employer may need to overlook some missed commitments or loose ends from co-workers in favor of focusing on the major projects and key tasks that produce business results.

In the end, each of us must decide what is most important, what is least important, and where we draw the line on what is allowed to slip between the cracks. Like Bob did with Gloria, who excelled in sales when she wasn't sick, it is important to consciously decide what will be allowed to slide past our attention. The sentiment that "everything is important" ultimately results in nothing being important because no priorities are established to direct our focus.

Becoming *pound wise and penny foolish* involves a significant degree of introspection and wisdom. However, for those who are successful in setting their goals and establishing their priorities, the rewards are truly great.

SMART PEOPLE CAN ACT FOOLISHLY TOO

Not only stupid people act foolishly. Smart people can act foolishly when they think they are so smart that it is beyond them to act foolish. I imagine you know people like this. They are smart, but in being smart, they think they're always right no matter what, even when they're not. They're what my mother called a *know-it-all*.

These people commonly turn up their noses at the thoughts and ideas of others. It's a type of conceitedness. They think they are so smart that they are above reproach. This is also being overly confident and arrogant, as we previously discussed. They display certain omnipotence about doing whatever they want, and they believe they can get away with whatever it is they want to do.

Brian was both smart and wise in his *Quietwind Adventure*. He listened to the advice he received about his established product price, and then modified the price accordingly. He avoided making a foolish decision on his own. Instead, he sought out, listened to, and appropriately responded to someone with more experience and wisdom. If Brian had been the arrogant know-it-all, he would have been a smart person acting foolishly.

Leaders need to know themselves well enough to understand whether or not they have the expertise to make certain decisions. If they have the expertise, they should feel free to go ahead and make the decision. If they don't, they need to consult with those who do.

It's kind of humorous when you think about it. No one knows everything and there is always something else to learn! We're always *chasing wisdom* in life and in business. Wise leaders understand this and know that they learn better by considering the thoughts and ideas of others than by expressing their own opinions.[123]

FEEDING THE BEARS

The following is a great story to illustrate how allegedly *smart* people can act foolishly. A story in the *Huffington Post* in 2011 explained that the Colorado Division of Wildlife was looking for two or more people. These people were seen feeding Burger King cheeseburgers to a black bear and her two cubs in Eagle, Colorado. The mother and cubs attracted a cluster of people while digging through the Burger King dumpster. Witnesses told the Eagle police they even saw people go in the fast food restaurant and buy food for the bears.

"This is an extraordinary example of stupid and irresponsible behavior of the people," said Northwest Regional Manager Ron

---

[123] Proverbs 18:2, (*New International Version*): Fools find no pleasure in understanding but delight in airing their own opinions.

Velarde. "Because of their reckless actions, the sow and the cubs now know that when people are around, this means food. This dramatically increases the likelihood that these bears will get into trouble in the future and have to be put down."

This is just another example of people acting foolishly. These people probably weren't stupid: instead, they were probably kind people and thought they were being good to the animals. They weren't wise in their decision to feed Burger King cheeseburgers to the bears. This was downright foolish. Foolish people lack judgment and do not consider the effects of their actions. They used no wisdom whatsoever in their decisions.

YOU AND YOUR CHASE

You've read Brian's *Quietwind Adventure* along with other stories and the discussions surrounding the *fool* topic. This section discusses practical ideas based upon this chapter that you can use as ideas for handling your own business and life challenges regarding fools and foolish acts.

> Keep in mind that a fool is often quick-tempered—a hothead.[124] When you are acting as a business leader or employee, you will have control of your anger and temper and not react as a hot head. This will diminish any tendency to act like a fool.
>
> The fool will often deny, disregard or rebel against God.[125] Keep strong in your faith, read the Bible, pray, contemplate and meditate. Keep God in your heart at all times. Trust me, this works. If you try to be in alignment with God's thinking, you'll stay on the right path. I think it's good to say: *What would Jesus do?*

---

[124] Proverbs 12:16, (*The Message*): Fools have short fuses and explode all too quickly; the prudent quietly shrug off insults.

[125] Psalm 14:1, (*New International Version*): The fool says in his heart, "There is no God." They are corrupt, their deeds are vile; there is no one who does good.

Be honest with yourself and others. Remember, when a person is dishonest, often others know, and if you're that person, you'll only end up looking like a fool.

Do not be a bragger, or be highly opinionated, or talk endlessly about yourself. I cannot think of anything more boring. Always think before you act.[126] Is what you are about to do truly wise?

Take responsibility for your actions even if you've made a mistake.

HAVE YOU ACTED LIKE A FOOL?

I imagine all people have acted like a fool at times. Many people act foolishly sometimes, especially young adults who haven't had a great deal of real life experience yet. We're human, after all, even though we strive to be so much more. If you've messed up and acted like a fool before, don't worry about it. Just remember the next time that an issue in business or your personal life arises, stop and think about it before you speak or act. Is the issue something petty? Is it worth making a big deal about?

Are you missing the forest for the trees?

---

[126] Proverbs 13:16, (*New Living Translation*): Wise people think before they act; fools don't—and even brag about their foolishness.

LISTENING

Wise men and women are always learning, always listening for fresh insights.

Proverbs 18:15 (*The Message*)

Wise people listen carefully. And this holds true for your place of business or with friends. It holds true for business meetings, especially. The people in the drawing above are attending a seminar. Are they listening to the presenter? Or, are they daydreaming about what they're going to have for dinner or where they're going on their next vacation? Many students *look* like they're listening to their teacher in a classroom, but they're not. Many employees *look* like they're listening to their manager or business leader, but they're not. Often, the words being spoken fall on deaf ears. Listening is an art, after all, and not everyone knows how to do it properly.

Do not confuse hearing and listening. Hearing is a sense by which sound is *received*. Hearing focuses on a mechanical receiving of sound. Technically speaking, it involves proper functioning of parts of the ear like the eardrum, the auditory nerve, and the anvil. People get hearing aids in order to better receive the sounds around them.

Listening is much different than hearing. Listening has to do with the way sound is *perceived*, not received. While hearing is more mechanical, listening is more perceptual and goes well beyond the mechanical receipt of sound. Listening involves interpreting what is heard. Listening involves hearing, but also includes comprehension and *understanding* of what is heard.

People can talk *at you* all they want, but unless you are listening, it does no good. There is one thing I have learned for sure–that knowing how to listen is one of the most important skills you can have when *chasing wisdom in business and life*.

A wise business leader knows how to listen and actually *get* what others are saying. Epictetus, the Greek philosopher, wrote: "We have two ears and one mouth—for a good reason." It's more important to listen than it is to talk—most of the time.

We've briefly mentioned listening from time to time in previous chapters. This chapter goes into great detail about listening and helps to answer questions like: *Should I be concerned with how people listen to my messages in business? How can I improve my listening? How do I know if people are truly listening to me? How important is listening in business?*

We all can improve when it comes to listening. There's always another step to being a better listener. Enjoy the following story about my son Brian and the related discussion throughout the chapter to gain deeper insight about becoming wiser by learning how to "listen."

BRIAN'S ADVENTURE OF VALUE AND QUALITY FOR FRIENDS

It was the day of the grand opening of Brian's second Eden's Fresh Company location. Everyone in the company was excited about the prospects of the new store given that it was at the corner of Church Street and Orange Avenue, one of the busiest intersections in downtown Orlando. In addition, the new store was at ground level in the Seaside Bank Building, one of Orlando's elite high-rise signature office buildings.

On the day the new store was to start serving customers, the doors of the new restaurant were scheduled to open in about thirty minutes. A few customers were milling around outside, waiting for the store to open. The buzz had been building for a week or so and everyone was excited about it. Eden's Fresh Company had a good reputation.

Brian stood gazing out the window at the waiting customers with quiet satisfaction. He remembered all he had to do over the last six months to get the new restaurant to this point. He did most of the work himself to cut down on expenses, things like redesigning the serving line, painting the store, choosing and installing coolers, as well as interviewing, training, and hiring new staff. After all his work, the store was now completely different than the one for which he had signed a lease.

Finally, as the doors swung open, the customers began filing in. As guests ate, they filled out review forms. Comments were positive and included:

"Wow, this place is so clean and bright!"

"The food looks so fresh."

"The best salad in town…"

Although Brian was pleased overall with the customer reviews, he wasn't as pleased with how he saw his new team operate. Brian had spent much time and effort *informally* explaining to employees how they should view customers and react to them. He had *informally* gone over customer service guidelines, but there hadn't been a formal training session per se. Instead, Brian had talked to each employee individually, giving insights to each about how to handle themselves when the store opened.

Brian's philosophy about how an Eden's Fresh Company should operate is encapsulated in a simple maxim: *Value and Quality for Friends.*

Brian was satisfied on that first day with the value and quality of the food provided, but the friendliness, smiles, greetings, politeness, and general customer service were lacking. Perhaps his staff was somewhat nervous and improved friendliness would come. He hoped. On the other hand, perhaps his staff really didn't know what he meant by *friendliness*.

Brian was asking himself some questions: *Had he clearly asked his employees if they understood what he was trying to tell them concerning customer service and friendliness? Had he asked them if they had any questions or concerns before the new restaurant opened? Had he listened well enough? Had they listened well enough?*

INITIAL REFLECTIONS ON THE ADVENTURE OF VALUE AND QUALITY FOR FRIENDS

Brian didn't want to jump to any conclusions about why customer service didn't seem up to par. Instead, he decided to gather data by listening carefully to what his new employees had to say about their level of customer service provided for their restaurant guests. Brian knew that his new employees wanted to do a good job. He just needed to find out why they weren't excelling in customer service. His initial hunch was that there had been a communication breakdown when he gave the employees one-on-one instructions about how to best serve customers.

What he learned was that many of the employees didn't truly understand how to provide optimal customer service. A wise move on his part, he asked the employees for suggestions on how to improve customer service and wrote down what they said. Some said that they didn't know just how friendly they should be. Did it mean asking the customer about their day? Did it mean complimenting them on the way they dressed? What was the most important thing that they needed to do when it came to customers? Brian addressed each of their questions and then decided to go a step further.

He then developed a training program so the employees could role-play. Some took turns being the customer while others honed their skills in providing superior customer service. Through role-playing, the employees understood better what a customer needed. It's always beneficial to put yourself in the other person's shoes. That's one of the best ways to understand what that person is experiencing.

After conducting a few of these sessions, and then working with his staff during their shifts, Brian was very happy to see that the customer service in his restaurant was building to be top-notch and that it matched his superior quality food. If he had not listened to his employees and addressed their questions and concerns, he could never have solved the problem and that could have eventually ruined the restaurant.

As stated by Dr. Ralph Nichols, a pioneer in the field of listening, "The most basic of all human needs is the need to understand and be understood. The best way to understand people is to listen to them."

Brian listened to his employees before he took action to solve a problem. Through proper listening, he better understood employee needs and was better able to develop programs to help them. Listen before you act.

BECOME A POWERFUL LISTENER

A *powerful listener* is a listener who avoids distractions when listening to another. Being a powerful listener is critical for a leader because listening can be as potent in leading others as speaking. In addition, leaders lead through conversations and a leader cannot have a useful conversation with another without being a good listener. The Bible tells us that wise leaders are listeners. [127]

---

[127] Proverbs 12:15, (*New International Version*): The way of fools seems right to them, but the wise listen to advice.

What do powerful listeners do? Here are some examples:

- *They shut out everything else around them—all the distractions and peripheral activities—and listen.* Really listen. As prompted by the Bible, wise leaders focus on their employees and listen to them without distraction.[128] As a wise leader, implement a listen-before-you-act mentality. Make it a continual part of your business life. When was the last time when you acted before you listened?

- *They focus on listening to you.* Someone who is a great listener will focus on the conversation and be "present" instead of daydreaming or thinking about themselves. There's nothing more rewarding than to have someone really listen to your ideas and thoughts. Likewise, if you do this with someone—*really listen to him*—then he will feel rewarded and validated, too.

  I have learned that most people do not listen well. And in this day when everyone carries around an iPhone or iPad, people don't even pay attention to their friends when they're having lunch or supposedly visiting one another. Especially the teens and college students. Instead, they stay glued to their iPhones and iPads, with very little awareness of what's happening around them. Listening requires putting your own needs aside when trying to interpret what another says.

- *They know that the speaker has a strong need to be heard and understood.* The wise person will listen and validate those who are speaking and will make sure that the speaker knows that whatever information or advice is being given, it is being heard, understood, and greatly appreciated.

---

[128] 1 Corinthians 7:32-35, (*The Message*): ...All I want is for you to be able to develop a way of life in which you can spend plenty of time together with the Master without a lot of distractions.

If you are asked to listen and do not have time to do so, then it's better to acknowledge this and ask, "Can we talk about this later? I really want to discuss this with you, but I have a prior commitment." The person who wants to talk will appreciate your honesty and understand.

Many people who have low self-esteem can often be the loudest in a crowd. They want to make sure their opinions are heard. It's their way of saying: "Hey, look at me! I'm important! Can't you see that?"

It would be difficult if no one ever responded when you spoke to them. You might start to feel invisible and that no one cares. It's important to have a voice that is heard by people both inside and outside the organization in which we work. When we have a voice and receive feedback, we begin to understand ourselves better.

LISTEN FOR MESSAGES

Powerful listeners listen for messages in what people say to them. Larry Allan Nadig, Ph.D., a clinical psychologist, marriage and family therapist, states that there is a real distinction between merely *hearing the words* and really *listening for the message*. If we are truly listening to someone else, then we can better absorb and understand what that person is trying to communicate. When we're not listening, we'll miss the entire message.

If we truly listen, then it's like we're putting ourselves in the other person's shoes. We look at the world from their viewpoint and we hear with their ears. No two people have the same viewpoint. And no two people always agree with each other. But, that doesn't mean you can't listen and try to understand the other person's perspective.

Generally, we'll learn something from the conversation. This requires being actively involved in the conversation and not just passively listening without interaction.

WISE LEADERS LISTEN TO THEMSELVES

Along with knowing how to listen to others, we must also listen to ourselves. As we chase wisdom, we accumulate more and more Biblical insights about how to deal with difficult situations. We become wiser as we accumulate these insights and need to listen to our hearts about how to handle challenging problems. In effect, we develop wise instincts about what to do. We need to trust our wise instincts that we develop. Listen to our hearts and trust them in telling us what's best to do.

Listening to our own hearts might not be as easy as it sounds. We're all operating from years of programming from TV, radio, our parents and friends. This programming often runs interference with what our hearts are trying to tell us. For example, a young man might take a job based on the fact that his parents think it is the right one for him.

In reality, he might like another job better, but he doesn't stop long enough to listen to what his heart says and, in a sense, makes a decision without listening to himself. And he makes one of the biggest mistakes of his life because he rushes into a job that someone else thought was best for him.

DAVID: A LESSON IN LISTENING
TO YOURSELF

The following is a true story, but the names have been changed to protect everyone's identity. David was the only son who grew up in an average home on a farm with three sisters. His father was excited about teaching David the family business—a real estate company that had excelled. In fact, it was one of the leading real estate companies in the state. But David was a musician and wanted to pursue music. While in high school, David often tried to talk to his father about his passion, his goals in music. But his father never *heard* him.

"Dad," David said one afternoon at the dinner table, "I think I'm going to go to this great music school in Boston and get a degree in music."

"Uh-huh," his dad said while cutting a piece of rib-eye with his knife.

"That's nice, honey," his mother piped in. "You'll have to tell us more about it." She, too, glossed over what David was saying. She was so used to her husband making the family's decisions that she didn't worry about much other than what to cook for dinner each night. She supported whatever her husband wanted.

The sisters looked at David and empathized with him. They knew their father wasn't really listening and that David would never get to go to music school as long as their father was paying the bills.

"It's a good program," David said. "And I might be able to get a scholarship."

"Uh-huh," the father said. "Hey, did you hear about Corey Smith's son, Derek? He just got accepted into Harvard's Business School."

"Yeah, I heard about that," David said, shoulders slumping. David knew that his father wanted him to go to Harvard, and then the Wharton School of Business for an MBA before taking over as the president of his real estate company. It was all he had ever talked about. Whenever David invited his father to a concert or a night playing music in a coffee shop, his father had always been too busy.

That night, David knew it was a lost cause. He finished his dinner while the family talked about Derek's admission into Harvard.

David ended up going to a local college and getting a degree in business. When he graduated, his father immediately made a place for him in the real estate business. David accepted the job, but turned to alcohol as a way to numb his pain, and ended up in rehab. It was only a couple years later that he was able to stand up to his father, quit the real estate business, and go back to his one true love: music. He is now a successful musician with several CDs and on the road to becoming a major superstar.

The fact that David's father never listened to him almost cost him his one true passion: music. However, because David had an inner strength that burned like fire, he was able to go through rehab, find the inner discipline he needed to stand up to his father and proceed with the life he was meant to live. He forced his father to listen.

Likewise, his father learned a good lesson. He never tried to instill his own dreams onto his daughters and let them choose the colleges of their choice.

So, while practicing the art of listening to others, also practice the art of listening to your heart. It only requires a few moments each day of honest reflection, and may save you wasted years, time and resources.

BARRIERS TO POWERFUL LISTENING
RELATED TO THE SPEAKER

Here's the situation. You're in a conversation with someone and trying to be a powerful listener. But in reality, there may be many factors related to the *speaker* that might make it difficult for you to be a powerful *listener*. Here are a few of these and hints on how to overcome them:

1. *The speaker may be speaking too softly.* Obviously, you cannot be a powerful listener if the person that you are trying to listen to is speaking too softly. Has this ever happened to you? You might move closer, but still have trouble hearing. Don't be afraid to simply ask the speaker to speak up a bit. Also, try eliminating competing noises like turning off background music.

2. *The speaker's message might be too complex.* Sometimes, messages that you're trying to listen to might be too complex or too detailed to understand. If you don't understand a message, you can't have a conversation about it. Don't fake understanding. The speaker will soon find out if you're faking. Don't be too embarrassed to ask for clarification so you can understand what the speaker is saying.

3. *The speaker might use vocabulary that is "above your head."* If you find yourself in this situation, ask for clarification. Think of it this way. If you go to see a physician and he explains a disease or sickness in medical terms, you might not understand what he's saying. You ask questions, right? In the same way, if someone is using vocabulary "above your head," ask that person to explain his statement in simpler terms. There's nothing wrong with admitting you don't understand something. Such clarification will ensure your role as a powerful listener.

4. *The speaker's body language may contradict the meaning of the words being spoken.* For example, one of the people that you lead may tell you how excited she is about her job. However, when she tells you this, her face shows no excitement and her voice is very mellow. Brian had to be alert to this when he trained his staff on customer service. Some of the employees weren't really interested, and he could easily determine which ones were and which ones weren't, depending on body language. Slouched shoulders, yawns, rolling of the eyes, etc. are all indicators that the person you're talking to isn't really listening.

   In order to be a powerful listener, you need to delve further into how the employee actually feels. Only through such exploration will you get the true meaning of contradictory messages.

LINDA: A LESSON IN POWERFUL LISTENING

A true story about a young lady named Linda who was an herbal expert in her state offers a lesson in powerful listening. She was hired to travel throughout the state one summer and present programs on wild herbs in the area. Linda was confident and dynamic. She created a PowerPoint program as well as a video for her presentations and set off across the state to conduct workshops and seminars. Her knowledge was outstanding and she could answer any questions regarding any kind of herbal plant there was in North America.

However, she had a problem with listening. After her programs, attendees would often come to her and ask her about various plants. And at times, they offered information to Linda about plants that she wasn't aware of. But, Linda didn't pay much attention to those who offered *new* information. Instead of listening to what people asked or said, she lectured them on what she thought they should know. This resulted in many dissatisfied participants because they couldn't get their questions answered.

After several programs, the program director told Linda he had received many complaints about her because she didn't listen to the audience's questions and/or disregarded information the audience had about herbs. For as far as Linda was concerned, she knew it all. She was the expert.

So, Linda had to change her attitude and accept the fact that maybe she didn't "know it all" and could use the insights of some of her attendees. And, she had to stop and really listen to the people who attended her seminars. After some practice—it took several months—she began to get positive feedback from the attendees because she stopped and listened.

Listening, in case you didn't know, is a powerful thing.

ACTIVE LISTENING: IMPROVE YOUR SKILLS AS A POWERFUL LISTENER

Wise leaders are always trying to become more powerful listeners and there are certainly several sound techniques available to do so. One fundamental and widely accepted technique is called *Active Listening*. Carl R. Rogers, one of the most historically well-known American psychologists, developed this technique. *Active Listening* is especially useful for listening in emotionally charged situations, and basically, it recommends that a leader take on an active role rather than a passive role when listening.

As a leader, you should practice *Active Listening*, which means you will:

Clarify: The *Active Listener* graciously asks the speaker to clearly define the problem or issue at hand and, if necessary, to elaborate upon the definition or answer specific questions related to it.[129] Only by establishing clarity about an issue or problem can one be a powerful listener in a conversation. And only then can one effectively answer the question. That's what my son, Brian, did at Eden's Fresh Company. He listened to what his employees needed, and in turn, created a training program that addressed their problems. And that's what Linda did when she listened to her attendees at her herbal programs. It took her a while, but she finally learned how to listen and respond appropriately.

Paraphrase: Here, the *Active Listener* repeats the speaker's message to affirm that the message sent was accurately heard or received. An example would be: "So, what you're saying is that you'd like a performance review and possible raise? Am I understanding this correctly?" The listener is communicating what he or she heard and the speaker has the opportunity to correct the message if not heard properly.

---

[129] Colossians 4:6, (*New International Version*): Let your conversation be always full of grace, seasoned with salt, so that you may know how to answer everyone.

Reflect feelings: The *Active Listener* inquires about, or acknowledges, overt or underlying feelings that seem to be reflected or projected within a message. The *Active Listener* might say, "You mentioned that you agree with what I just outlined, but I have a feeling you're still a bit frustrated and concerned. Would you like to talk about it?"

If you pay attention to people's nonverbal actions like rolling their eyes or shrugging their shoulders, you can more easily detect their feelings. Often, a person won't look you in the eye if they disagree with you. This is a cue that they're not really agreeing with what you're saying. If you watch the person, you will be able to more accurately ascertain his or her feelings.

Summarize: At the end of a conversation, an *Active Listener* will often summarize what has been said just to make sure that both parties are communicating accurately. In addition, these summaries will help identify agreements, differences, timeframes for accomplishing goals, and outline specifics about follow-up activities.

EFFECTIVE LISTENING

Effective listening is *getting* what someone tells you. It is accurately absorbing information projected to you by the speaker. Becoming an *Active Listener* will enhance your effectiveness as a listener. Effective listening is a tool for becoming wiser in business, not just a technical skill.

Remember that effective listening is also a vehicle for learning about team members, becoming a better leader and, ultimately, making sure that you are accurately communicating your thoughts and ideas. Brian was able to learn more about his team members when he started effectively listening to them about what they needed from him regarding customer service at Eden's Fresh Company.

Linda learned that she had to become an effective listener if she wanted to continue doing herbal programs for her state. Brian learned that he had to become an effective listener if he wanted to learn why his employees weren't providing optimal customer service at his restaurant. Both of these people benefitted from learning how to become more effective listeners. And you can, too.

A wise leader is an *effective listener*. To enhance their effectiveness as listeners, wise leaders build a climate within which a speaker will give you honest information. Here are three of my personal tips for creating such a climate:

1. *Empathize with the Speaker*. Demonstrate that you have an understanding of people's positions and predicaments, pains and passions. In other words, I try to put myself in their shoes. This always helps. When people genuinely feel that you understand them, they are more open to communicating with you and help you as a listener to understand them.

2. *Minimize Status Differences*. To help you become an effective listener, it is useful to minimize any obvious status or hierarchy differentials between yourself and those with whom you are communicating. I can't think of a situation in which flaunting that you're "the boss" will encourage people to communicate honestly and openly. Listening to others under such circumstances will not help a listening manager to gather the best data. Linda had to stop acting like a know-it-all and as if she were superior to everyone else at her herbal seminars.

3. *Do not make it Risky for Employees to Discuss Mistakes*. When listening leaders are trying to find out why customer orders are not being filled on time, for example, employees have to feel secure that the leaders will solve any related problems without penalizing them. Without this trust, this security, employees may not be quite as open or honest about discussing mistakes for fear of punishment.

REFLECTIONS ON LISTENING

Have you ever wondered what would happen if you stopped and really listened to what someone was saying? I mentioned this earlier when I discussed how rewarding it was when someone stopped what they were doing and focused *on you* when you talked to them. And, how that person also felt validated and rewarded when you focused *on him or her*. When you *listen*, there's nothing like the feeling of being *heard*.

Whenever you talk to someone and know that they're truly listening and understanding what you're saying, there is a bonding and understanding between you. As you understand the words, you also understand the feelings. This is true communication and it's important because your overall effectiveness in life and in business as a leader and member of the human race depends on your ability to deal well with people in your communication skills.

This discipline of listening will increase your ability to make an impact on other people, and in turn, help you *chase wisdom in business*.

MATTHEW LISTENS AT WEBSOLVERS

One of my experiences with my son, Matthew, represents a good example of powerful listening. After a few years in business, Matthew moved his company, Websolvers, from a 100-square-foot space on the second floor of an office building in Winter Park, Florida, to a space of about 1,800 square feet on the first floor of the same building.

Given that Matthew had not undergone such a change previously, we had extensive conversations over several weeks about how such a change should be made. Based upon these conversations, Matthew decided to try to make the change in such a way that would help build his employees into a better team while at the same time creating a more positive company culture.

All employees had the opportunity to share their opinions about issues like what color the office walls should be, the type of furniture that should be purchased, and the way the space would be filled in order to promote efficiency.

Through listening to employees, Matthew finally implemented workspace features that were not what he had initially envisioned. But the entire process ended up creating a workspace that promoted efficiency and effectiveness. In some instances, employee input helped to create a workspace that was even better than what Matthew had originally envisioned. Perhaps best of all, the process brought him closer to his employees and employees became committed along the way to making the workspace design successful because Matthew—their boss and leader— *truly listened.*

This is an example of the way listening can empower everyone and shows that wise leaders who listen to employees can make changes more successful.

LISTEN WITH FULL ATTENTION

A man once said of Sigmund Freud, "He struck me so forcibly that I shall never forget him. His eyes were mild and genial. His voice was low and kind. His gestures were few. But the attention he gave me, his appreciation of what I said, even when I said it badly, was extraordinary. *You've no idea what it meant to be listened to like that.*"

This story about Freud, from Dale Carnegie's *How to Win Friends and Influence People*, shows how powerful it is to listen and give someone your full attention. In the Bible, Job makes this same point by telling God how honored he was by people in his town because when he spoke they listened and hung on his every word.[130] You never know what kind of influence you have upon another person.

Whether you're speaking at a seminar or training your employees and getting feedback from the audience or a person in the audience, always focus your attention on the speaker. Focusing attention in this manner is an important part of the listening process. It's the beginning of the listening process and as important as putting a good coat of primer on a piece of wood before you paint it. Remember that focusing attention in this fashion is not listening, but the beginning of listening. To be a first-class listener and wise business leader, you will always encourage the speaker. You will provide affirmations to the speaker by nodding and eye contact and general body language, showing appreciation and respect for what is being said. Some people think if they're quiet while listening that they're not engaging in the conversation or participating. But, that's not true. You'll actually be an *Active Listener*, which we discussed earlier. Your focus on the speaker, your body language, and your eye contact will all communicate to the speaker that you're listening and understanding. You are taking the time to focus and *hear* with your whole being. Carefully consider how you implement all aspects of listening – from asking clarification questions to having positive body language.[131]

Giving the speaker this undivided attention is priceless. You are taking care to listen not just for the sake of the speaker, but for the sake of others to whom you may have to pass on the meaning of the message.

---

[130] Job 29:6-20, (*The Message*): …When I walked downtown and sat with my friends in the public square, young and old greeted me with respect; I was honored by everyone in town. When I spoke, everyone listened; they hung on my every word…

[131] Luke 8:18, (*New International Version*): Therefore consider carefully how you listen. Whoever has will be given more; whoever does not have, even what they think they have will be taken from them.

YOU AND YOUR CHASE

You've read about Brian's listening activities in his *Adventure of Quality and Service for Friends*. You've read about Linda's listening weaknesses related to presenting programs on herbal plants at statewide parks. You've also read Matthew's story about the role of listening in planning an office move at Websolvers. You've studied many different comments about listening related to each of these stories.

As a result, you've learned many fundamental principles of powerful listening. You've learned that wise leaders become *Active Listeners* and focus on developing their listening abilities. Here, listening involves not only hearing messages, but gaining a complete understanding of them. Wise leaders know of the high importance of listening and try to balance the time that they spend listening and speaking. It's not unusual for wise leaders to strive to listen *more* than they speak.

Wise leaders emphasize not only listening, but *powerful* listening—focusing on what another is saying without being distracted. To be a powerful listener, you must take steps like shutting out all distractions to a conversation, intensely focus on listening, make the speaker feel heard and understood, and listen for a *message,* not simply the words. Don't forget, however, that in order to listen well, you may have to deal with issues like a soft-spoken speaker, complex messages, advanced vocabulary, and even contradictory body language. To help overcome such barriers, be an *Active Listener.* Clarifying, paraphrasing, defining feelings, and summarizing what you hear will help you to be a powerful listener.

Empathizing with the speaker, minimizing status and socioeconomic differences between you and the speaker, and minimizing the risk that the speaker feels in talking to you will all help to overcome such issues, as well. And don't forget to listen with full attention to help you deal with such difficult listening issues. And also don't forget that as a wise leader, you must listen to yourself. Trust and guard your accumulated wisdom.

In addition to all of these insights about how to be a better, more powerful listener, the following practical steps should help as well:

1. *Document your values related to being a powerful listener.* Focus on keeping yourself motivated to be an outstanding listener. Forcing yourself to describe the high value of listening to yourself will help to keep you motivated. Refer back to what you've written from time to time in order to maintain your motivation to listen.

2. *Write a plan for increasing your skill as a powerful listener.* Develop a plan for making yourself a better listener. Such a plan will help to ensure that your efforts to become a better listener will indeed be successful.[132] Be proactive in asking for advice in developing and carrying out your plan. The advice of others can be invaluable in forming and carrying out your "better listening" plan. The Bible tells us that this advice could be the key to making your plan a success and in making you a wiser, more respected leader. [133]

3. *Listen to learn.* The wise add to their learning by listening.[134] If you truly listen to someone, you will learn something. So, don't waste the time you spend listening. The more carefully you listen, the more you'll understand the meaning of what's being said, and the more you will

---

[132] Proverbs 21:5, (*New International Version*): The plans of the diligent lead to profit as surely as haste leads to poverty.

[133] Proverbs 11:14, (*New International Version*): For lack of guidance a nation falls, but victory is won through many advisers.

[134] Proverbs 1:5, *(New International Version):* let the wise listen and add to their learning, and let the discerning get guidance—

learn. As the verse from the Bible at the beginning of the chapter indicates, wise men and women are always learning, always listening for fresh insights.

4. *Slow down. Let there be silence in the conversation.* You don't have to fill every second with chitter-chatter. People who move at a fast pace often try to hurry a conversation along, so they can move on. Or, they become uncomfortable with pauses. Sometimes, a pause or moment of silence can help you gather your thoughts and reflections on what's being said. This was one of Linda's faults; she didn't like slowing down long enough to glean the information that the speaker was trying to provide.

5. *Listen with respect.* Stay in the moment and focus on your conversation with someone. Treat each conversation as an opportunity to respect and value the other person. This gives the other person validation that he or she is important to you. If you don't respect others, then you won't *listen* very well. People who *judge* others don't listen to them. They disregard their opinions.

6. *Listen for intent.* Words alone may not fully convey a person's true message. There could be a hidden message in what someone is telling you. Observe what speakers say, how they say it, their body language, and emotion behind their words.

Remember that learning the *true art of listening* is perhaps the most valuable tool that you can acquire in order to become wiser and as you *chase wisdom in business.*

As I conclude this chapter, let me remind you to focus and listen in the *moment.* As Dan Millman, the author of *The Four Purposes of Life: Finding Meaning and Direction in a Changing World,* said, "*This moment deserves your full attention, for it will not pass your way again.*"

THE HEART

Guard your heart above all else, for it determines the course of your life.

Proverbs 4:23 (*New Living Translation*)

The purpose of this chapter is to help you to become wiser by embellishing your understanding of *heart*. In this chapter, you will learn what heart is, how to build it, and how to recognize it. As you can see in the chapter opening verse, understanding heart is critical because it determines everything that happens to you in life.

This chapter will help you to understand how the heart affects business and life. Through studying the Bible, God's Word, you will gain deeper insights about how to consider heart issues in business and life situations and whether it's important or not. *Can you define heart? Do you know the importance of heart in your business life? Can organizations have heart? Can you see the heart of a business?*

Hopefully, by the end of this chapter, you will be able to answer these and other heart-related questions and to gain insights about how to consider heart issues in business situations. And hopefully, you'll be able to become wiser in business by gaining deeper insights about heart. For now, gain greater insights by thinking about Brian's *Adventure of the Right Heart* that follows, as well as how concepts throughout the chapter relate to it.

ADVENTURE OF THE RIGHT HEART

Brian had just hired a new employee, Sally, for his Winter Park Eden's location, and was very excited about the quality of the person he had been able to recruit. This woman was 23 years old, had four years of experience in working in other privately-owned restaurants around town, a degree in business from a local community college, and personal and business references from a number of prominent local business and community leaders.

Brian was excited about hiring Sally and designed a special job just for her, similar to that of an assistant manager. She would work with suppliers to order salad ingredients, as well as service customers by mixing salads as customers ordered them.

As time went by, Brian began to get unsolicited feedback about this new hire, Sally, from what seemed like almost everybody: customers, employees, and suppliers. From the tone of the feedback, Sally was not quite as good as he had anticipated. She was harsh with the employees and reprimanded them for almost anything that she thought was out of line. Things like not leaning on the counter, not wiping down a counter every five minutes—that kind of thing. She even reprimanded employees in front of customers.

Customers became upset because she was short with them and never seemed to be in a good mood. Even suppliers complained to Brian about the harshness and lack of cooperation she demonstrated toward them.

Brian was confused and befuddled by this feedback. Everyone seemed to be dissatisfied with Sally. He found it hard to believe that he had made a mistake in hiring her, given her outstanding education and work credentials. Everything "on paper" was exceptional.

As we spoke about the situation, Brian searched for ways to improve Sally's behavior. Maybe she needed some training in customer relations? Maybe she needed some advice and guidance from him regarding employee relations and teamwork, or in building organizational community?

INITIAL REFLECTIONS ON THE RIGHT HEART

Eden's, like any other business, will stop dead in its tracks if its people, its employees, don't show the right heart in everyday business. In general terms, people with the *right heart* treat others respectfully and with dignity. They treat others in a fashion that is consistent with Biblical principles, morals, and ethics. They do this without thinking—almost reflexively—because of their own personal beliefs and values that they possess.

Living one's life and practicing business the *heart way* is not easy to define because the heart is an intangible quality of one's being. It is the deep essence by which one exists. Some people have the right heart and others don't. Some businesses have the right heart and others don't. But one thing is for sure: if a business owner does not have the right heart, then most likely, his or her business will not either. If the business owner does have the right heart, then it is most assuredly reflected in the business.

People will always be the primary engine that makes businesses work. Maintaining the right people with right hearts is critical for building positive interpersonal relationships and teams that make organizations run successfully.

It's a very serious matter if a staff member like Brian's new employee is consistently causing disruptions among other employees, customers, and other stakeholders. If an employee like Sally is belittling and causing undue stress on other employees and customers, then there's a major problem and the business owner needs to identify it and resolve it quickly before it's too late.

Sally is certainly not treating others with respect and dignity—with the right heart. Quite the opposite. In this situation, she may be called *wrong-hearted*. Someone who is mostly inclined to treat others with disrespect. This is inconsistent with Biblical principles. If allowed to continue, such behavior would become a major barrier to Eden's success.

If you are in a position like Brian was, you cannot base your opinion of Sally simply on hearsay. That wouldn't be fair to her. Instead, you would need to monitor Sally to assess the situation and determine your own opinion of her behavior. Perhaps you could also set up a meeting and talk to her about her performance and the way she interacts with people. From there, perhaps you could advise her on the appropriateness or inappropriateness of her actions and on ways to improve.

On the other hand, not all people are necessarily good fits for working in a company and in Brian's company, Eden's Fresh Company. Perhaps Sally just didn't have a *right heart*, a prerequisite for working at Eden's. Maybe her values regarding people and how to handle them were inappropriate given company values. Maybe her beliefs about how to react to others simply didn't fit the corporate culture at Eden's because Eden's Fresh Company is a company with heart.

If this is the case, sometimes it makes more sense to hire a different employee, rather than to try to change a heart. Why? It's possible that an employee can change his or her own heart, and you can help in that process, but it may take a very long time and, from a business viewpoint, may not be worth the time and effort. It's very difficult for people to significantly change their hearts. The core of their beings. The essence of who they are.

A person with the right heart always strives to remember who he or she is in relation to God, and that he or she has a spiritual purpose in life. Such people will always try to keep their hearts on the right path.[135]

---

[135] Proverbs 23 :19, (*New International Version*): Listen, my son, and be wise, and keep your heart on the right path.

Brian thought long and hard about the situation and what to do when a person's heart seemed to be in direct conflict with Eden's needs. Perhaps more importantly, Brian used this situation as a catalyst to think about his own heart and how to build it in a way that made sense for him and his company.

WHAT IS HEART?

At this point, you're probably wondering just exactly what heart is since it is clearly an intangible thing. In trying to think about what heart means in the context of this chapter, eliminate any scientific notion that it means the organ in your body that pumps blood.

As already explained, the heart is hard to define and grasp because it's intangible. Read, reread, and carefully study this section on defining heart. Go within and examine your own heart. It may be as difficult for you to understand as it will be valuable for you to know.

Heart is your inner self, the spirit of who you are. Heart appears in the Bible more than one thousand times and is used to refer to a person's intangible nature. Heart is discussed in the Bible as the center of spiritual activity as well as all operations of human life. Heart is the home of all personal thought and activity. Emotions such as joy, love, and desire are emotions said to emanate from a good, cheerful heart.[136]

In essence, heart is at the very core of a person and influences all that a person does and how he or she does it. Even something as simple as the smile on one's face can be determined by one's heart. In fact, that smile *reflects* one's heart. The smile is the mirror of the heart. In the same way, if someone is angry, then that look of anger will reflect what's in the heart. Make sure that what's in

---

[136] Proverbs 17:22, (*New International Version*): A cheerful heart is good medicine, but a crushed spirit dries up the bones.

your heart is love toward your fellow man, your workplace and your life.[137]

The Bible teaches that one can be right-hearted or wrong-hearted depending upon what comprises one's heart.[138] You are right-hearted if your heart is comprised of thoughts and beliefs that are consistent with Biblical thought. You are wrong-hearted if your heart is comprised of thoughts and beliefs that are contrary to, or inconsistent with, Biblical principles.

You can tell the type of heart one has by watching what he or she does. A heart spawns behavior that reflects what a person values or treasures.[139]

A *right* heart treasures Biblical principles and spawns behavior consistent with carrying them out. A *wrong* heart values worldly possessions and spawns behavior aimed at attaining them—sometimes at almost any cost. Wise leaders are right hearted and focus on reflecting Biblical principles in all that they do.

Is it important for leaders to understand their own hearts? Well, of course. Business is business, but without heart, it is just a rather flat, cold environment that does not encourage growth and productivity.

I regularly walk on my treadmill while listening to teaching tapes of Pastor David Uth of the First Baptist Church of Orlando. One morning while walking and listening, I heard Pastor Uth say that our hearts are critically important to all of us. According to Pastor Uth, our hearts determine what we do, and how well we

---

[137] Proverbs 3:3, (*New International Version*): Let love and faithfulness never leave you; bind them around your neck, write them on the tablet of your heart.

[138] Matthew 19:8, (*New International Version*): Jesus replied, "Moses permitted you to divorce your wives because your hearts were hard. But it was not this way from the beginning."

[139] Matthew 6:21, (*New International Version*): For where your treasure is, there your heart will be also.

do it. Not only that, our hearts determine our destinies. To me, that sounds like heart is pretty important. *Do you agree?*

You have probably heard people say: "Oh, she has a good heart." Or, "He may have done something that was bad, but he really has a good heart." If you stop and think about this, people innately recognize others who have good or bad hearts. But when it comes to business, the heart is often put on the back burner and not used when it comes to business decisions.

A CEO LISTENS TO HIS HEART

One executive I know is the CEO of a small hospital in Kentucky. Years ago, when his two sons were in kindergarten, he was given the opportunity to move to New York and serve as president of a major medical group. He would be given a new home, car, and a salary that was close to a million dollars with bonuses and benefits.

As the CEO at the small hospital, he already earned six figures, but the promise of the million dollars, the new home, and car was very tempting. However, this CEO knew that his children were receiving one of the best gifts he could give them. They were growing up with both sets of grandparents, numerous cousins and aunts and uncles, and would be receiving a good education in a smaller environment that had less students than a school in a large city. He also knew that if he took his children to New York, his parents as well as his wife's parents would never have the opportunity to get to know their grandchildren and the grandchildren would never know their grandparents.

So, while his *head* told him to take the new job in New York, his heart told him that he would not be as happy and that his children would not be as happy. Ultimately, he decided to stay in Kentucky and to this day, he has said that it was one of the best decisions he ever made. He listened to his heart and made the decision that made everyone happier. It was, ultimately, a decision of love. Such decisions are sometimes hard to make. Listening to and trusting God's Word will help all of us to make such difficult decisions correctly.[140]

Heart may be important to you as a leader in business, but is it a practical concept? You may be thinking that the idea and definition of heart seem too broad and vague to be of any practical use. If that's the case, you're probably *overthinking* it. Reflecting back on the Adventure of the *Right Heart* and the story about the CEO at the small hospital, can help you understand the heart in all avenues of life.

Brian was faced with a new employee who was harsh and uncooperative with workers, suppliers, and customers. This new employee didn't have a good heart. Even though she looked great on paper, had excelled in school, she was lacking in her people skills and in her *heart-thinking* abilities. Her heart—her inner being—was the springboard for how she acted. How she thought about people, her values regarding people, and her conscience shaped her behavior in a way that was inappropriate for the culture at Eden's.

Brian said to me, "What do I do with a wrong-hearted employee? With someone who treats people so badly?" He knew that he might be able to help Sally have a *change of heart*, but maybe not.

Perhaps you've had the same kind of problem in your business or in life. Most people have encountered this problem because that's just the way life is. There are good-hearted and wrong-hearted people everywhere.

The rest of this chapter contains thoughts and ideas that Brian and other leaders like you might be able to use to meet heart-related challenges in business and ultimately, in life.

---

[140] Proverbs 3:5-6, (*New International Version*): 5 Trust in the LORD with all your heart and lean not on your own understanding; 6 in all your ways submit to Him, and He will make your paths straight.

SPECS FOR A RIGHT HEART

Technically speaking, specifications or *specs* are meticulous explanations of the design and resources needed to make things. Specs are outlined to ensure that items are produced properly, ensuring desired performance levels. There are specs for electric systems to make sure that houses are safe. Specs for iPhones are used to ensure required functionality. There are even specs for bolts to make sure that they have necessary strength when used. This section discusses specs for a right heart, components that will ensure that your heart is *right* and functioning in a way that is consistent with God's Word.

As you might suspect, it's not easy to determine specs for a right heart. It's difficult because what makes up a right heart is essentially intangible. It's impossible to see the actual components of a right heart and their relative associations.

There are some clues about what constitutes a right heart for people in business, though. One set of clues comes from the experience of simply studying the actions of successful leaders and then inferring what characteristics of heart result in those behaviors. Remember to watch how successful leaders act, determine what characteristics of heart might lead to those behaviors, and then try to include those characteristics in your own behavior of the heart.

Over the years, I've observed successful leaders respond quickly and passionately to helping employees meet personal, unforeseen problems like dealing with a death in the family or illness of a child. As such personal circumstances arise needing employee attention, successful leaders tend to go out of their way to help employees deal with such issues—even if it requires that employees be away from their jobs for a time. To me, this behavior suggests that a right heart is characterized by that leader's respect for his or her employees as people. It is revealed by treating the employees with decency and dignity while they're trying to handle their personal issues. And this is vital in *chasing wisdom in business and life*.

One young man named Tyler worked at an accounting firm. It always gets super busy during tax time. In late March one year, his father was killed in an auto accident in another state near Tyler's family home. Tyler was devastated and heartbroken, and asked for a week off from work so he could be with his family and go to the funeral. His boss told him that he could have one day off for the funeral, but that they were simply too busy during tax season for him to take any additional days. This manager was not operating from a good heart. Rather, he was operating from greed and control. He simply couldn't understand why Tyler needed more than one day to go home and go to the funeral. Tyler, who had always been a punctual, hardworking employee, ended up resigning from his accounting job because the stress and heartbreak of his father's car accident was too much to bear.

Other clues about what constitutes a right heart are clearer and more explicit in God's Word in the form of Biblical thought. For study and contemplation, God's Word is your best source of insights about what a right heart looks like. If you gain strength in God's Word, then you will have the right heart and strength of heart.[141] Seemingly endless insights are nested within the Bible about what constitutes a right heart.

Combining knowledge of Biblical principles regarding heart, along with personal study and experiences of successful leaders and people in general, I've prepared a useful, but certainly not complete, list of important components of a right heart. Think of a right heart as containing:

A Faith Built Upon God's Word. Think of *faith* as a belief, trust in, and loyalty to God. Faith comes from hearing God's Word. [142]

---

[141] Psalm 73:26, (*New International Version*): My flesh and my heart may fail, but God is the strength of my heart and my portion forever.

[142] Romans 10:17, (*New International Version*): Consequently, faith comes from hearing the message, and the message is heard through the Word about Christ.

Faith reflects an admiration and respect for God's Word. With such admiration and respect as a foundation characteristic of a heart, the behavior that flows from that heart will follow Biblical principles naturally. Build your heart to be "right" by building your faith and acting accordingly, using Biblical principles. Following such principles is a fundamental mark of wisdom.

A True Appreciation of Recognition.[143] Wise leaders do not boast of their accomplishments because such behavior offends others, and most of all, because such recognition truly belongs to God for the gifts that He has bestowed. The right heart knows where recognition rightfully belongs.

Generally, leaders who are successful in business receive various awards throughout their careers. Awards like: *The Highest Annual Sales in a Territory, Manager of the Most Productive Department for the Quarter*, and *Most Socially Responsible Community Project* are commonplace. Wise leaders and business owners make sure that their employees receive the recognition that they deserve in their company.

Remember that such awards carry with them a bit of fame for the recipients—either inside or outside the organization, or both. Such successful leaders accrue a bit of celebrity. If not careful, this fame can result in successful business leaders becoming arrogant and unrealistic about how and why they've achieved their success. Such conceit does not allow credit to be given to where it most rightly and most fundamentally belongs—*to God*—for bestowing talents and other gifts upon us that enable success.

If business leaders grow more and more arrogant over time as they receive more and more recognition, then they will become intolerable to others and such leaders will eventually bring more harm than good to a business.

---

[143] Proverbs 27:2, (*New International Version*): Let someone else praise you, and not your own mouth; an outsider, and not your own lips.

Humility.[144] Think of *humility* as a conservative view of one's own value. If you are humble, you are not arrogant. In humility, you are not vain, conceited, or focused on self-ambition. The humble do not see themselves as being better than others. They are not judgmental. As a result, the humble are able to respect God's Word to the fullest.

On the other hand, if you are without humility, you see yourself as being so important that God's Word is inconsequential to your success. Without veneration for God's Word, it's impossible for anyone to have a right heart.

Forgiveness. A right heart is forgiving. *Forgiving* means pardoning others for offenses that they commit. A *forgiving heart* is one that is willing to reflect on wrongdoing and forgive it. The wise forgive others for wrongdoings in order to follow God's lead and to gain God's forgiveness for themselves.[145]

Forgiveness is based upon the principle that one must often hold back anger at an offense in order to forgive it. The Bible teaches that it is our duty to forgive others for offenses that they commit. It's honorable. On the other hand, those who do not forgive dishonor themselves.

As a business leader, you certainly will have people who offend you. The offenses can be varied and involve many different facets of your business life and maybe even your personal life. As an example of such an offense, perhaps someone is gossiping about your business travel with a co-worker of the opposite sex. Or, perhaps someone has lied about an action that you have taken.

---

[144] Philippians 2:3, (*New International Version*): Do nothing out of selfish ambition or vain conceit, but in humility consider others better than yourselves.

[145] Matthew 6:14-15, (*New International Version*): 14 For if you forgive other people when they sin against you, your heavenly Father will also forgive you. 15 But if you do not forgive others their sins, your Father will not forgive your sins.

As another, someone might be openly disrespecting you in front of other organization members.

Give serious and careful thought to your forgiveness as a business leader. Biblical principles require that you forgive others for offenses. These offenses, although occurring in a business environment, are typically personal offenses against you. You are required such forgiveness, but must still be diligent about the wellbeing of your business.

For example, suppose that someone has been openly and disrespectfully confronting you and your ideas in front of others during business meetings. The confrontation is getting to the point that you're finding it difficult to maintain the respect of others at meetings. It's your responsibility to forgive this misconduct against you, but you must do whatever is necessary to have the transgressor understand the problem and to stop disrespectfully confronting you for the wellbeing of the company.

You do not hold any personal animosity for the transgressor. You are just trying to solve a problem. If the transgressor continues to confront you in meetings, you may need to terminate the person because of the negative impact that his or her behavior is having on others at the meetings. The termination is the result of the transgressor not changing behavior, not a result of your lack of forgiveness. Here, the right-hearted business leader forgave the transgressor, but eventually had to fire the transgressor anyway.

Think back to Brian's *Adventure of the Right Heart*. Perhaps the newly hired employee is indeed wrong-hearted. Perhaps she has a heart that is not consistent with *God's Word*. If so, insights about what Sally can do to become more right-hearted seem clear. Having a reverence for God's Word, knowing how to recognize the contributions that others make to her personal success, being forgiving, and being humble, could go a long way to improve the way she interacts with customers, suppliers, and other employees.

EGOTISM: RIVAL TO A RIGHT HEART

To be a wise leader, you must make your heart *right* by thinking and acting in ways consistent with Biblical teaching. One factor that often prevents or slows the building of a right heart is called egotism. *Egotism* is a tendency to think of oneself as having inflated talent and self-importance.

It makes sense that an egotistic heart is a wrong heart since individuals with such hearts genuinely view themselves as much more important than others, which is a non-Biblical viewpoint. History shows that individuals with egotistic hearts often avoid making decisions or doing anything else that will diminish their own sense of high self-importance.

JOHN ROCKEFELLER & SAM ANDREWS

Here's an historic example of the negative influence that egotism can have on business decisions. In 1874, Sam Andrews was becoming increasingly upset with his partner, John Rockefeller. Rockefeller's domineering personality and enormous ambition to build Standard Oil constantly overruled Andrews' desire for greater personal profits.

One day Andrews reached his limit with Rockefeller and exclaimed, "I wish I was out of this business!" Rockefeller asked him his price. It was one million dollars. Rockefeller paid it to him the following day. Andrews boasted that someone had finally bested Rockefeller in business. Then Andrews learned that Rockefeller turned right around and sold Andrews' former shares to William Vanderbilt for 1.3 million dollars.

Andrews was incensed and claimed he was cheated. Rockefeller offered to sell Andrews the same number of shares at the original price, but Andrews proudly refused. Historians estimate that by the 1930s, Andrews' shares would have been worth over 900 million dollars. A biographer concluded, "This rash decision, motivated by pure ego, kept him from becoming one of America's richest men."

This story shows how a heart characterized by egotism can prevent you from making a rational decision. Andrews was not about to admit that, in this situation, Rockefeller was right and had better business sense. If he had not let egotism interfere with business decisions, Andrews could have made millions instead of his one million dollars. For a business leader, doing business with an egotistic heart is like trying to swim with a pocket full of rocks.

Reflecting back on the *Adventure of the Right Heart* it could be that the harsh interactions of Sally, the newly hired employee, were caused by her egotism. Perhaps she felt so much more important than others at Eden's that she didn't see the need to focus on respecting them as people.

Wise leaders know that egotism is an obstacle to being right-hearted and shy away from egotism in all situations as best they can. In addition, wise leaders work on eliminating any inflated feeling of self-worth or importance that they might have.

CAN BUSINESSES HAVE HEART?

Heart was defined earlier as the inner self, the core of an individual. One's heart is characterized and exposed to others by actions. What people say, what they do, and how they do it, is driven by what's in their hearts. Biblical references to heart seem to focus more on people than on business.[146]

This leads us to an interesting question. *Can a business have a heart?*

Yes, a business can, and does, have a heart. It's because the business is a reflection of the business owner, managers and employees. It's a special heart, however. A *business's heart* is made

---

[146] Proverbs 27:19, (*New International Version*): As water reflects the face, so one's life reflects the heart.

up of the collection of the hearts of all the people who exist within the business. The sum total of what people say, what they do, and how they do it reflects the *collective heart* of all who exist within the business.

Wise leaders focus on developing a *right business heart* as well as monitoring and improving it over time while *chasing wisdom in business and life.*

MARY KAY ASH

Mary Kay Ash is an example of an internationally known business leader who intently focused on making the heart of her business right. In 1963, she founded a cosmetics and skin care company that has grown to become a globally trusted name in the industry. The company's world headquarters are in the town of Addison, a suburb of Dallas, Texas.

According to Jim Underwood's book, *More than a Pink Cadillac*, at the Mary Kay Ash memorial service after her death in November 2001, the main focus was not on the global business that she had developed, her outstanding philanthropic work, or any other of her remarkable achievements in life. Rather, the focus was on her strong faith and how it supported her in building her company and helped her to develop positive and strong personal relationships with others. Mary Kay always put faith in God above all else. She respected God's Word. In essence, Mary Kay's focus on building the right business heart in her company was reflected in a clear set of priorities which she implemented into her vision statement: God first, family second, and the career third. At the outset she made this belief system a central part of her business.

While Mary Kay was open about her personal faith, she did not use her position in the company as a way to evangelize on behalf of her faith. She prayed, she read the Bible, and she faithfully worshipped God. She always spoke about the importance of religion in her life. When television's *60 Minutes* came to interview her and Morley Safer asked Mary Kay if she wasn't just *using* God, she looked Safer squarely in the eye and said: "I sincerely hope not. I hope instead that God is using me."

BUILDING YOUR HEART

How do you become more right-hearted? Is it complicated? Is it possible? Remember that heart is your inner self—your beliefs, values, etc. You build your inner self, your heart, through the thoughts and ideas that you put inside yourself and believe in.

Your senses can help you. Things you see and hear, and how you think about those things, can contribute to your heart. The Bible supports this point by indicating that you should listen to the sayings of the wise to make them a part of your heart.[147]

I regularly perform several activities to try to become more right-hearted. I'm not sure that these activities are advisable for everyone to perform in building right hearts, but performing them seems to help me build mine. Remember, everyone is different and what might be right for me isn't necessarily right for you. Do not simply mimic my *heart-building* activities. Instead, develop a heart-building plan that best suits *you* and then implement it. My activities are merely examples of what you *might pursue* to build your heart.

Perhaps the most fundamental activity that I pursue to make my heart right is to read Bible Scripture regularly, and daily, if possible. If I don't become clear about what Scripture says, it's impossible to make sure my heart is in alignment with the Word of God. I try to maintain an understanding of individual Biblical verses, themes of various books of the Bible, and the relationship between *Old* and *New Testament* writings. To help me better

---

[147] Proverbs 22:17, (*New International Version*): Pay attention and listen to the sayings of the wise; apply your heart to what I teach.

understand the meanings of Biblical writings, I use a Study Bible with explanatory footnotes and reflect on interpretative comments as they appear in books like *Matthew Henry's Commentary*.

Attending church regularly is also a major asset in making my heart *right*. My wife, Mimi, and I, are members of Northland - A Church Distributed, a nondenominational church, in Longwood, Florida. We attend regularly to listen to the Biblically based sermons of our pastor, Dr. Joel Hunter. His weekly sermons inevitably focus on issues that are critical in building right-heartedness.

During church services, singing and listening to the words of traditional spiritual hymns, as well as contemporary Christian songs, helps me to understand God's Word in a much different context. Pastor Vernon Rainwater and the rest of the worship team use music to help me understand the teachings on a deeper level and make Biblical principles a part of the heart that I'm trying to build. I download various songs and hymns from the services and listen to them throughout the week to help me become more right-hearted as I bike or walk during my daily exercises.

Church-sponsored trips also help me to make my heart *right* and from time to time, Mimi and I take trips sponsored by Northland - A Church Distributed.

One such trip followed a teaching journey of the Apostle Paul through Turkey and Greece. Another trip led by Pastor Gus Davies took us throughout Israel. We read the Bible while visiting the places mentioned in our readings. Our activities included exploring the Jordan River, taking a boat ride on the Sea of Galilee, praying in the Garden of Gethsemane, touring Jerusalem, and visiting Bethlehem and Nazareth as well as Jericho. I don't think there's anything more moving than praying in the Garden of Gethsemane, where Jesus prayed with His disciples. It is a life-altering experience.

I have found these trips to be very powerful in helping me to know and understand Biblical Scripture, and very instrumental in building right-heartedness.

It's really all about stopping and getting in touch with God on a regular basis. Our world is so busy these days, people don't take the time to stop and reflect. To honor and acknowledge. To let one's heart *listen*.

In addition to church activities, I participate in other activities to help me to make my heart *right*. For example, I attend a Bible Study with ten other men representing many different walks of life. Don Bjork, a retired Baptist minister we affectionately call Rabbi, leads this small group. His broad experiences with the Moody Bible Institute, involvement in the Billy Graham ministry, pastoring churches, and being an army chaplain all contribute to the richness of his messages to our group. This group meets once a week early in the morning before work and focuses on interpreting Biblical passages.

I've been attending this group for over 13 years—more recently not as regularly as I should. I have found my experiences in this group to be invaluable in becoming more right-hearted. I consider Don my *personal pastor* and guide. His teachings are invaluable and I could find no way to repay him for what he has given me.

I also belong to a discussion group called The Spirit of Business Forum at the Crummer Graduate School of Business at Rollins College, where I teach. This group meets monthly and is made up of faculty, students, alumni, and administrators who meet over lunch in the school's board room. The meeting lasts an hour and is very informal. Each person comes to the meeting prepared to discuss a Bible verse of his or her choice that has significant implications for how to run business affairs. I find that listening to the ideas of this diverse group helps me to clarify and crystallize what I want to include in my heart.

As last examples, I also pursue a number of Internet activities to help make my heart *right*. On Twitter, I follow the thoughts and ideas of many people who tweet about Biblical principles. Occasional messages from such people help me to clarify, crystallize, and retain Biblical ideals that I want to include in my heart. These Twitter messages remind me of who I am and what I want to accomplish with my heart. They remind me to stop and remember. I try to *pass these messages forward* with my own thoughts through my own tweets at twitter.com/wiseleaders.

I subscribe to daily email newsletters sent out by various Christian writers. I find that these newsletters help to keep heart in the forefront of my mind on a daily basis and provide sound thoughts and ideas for heart building. *Daily Hope* is one such newsletter written by Rick Warren that is of immense help to me in making my heart right. Take a look at it. It may be valuable for your heart-building as well. I only mention these activities as a way to offer you some suggestions that you might utilize in your own life.

Think back to Brian's *Adventure of the Right Heart*. Perhaps Sally could improve the quality of her interactions with others by becoming more right-hearted. She could focus on becoming more right-hearted through activities like reading and studying Scripture more regularly, becoming more active in a church, participating more in Bible study groups, and subscribing more to various Internet newsletters and blogging sites that focus on Christian education. Improving her heart will take time and effort. And she has to want to do this. No one can force beliefs on anyone. No one can force a person to change.

GUARDING YOUR HEART

Like building a house, as you are building your heart—and you never really finish building it—you must protect it as you go. You are continually building your heart as you *chase wisdom in business*.

Like most of us, you probably invest significant amounts of money protecting your earthly possessions. People buy insurance on houses to protect their investments. They buy liability insurance to make sure that if someone is injured on their property the injured party cannot sue for damages. People buy security systems and even guns to protect themselves from thieves. You also buy insurance to protect your health and body. There's dental insurance, health insurance, car insurance. All important insurances to protect yourself.

Guarding your heart is even more important than guarding your earthly assets. The Bible teaches that it is more important for you to guard your heart than anything else.[148] Why? Because our hearts guide and direct all our behavior, all our thinking. Everything that we say and do is guided by our hearts. Because, really, the *heart* is *you*.

We should keep vigilant watch over our hearts because, as the verse from *Proverbs* at the opening of the chapter indicates, the heart is where life begins, the origin of everything we do.

Depending upon our heart, whether it's right-hearted or wrong-hearted, we will demonstrate either desirable and undesirable behavior.

Not guarding your heart can lead to ruin. Not guarding our financial assets can lead to financial ruin. Not guarding our bodies can lead to physical ruin. Not guarding our hearts can lead to spiritual ruin. If we allow our hearts to be filled with ideas and images that are contrary to God's Word, we'll tend to act in immoral ways. Filling our hearts with thoughts and ideas that are consistent with God's teachings will help to ensure that we'll act morally. That's why my church trips abroad have been so powerful. They filled my heart with thoughts and ideas that are consisted with God's teachings.

---

[148] Proverbs 4:23, (*New International Version*): Above all else, guard your heart, for everything you do flows from it.

Be sure that you understand how to guard your heart. Think of your heart, your inner self, as an empty test tube that has no allegiance to anything until you start to build or fill it with God-given thoughts and ideas. Think of the thoughts and ideas that build your heart as drops of food coloring. Each thought or idea that you allow into your test tube—your heart—that is *consistent* with God's Word is a drop of blue food coloring. Each thought or idea that you allow into your test tube—your heart—that is *inconsistent* with Biblical principles is a drop of red food coloring. If you allow one drop of blue and then one drop red into your heart, your heart becomes purple. We all know that mixing blue and red makes purple.

The color of your heart tells you how well you are guarding your heart. If your heart is primarily red, you are not guarding well and letting in too many thoughts and ideas that are inconsistent with God's Word. If your heart is mostly blue, you are indeed guarding it well and are mostly using thoughts and ideas to build your heart that are consistent with God's Word.

If your heart is clearly purple, you are inconsistent in guarding your heart. You are using equivalent doses of thoughts and ideas that are both consistent and inconsistent with God's Word. If you have a purple heart, it will be difficult for you to consistently act with a good heart. A right heart. Others will have difficulty understanding what you stand for.

In guarding your heart, make sure that it is blue, not red or purple. A blue heart will help to ensure that every action you take is *consistent* with God's Word. A red heart will help to ensure that the action you take is *inconsistent* with God's Word. If your heart is red, you are not guarding it at all. Purple hearts are poorly guarded and are springboards for sparking an action or behavior that is sometimes consistent and sometimes inconsistent with God's Word. Again, above all else, guard your heart. Nurture it. Build it. Feed it. *Be blue!*

As stated earlier, the purpose of this chapter is to help you to become better at chasing wisdom in business and life through a better understanding of heart and the role it plays in business and in your life. You already know from earlier chapters that wisdom is insight about what's right and wrong in solving problems. Wisdom involves being right-hearted. Wisdom's insights mainly come from knowing and understanding God's Word.

From this chapter you know that your heart is your reservoir for storing insights about God's Word. More simply put, insights that you use to become wiser over time are stored and accumulated cumulatively in your heart. Because the heart stores and accumulates these insights, many wise leaders say that wisdom actually resides in the heart. The bluer your heart, the wiser you should be able to become.

MISSION STATEMENTS AND THE BUSINESS HEART

A *mission statement* is an expression of the overarching purpose of an organization. An organization's purpose is stated in one or a few paragraphs and then all organization members focus together in trying to achieve that purpose. A mission statement should reflect the heart of the business, and the heart of its owners and managers.

Over the years, management theorists have consistently argued back and forth about issues like the value of mission statements, what they should include, and even how long they should be. Although some theorists even question if an organization needs a mission statement, most agree that they serve a worthwhile purpose in helping business leaders set the general, unified direction of organizations.

CHICK-FIL-A

Chick-fil-A is fast-service restaurant chain headquartered in College Park, Georgia. The chain specializes in chicken sandwiches and various chicken-related entrees. S. Truett Cathy, the founder of Chick-fil-A has a very clear mission in mind for his company. According to the corporate website, the company mission: "To be America's best, quick-service restaurant." Cathy believes that the purpose of his company is: "To glorify God by being a faithful steward of all that is entrusted to us and to have a positive influence on all who come in contact with Chick-fil-A."

It is common knowledge that Chick-fil-A is built upon and upholds the Christian values of its founder. Cathy is an example of a business leader who uses mission statements to help him build the right business heart for his company.

What I think is interesting is that Chick-fil-A is one of the best fast food restaurants in America. Their food is delicious. It's always busy because its food is fresh and it uses the highest quality ingredients. It also uses chicken that is farm-raised and doesn't have harmful chemicals or hormones added. I don't think it's a coincidence or accident that Chick-fil-A's food is good and that the business is thriving. It reflects the heart of its owner.

Cathy founded Chick-fil-A more than sixty years ago. In 1982, according to the website, www.WinShape.com, Cathy created the WinShape Foundation that promotes the theme, "This is about life on purpose." The foundation is designed to create life-changing experiences which help individuals, including youth, develop personally and spiritually through summer camps, scholarships to Berry College, and retreats to help enrich married couples' lives. This is a perfect example of how S. Truett Cathy is building the right business heart at Chick-fil-A.

As a business leader, you need to find ways to build the right business heart for your organization the way S. Truett Cathy has done. This means that you must determine how you would like for all organization members—all employees—to collectively act and then go a step further. You must implement activities and programs which encourage your employees to collectively build and nurture the right business heart.

Wise leaders know that a right business heart, as evidenced by the collective behavior of all organization members, must be based upon Biblical teachings. Chick-fil-A provides an excellent example of this.

Think back to Brian's *Adventure of the Right Heart*. A leader like Brian needs to realize that handling Sally, the newly hired employee, is critical not only because of the negative impact of her individual interactions with people, but because she seems to be negatively impacting Eden's business heart, the collective hearts of all Eden's Fresh Company employees. To help improve the behavior of the newly hired employee, perhaps Brian could use a well-crafted mission statement that defines a right business heart for Eden's, and guides employees on how to act in ways that are consistent with it.

BUSINESS HEART AND PROFIT

In creating the heart of your business and making it *right*, don't shy away from emphasizing profit. In other words, don't be reluctant to focus on profit. Businesses exist to make a profit. They continue to exist only if they are profitable.

Keep in mind that making a profit is consistent with Biblical teachings. The Bible mentions that King Solomon earned funds not only from taxes, but from profit from business dealings with merchants, kings, and governors.[149] Whether your business manufactures products or offers services, it is in business to generate a profit. You are in business to profit from your work and making a profit is honorable.

Without profit, businesses become extinct.

Study the Bible for insights about how to make a profit. First, don't expect to make a profit easily. Expect to work hard

---

[149] 1 Kings 10:14-15, (*The Message*): 14 Solomon received twenty-five tons of gold in tribute annually. 15 This was above and beyond the taxes and profit on trade with merchants and assorted kings and governors.

for it. Don't simply talk about making a profit, but make it by maintaining a concentrated and continual effort.[150]

God's Word also says that if you really want to make a profit, you have to plan diligently—setting profit goals, outlining the steps you need to take to reach the goals, and then take the steps. Be patient. Being hasty in working for profit—without a plan—usually leads to failure in reaching profit goals.[151]

Do not try to avoid risk altogether when trying to make a profit.[152] Instead, *manage* risk. Calculate the risk of taking various actions in pursuing profit. Do not take unnecessary risk. However, keep in mind that the lower the risk associated with pursuing profit, the lower the profit usually made from the pursuit. On the other hand, the higher the risk, the higher the possible profit. Be cautious in facing risk. It's usually wise to follow the guideline of incurring a reasonable amount of risk to gain a reasonable profit.

The Bible also advises us about how *not* to make a profit. Be careful from whom you make a profit. Do not profit by exploiting the poor.[153] Making profit from transactions with the poor should not be condoned. Instead, the poor should be the recipients of gifts and contributions to help them function better as human beings and members of the community.

---

[150] Proverbs 14:23, (*New International Version*): All hard work brings a profit, but mere talk leads only to poverty.

[151] Proverbs 21:5, (*New International Version*): The plans of the diligent lead to profit as surely as haste leads to poverty.

[152] Matthew 25:28-30, (*The Message*): Take the thousand and give it to the one who risked the most. And get rid of this "play-it-safe" who won't go out on a limb. Throw him out into utter darkness.

[153] Leviticus 25:35-37, (*New International Version*): 35 If any of your fellow Israelites become poor and are unable to support themselves among you, help them as you would a foreigner and stranger, so they can continue to live among you. 36 Do not take interest or any profit from them, but fear your God, so that they may continue to live among you. 37 You must not lend them money at interest or sell them food at a profit.

ESTABLISH VALUES: ONE AVENUE FOR BUILDING BUSINESS HEART

One path that a wise leader can take to help build the right business heart is to openly establish and promote important values within a business. *Values* are essential beliefs about how people should handle themselves, and in this case, how people should conduct business.

Of course, wise leaders establish and promote values that are based upon Biblical principles. These values serve as a guide that organization members internalize and follow about how to do their jobs. The wise can discern between what is upright or appropriate and what is not. Such values include being honest and open in business dealings, listening intently to the opinions of others when solving problems, and avoiding anger as a vehicle for dealing with others.

Remember that a *business heart* is made up of the collection of the hearts of all the people who exist within the business. The sum total of what people say, what they do, and how they do it reflect the collective business heart. As individuals within a business internalize and act upon established Biblical values, the collective right business heart grows and flourishes.

CNL FINANCIAL GROUP

CNL Financial Group is a nationally known private investment management firm headquartered in Orlando, Florida. The company was started by founder James M. Seneff, Jr. in 1973. His entrepreneurial father loaned him $5,000 to start the business. Seneff used that loan to grow CNL Financial Group into one of the largest and most respected private real estate investment companies in the country; it is now worth more than $25 billion in assets. By almost any financial measure, the company has been extremely successful.

CNL Financial Group is an example of a company that has established and operates according to clear and straightforward values that reflect Biblical principles. The company website alludes to several such values. For example, according to the website, CNL holds the value of *serving* others. This service value is consistent with Jesus' instruction that it is our duty to serve one another and to help one another meet challenges, grow, and improve.[154]

The company website also indicates that CNL holds the value of respecting the dignity of every individual associated with CNL, whether they are shareholders, customers or employees. From a business viewpoint, establishing and promoting such values at CNL can be extremely worthwhile. How can it not help CNL to be successful if employees are continually focused on upholding the dignity of all company stakeholders and helping them to meet challenges, grow, and improve?

ENSURING VALUES IN INDIVIDUAL HEARTS

Here's the central question. What can leaders like those at CNL do to ensure that targeted Biblically based values get into the hearts of individual employees so that the collective business heart can grow in the right way? The following are steps you can take to help ensure that employee hearts contain the right values:

Establish "Values Training Programs." This step involves training people about what *values* are and listing those values that the company holds as important. Don't simply assume that because you state what you'd like the company values to be, that employees have an adequate understanding of what you mean. Training could include discussing the established company values as well as illustrating actions that would be consistent with those upholding those values. It's also usually worthwhile to

---

[154] Matthew 20:27-28, (*New International Version*): 27 And whoever wants to be first must be your slave; 28 just as the Son of Man did not come to be served, but to serve, and to give His life as a ransom for many.

point out employee actions that are inconsistent with upholding those values.

Recruit and hire employees whose hearts already uphold company values. God sees people based upon their hearts, not like man, who tends to see people based upon outward appearance or physical stature.[155] All too often, companies think about hiring new employees based mainly upon more easily observed factors like technical skills and experience. Hiring new employees should not exclude technical skills and experience as important criteria for hiring, but should also include trying to determine what's in a candidate's heart.

Many employers shy away from evaluating a candidate's heart because it's much more difficult to evaluate than a candidate's skill and experience. Do not shy away from evaluating a candidate's heart simply because it's difficult. Instead, recognize that evaluating heart is difficult and conscientiously prepare to do it. Perhaps measuring a candidate's heart should include reference letters from individuals that the candidate supervises, a profile of a candidate's philanthropic or church activities, or even evidence of a candidate's volunteerism.

You can also learn about a candidate's heart by being very attentive in an employment interview. The Bible tells us that the way people act, perhaps in an employment interview, can give us important clues to the composition of their hearts. For example, someone who acts conceited or arrogant in an interview probably has a heart consumed with self-glory and personal success.[156] Regardless of candidates' skills or experience, you may not want

---

[155] 1 Samuel 16:7, (*New International Version*): But the LORD said to Samuel, "Do not consider his appearance or his height, for I have rejected him. The LORD does not look at the things people look at. People look at the outward appearance, but the LORD looks at the heart."

[156] Proverbs 21:4, (*New International Version*): Haughty eyes and a proud heart—the unplowed field of the wicked—produce sin.

to hire them if their hearts are filled with narcissistic values that would promote self-glory or personal success.

Link performance appraisal to upholding values. A third possible step to help ensure that values are ingrained in the hearts of individuals is to make "upholding company values" a formal part of the company's performance appraisal process. In this situation, all those within the business would know the established company values, and employees would be rewarded and promoted, at least partially, based upon on how well they upheld the company's values through their actions.

YOU AND YOUR CHASE

Remember Brian's *Adventure of the Right Heart?* If you were in such a situation, in addition to improving the way that Sally interacts with others, what would you do? It would be wise to focus on encouraging her to conform to a business heart that supports making a profit. This business heart should uphold working hard to earn a profit along with plans on how to make a profit, but should discourage making a profit off of the poor. Providing appropriate training, and linking the *upholding of values* to performance appraisal, will help to ensure that Sally internalizes, and acts upon, established right business heart" values.

This chapter has focused on becoming wiser by understanding heart, a prominent Biblical theme. Remember to think of heart as your *inner self,* and among other things, your beliefs and values. Your heart is you. It is everything you think, believe, and do. It is your very core and influences all that you say and do. Your heart determines how you live your life personally and in business. Your heart is the reflection—the mirror—of your inner self.

Given its importance, you must continually focus on building the right heart—the heart that reflects Biblical principles. Among other things, build your heart to include a reverence for

Jesus Christ, for God's Word, an understanding of how to handle recognition, humility, and forgiveness.

Build your heart by putting the right ideas inside yourself and believing in them. Such ideas are the basic principles of God's teachings. Think about using your senses to input your ideas. What you hear, see, smell, touch, and taste are the highways on which critical thoughts travel from outside yourself to inside yourself, inside your heart.

In building your heart, don't forget to guard it carefully. Your focus should be on inputting thoughts and ideas that are consistent with God's Word into your heart and not those that are inconsistent with it. Remember to avoid egotism—a factor that makes it especially hard to build right-heartedness.

Also, remember that you need to be attentive to the heart of your business—the collection of all hearts of those individuals within it. As a business leader, you are responsible for building and monitoring the heart of your business. Use mission statements to establish overall company direction and to help ensure that a right business heart develops.

The following are some practical hints that you might use to help build right heartedness for you and your business:

1. *Value discipline and accept correction.* When we receive sound advice about mistakes we're making, accept the advice, internalize it, and use it to modify and strengthen your right-heartedness. Discipline provides insights about discriminating good from the bad and defending right against wrong. Discipline is an asset of the wise. We all make mistakes. Learn from them.

2. *Do not covet what belongs to others.*[157] It's impossible to build a right heart if you covet what others possess. When you covet something it means that you have a desire to possess

---

[157] Exodus 20:17, (*New International Version*): You shall not covet your neighbor's house. You shall not covet your neighbor's wife, or his

it. This desire comes from a longing to enjoy something—in this case, something that belongs to another.

Coveting is immoral because it results in the deprivation of another to enjoy what he or she owns. Coveting is wrong-hearted. Avoid it at all costs.

Think about coveting and your business life. Coveting what other people in an organization possess could include desiring their high salaries, premium office space that they're occupying, titles that they possess, close relationships that they have with bosses, and awards they receive.

When coveting becomes strong enough, people are motivated to do whatever is a necessary—sometimes morally questionable actions—to obtain coveted items. Heart should never accept the worthwhileness of being covetous.

3. *Build heart over a lifetime.*[158] Stay dedicated throughout your life to building your heart. Pay special attention throughout all of your days to building your inner self. Do not forget your lessons, and all you've learned.

Don't be satisfied with simply remembering God's Word. Study it. Retrieve it for review. Pray about it. Commit to it. Follow it. Store it in your heart—your inner self. Only in this way will your behavior follow God's Word. Your heart will put God's Word into action. And that is what chasing wisdom in business and life is all about.

---

male or female servant, his ox or donkey, or anything that belongs to your neighbor.

[158] Deuteronomy 4:9, (*New International Version*): Only be careful, and watch yourselves closely so that you do not forget the things your eyes have seen or let them fade from your heart as long as you live. Teach them to your children and to their children after them.

4. *Follow your heart.*[159] Get in the habit of listening to your heart and doing what it suggests. You will soon find out that there are many benefits to following your heart—doing what is consistent with Biblical principles. Receiving these benefits will encourage you to continue building and relying on your heart.

It may take courage to follow your heart knowing that it is always under construction. One's heart is never really completed. It's always in the process of developing. Your heart will never be perfect. In building your heart, however, you must have confidence in it along the way as it grows and develops. Follow it!

Overall, remember that following the Biblical principles housed in your heart is the foundation for your wisdom. It will help you in every step of chasing wisdom to becoming wiser.

---

[159] Proverbs 13:19, (*The Message*): Souls who follow their hearts thrive; fools bent on evil despise matters of soul.

TRUST

Those who trust in themselves are fools, but those who walk in wisdom are kept safe.

Proverbs 28:26 (NIV)

The purpose of this chapter is to help you to become wiser by helping you to better understand the concept of *trust*. Trust in yourself and others. Yes, understanding *trust* will help you to become wiser because it will help you to develop sound insights about how to handle difficult situations or problems in business or in life, and it will help you be confident of those insights.

What is trust? How do you become trusted by others? How do you trust yourself? Should wise leaders trust others? Can trust help to ensure the success of the business?

Begin learning about how the wise handle trust by reflecting on *The Adventure of the Pocketer*, an experience that Brian had at Eden's Fresh Company. This will give you some helpful insights about handling trust issues in business organizations.

THE ADVENTURE OF THE POCKETER

As is the practice in most retail establishments, immediately after a workday ends, someone at each Eden's Fresh Company location closes out the register to make sure that all customer transactions during the day are accurate. A particular employee at each restaurant is assigned this responsibility, enters the results of the day online, and then Brian reviews these results online for all stores each evening.

In tracking trends for each restaurant, Brian began to notice that there was a cash shortage that was consistent and growing almost every day at one particular restaurant. The shortage started as only a few dollars each day, but grew over several months to a level of a few hundred dollars each week. Brian's worries grew from being *somewhat* concerned about the shortage, to being more and more alarmed over time.

In trying to explore this problem of cash shortages, Brian began to realize that his internal systems needed to be improved if his company was to grow to fifteen or twenty restaurants. Since all employees at the *problem* restaurant checked out customers from time to time, there was no way to attach the shortages to one particular employee. Since there were no security cameras in the problem restaurant, there were no visual records of employee activity to review.

The more that Brian explored this problem, the more he began to feel that it was an issue of an employee pocketing money and not an issue of inadvertent mistakes by employees as they made change for customers. He was very concerned about the loss of revenue, but more importantly, he was also extremely disappointed that it seemed someone he trusted very much was betraying him. It was difficult to tell which issue was more disappointing to Brian, the loss of revenue or the betrayal of trust.

INITIAL REFLECTIONS ON THE POCKETER

Most leaders can identify with Brian's disappointment. They commit to people who work with them. They very carefully recruit and select just the very best people to join their organizations. They reward people who contribute to the success of organizations and discipline them with genuine care in order to help them do better in the future. They support people who need help in achieving what is expected of them. They try to demonstrate genuine and worthwhile commitment to the overall well-being of those who work with them. Overall, leaders feel that they have made not only a professional commitment, but also a personal commitment to those who work with them.

In Brian's case, an employee repaid this professional and personal commitment by stealing money. Brian's feelings of disappointment and even infidelity as a result of this theft seem only human.

Other leaders probably have the same feelings in dealing with other types of employee behavior. Some people habitually arrive at work fifteen to twenty minutes late while others commonly take long lunch breaks. Others surf the Internet when they should be working or help themselves to pens, printer ink, or anything else they can take home. Still others are in the habit of making personal calls on company time.

Perhaps leaders in these situations become disappointed because they place trust in others and this trust is betrayed. Brian trained his employee in how to close the restaurant at the end of the day and to count and deposit sales revenue accordingly. He trusted his employee to follow through on the training. Brian's trust was betrayed. Other leaders inform their employees about when to arrive at work, how long to take for lunch, proper use of the Internet, and the undesirability of personal calls during work hours. These leaders trust that organization members will follow through on this training. Their trust in these matters is commonly betrayed.

All of us feel disappointment when trust that we place in others is betrayed. Wise leaders understand both the positive and negative impacts that trust can have on business operations and life. They understand who to trust and how to be trusted. Read on for insights on how to become a wiser leader by understanding more about trust in organizations.

TRUST OR MISTRUST

Define *trust as* a firm belief in reliability of something or someone. When you trust someone you believe that he or she is going to do what you expect. Trust isn't limited to what people do, however.

The King James Dictionary defines trust as reliance or resting of the mind on the integrity, veracity, justice, friendship or other sound principle of another person. This belief could be related to one's character, skill, or strength. The drawing that opens this chapter shows two mountain climbers in action. In a mountain climbing situation, one believes in the character, skill, and strength of another to a maximum extent. In this situation, one trusts the other with his or her life.

Mistrust, on the other hand, is suspicion or doubt about the reliability of something or someone. When you mistrust someone, you have doubts about what to expect from that person. This doubt relates not only to what a person will do, but extends to who the person really is. Is the person just? Is the person a friend? Is the person full of anger? In essence, this doubt can extend to the whole person—a person's character, skill, or strength.

From my experience, people develop mistrust for leaders for several different reasons. Leaders taking action like downsizing for selfish reasons, making arbitrary decisions, or disciplining unfairly lead employees to becoming cynical about leaders, and as a result, developing mistrust for them.

Most of the time, I find leaders to indeed be trustworthy. However, if leaders do not take the time to explain issues like why downsizing must take place, why certain decisions must be made, or why discipline is necessary, they create an information vacuum that often leads their employees to mistrust them. Wise leaders explain their actions carefully and thoroughly in order to give others complete information about their actions and to eliminate any information vacuums that could lead others to mistrust them.

WHY WISE LEADERS FOCUS ON BEING TRUSTED

Essentially, wise leaders know the impact that both being trusted and being mistrusted can have on a business and life. When wise leaders surround themselves with people who trust them, then everyone within their organizations can focus on being productive—in solving problems without any need to be personally protective. They won't hinder progress because of fear of reprisal, or being punished.

Why do wise leaders focus on being trusted by their followers? When employees trust leaders they become more fully engaged in their work. They also tend to support changes that leaders attempt to make more quickly and more completely than if they mistrust leaders. Overall, when employees trust their leaders they tend to be more fully engaged in making contributions that ignite business success.

Wise leaders also know, however, that *mistrust* can have a devastating effect on organizational success. When an organization is characterized by mistrust, people are not wholly committed to solving problems because they are somewhat preoccupied with protecting themselves from others as well as fear of retaliation or punishment. People in organizations characterized by mistrust might even become defiant. Wise leaders understand that the more mistrust that exists in an organization, the lower the probability that the organization will be successful in the long run.

Mistrust has a significant impact on organizations. It tends to lower morale and increase absenteeism, which increases costs. It tends to lower overall employee satisfaction in the workplace. Employees tend to leave organizations characterized by significant mistrust among organization members, especially the leaders. It also tends to lower the efficiency of organizations because employees become focused too much on self-protection, self-preservation, and not enough on creativity and innovation.

Wise leaders focus on being trusted because they understand how much trust contributes to business success. They also understand how mistrust is a major deterrent to business success. In a nutshell, wise leaders focus on being trusted in organizations—not mistrusted.

CREATING HIGH TRUST BUSINESSES: JOHN MACKEY AND WHOLE FOODS MARKET

As discussed earlier, there are many business advantages to leaders being trusted by their followers, as well as trusting one another regardless of positions held. As a result, wise leaders focus on developing *high trust organizations*—organizations characterized by significant levels of trust among all organization members.

John Mackey, co-founder of Whole Foods Market, a grocery store chain that focuses on selling health-conscious foods, has several good ideas on how to create a high trust organization. Many of Mackey's thoughts in this regard are captured in a YouTube video, "John Mackey of Whole Foods Market on Creating High Trust Organizations."

In this video, Mackey indicates that in order for a leader to create a high trust organization, the leader must discover or rediscover the organization's purpose—why the company exists—and to communicate this purpose to all organization stakeholders. Leaders have to continually act in ways that are consistent with this purpose in order to avoid criticism, which in turn, can develop stakeholder mistrust for leaders—including employee mistrust.

Mackey also believes that organizing workers into small teams can help build high trust organizations. According to Mackey, people work best in small groups. When employees see that their leaders trust them to work in small-group settings, they know they are trusted to be productive and, as a result, they will reciprocate by trusting their leaders.

Mackey indicates that building a business culture wherein leaders give employees the necessary tools and other support they need to accomplish the mission of a business also helps build high trust organizations. When employees see that leaders are there to serve *them* and help *them* succeed, then the employee trust for the leader builds and accelerates.

In addition, when leaders are forthright, according to Mackey, employee trust for leaders will grow. Leaders are transparent, when they explain why they make certain decisions, discuss mistakes that they have made, and clarify why they have to make changes. Leaders should keep in mind that they might as well be transparent since it's very difficult to conceal facts or issues.[160]

When employees see and understand sound reasons why leaders take action, employees will understand that the motives of leaders are fair and for the benefit of all organizational stakeholders, including employees. When this happens, employees' trust for leaders will grow.

WISE LEADERS TRUST GOD COMPLETELY

As the Biblical verse that opens this chapter says, wise leaders do not trust completely in themselves. It would be foolish to do so. After all, leaders are human beings with strengths *and* weaknesses.

Instead of trusting themselves, wise leaders possess an absolute trust in God. This trust and having a firm view of who God is gives wise leaders insights about what to do to handle difficult problems and challenges. And how do wise leaders get to know God so that God will be trusted? Everyone comes to know and trust God through His Word, the Bible. The Bible is inspired by God and is useful in helping us be equipped to do good work and be good leaders. Wise leaders internalize and reflect on what

---

[160] Luke 8:17, (*New International Version*): For there is nothing hidden that will not be disclosed, and nothing concealed that will not be known or brought out into the open.

God says to improve, that is, to acquire discipline and knowledge about how to teach and treat followers.[161]

Wise leaders not only study and internalize God's Word, but they trust it completely and act, without reservation, based upon what it says. They trust in the Lord with all of their heart and do not rely simply on their own insights. These leaders believe that if they follow God's Word, problems will never be obstacles that cannot be overcome.[162]

SHOULD WISE LEADERS TRUST OTHERS?

The previous section focused on wise leaders trusting God. This section explores whether or not wise leaders should also trust other human beings. Of course, wise leaders should focus on trusting their followers!

All business activities in organizations are the result of human interaction. The usefulness of this interaction is influenced by the effectiveness of the relationships that people have with one another within the organization. Management books show that relationships in organizations that are characterized by mutual trust tend to increase the effectiveness of business relationships within organizations, thereby enhancing the organization's chances for success.

Mutual trust in organizations is typically characterized by several factors that help organizations to become successful. For example, when there is mutual respect among people in organizations, the people tend to collaborate more openly with one another and are

---

[161] 2 Timothy 3:16, (*New International Version*): All Scripture is God-breathed and is useful for teaching, rebuking, correcting and training in righteousness.

[162] Proverbs 3:5-6, (*New International Version*): 5 Trust in the LORD with all your heart and lean not on your own understanding; 6 in all your ways submit to Him, and He will make your paths straight.

more focused on directly attacking organizational problems. In addition, organizational environments characterized by mutual trust tend to enhance the flow of interpersonal communication within the organization as a means for making sure that no one is left out of the loop. These organizational characteristics are all excellent forerunners of organizational success.

Wise leaders understand that these factors precipitated by mutual trust in organizations can only increase the probability of organizational success and focus the effort of wise leaders on building mutual trust in organizational environments. They also understand the importance of mutual trust but understand that trusting other human beings is different from trusting God. The following section explains these important differences.

TRUST, BUT VERIFY

As the previous discussion explained, it's very beneficial for leaders to trust their followers whether in a workplace or other setting. There are many benefits when an organization is a high trust organization.

When trusting people, though, leaders must be very careful. Leaders need to remember that human beings are not perfect and sometimes do things that are inappropriate even if the leader trusts them. Consistent with this thought, the Bible teaches that leaders must keep a sharp eye out for inappropriate behavior since people sometimes find it difficult to do the right thing all of the time.[163]

Remember Brian and *The Adventure of the Pocketer*? Brian trusted his manager to properly close out his restaurant at the end of each day. Brian trusted this employee to do the right thing. Initially, the manager gained Brian's trust to do the job. Brian

---

[163] Proverbs 20:8-9, (*The Message*): Leaders who know their business and care keep a sharp eye out for the shoddy and cheap, for who among us can be trusted to be always diligent and honest?

viewed the manager as trustworthy because he carried out his job as Brian expected. Over time, however, Brian needed to be more vigilant in making sure that the manager maintained his trustworthiness. Some people may start out great in a job, but lose steam somewhere down the line.

President Ronald Reagan gave us useful insight about what to do in trusting people. In discussing business between himself and Mikhail Gorbachev, Secretary General of the Communist Party of the Soviet Union, Reagan often characterized his position in dealing with Gorbachev as being consistent with an old Russian saying: *Trust, but verify.*

Does this mean that Reagan didn't really trust Gorbachev? Perhaps. But, as another way to view Reagan's position, Reagan could have trusted Gorbachev at the time that their business agreements were drafted and finalized. However, he knew the tremendous pressures that Gorbachev would be under, over time, to disregard the agreement. Reagan simply wanted to periodically gather evidence that Gorbachev would be able to handle the pressure and conform to the principles of the agreements.

HONESTY BUILDS TRUST

Many would say that honesty is telling the truth—not lying. [164] Although the definition of honesty includes telling the truth, it goes well beyond simply *telling* the truth. According to *The King James Dictionary, honesty* is a disposition to conform to justice and correct moral standards in all social transactions. Fairness, candor, and sincerity are all characteristics of honesty.

Emphasizing the point that honesty goes well beyond telling the truth, the Bible points out many different ways that businesspeople

---

[164] Proverbs 12:17, (*New International Version*): An honest witness tells the truth, but a false witness tells lies.

can be honest.[165] Businesspeople should use accurate measurement instruments in order to be fair with customers and sell them exactly what they pay for, like using honest scales for weight and honest container sizes measuring quarts, gallons, and bushels.

Why does honesty build trust? Remember, as stated earlier, *trust* is reliance on the integrity or other sound characteristic of another. This belief could be related to one's character, skills, or strength. Honesty is a trait of an individual's character that encourages others to trust that individual. Because honesty is such a valued dimension of one's character, being honest is a very effective tool in gaining trust from someone else.

Honesty is so valued in our society, it has given rise to the axiom that "honesty is always the best policy." Yes, it is always the best policy because it is the way you earn trust.

Wise leaders are always honest. This is not as easy as it sounds. A leader has to constantly think of his or her employees' feelings. And, a wise leader has to be diplomatic and balanced in making decisions. Being honest takes courage and accountability.

ALWAYS TELL THE TRUTH

Wise leaders always tell the truth.[166] They realize that people find truth pleasant and refreshing.[167] Not only is it morally correct to be truthful, but speaking the truth is a powerful tool for earning the respect of those around you.

---

[165] Leviticus 19:35-36, (*New International Version*): 35 Do not use dishonest standards when measuring length, weight or quantity. 36 Use honest scales and honest weights, an honest ephah and an honest hin. I am the LORD your God, who brought you out of Egypt.

[166] Leviticus 19:11, (*New International Version*): Do not steal. Do not lie. Do not deceive one another.

[167] Proverbs 24:26, (*New International Version*): An honest answer is like a kiss on the lips.

Don't lie to others. If you tell a lie, even a little one, people will lose respect for you.[168] How can they trust you if you lied to them? If people catch you in a lie they will find it hard to believe you in the future. Friedrich Nietzsche, a 19th century German philosopher, may have said it best when he stated, "I'm not upset that you lied to me, I'm upset that from now on I can't believe you." Although I disagree with much of Nietzsche's thoughts about religion and morality, this statement about lies and trust is insightful.

Liars are not considered trustworthy. Wise leaders simply do not lie because the consequences for lying are simply too great. People do not expect their leaders to lie.[169] As a result, wise leaders find that when their thoughts and arguments are characterized by truth alone, they can become difficult, but are recognized as logical and therefore, beyond criticism.[170]

I think that's why that so many people become disillusioned with some of our politicians and top athletes and other celebrities today. It is very difficult for anyone to lie to the public because the news media is very skilled at uncovering truths. And with YouTube, Facebook, and Twitter, news spreads like wildfire. So, when a politician tells a lie, you can bet he's going to be caught and held accountable for his actions.

It is the same way with some of the famous athletes and celebrities. Some of them lie, but most of them generally get caught. When this happens, the general public loses respect for them and it's hard for those celebrities and politicians to ever gain favor with the public again. In fact, there are so many lies allegedly touted by politicians (especially in election years)

---

[168] Luke 16:10, (*New International Version*): Whoever can be trusted with very little can also be trusted with much, and whoever is dishonest with very little will also be dishonest with much.

[169] Proverbs 17:7, (*The Message*): We don't expect eloquence from fools, nor do we expect lies from our leaders.

[170] Job 6:25, (*New International Version*): How painful are honest words! But what do your arguments prove?

and by celebrities that it's hard to know the truth from the lies these days. This makes it even more important for leaders to be honest—to embody wisdom.

Wise leaders not only do *not* lie, but they are honest in all possible ways. Consider Abraham Lincoln, president of the United States from 1861 to 1865. Lincoln became famous for going to great lengths to be honest by taking great pains to return only a few cents that did not belong to him. Through actions of this sort, Lincoln was dubbed with the nickname "Honest Abe." His honesty undoubtedly helped him to earn the trust of many American citizens and all of the benefits of a trusted leader. In your life, in *chasing wisdom*, be an *Honest Abe*.

I remember one friend of mine, Darren, who had a six-year-old daughter named Chloe. She was an adorable little girl but very rambunctious. She learned that if she lied about her *bad* actions, she could save herself punishment of going to *time out*. Of course, her parents caught her in little lies over and over again. Finally, her father, Darren, sat down with her and said, "Chloe, you have to stop lying. Why do you lie to me and your mother?"

"I don't want to get punished," Chloe said.

"But you know it's wrong to lie, right?" Darren asked.

"Uh-huh," Chloe said. "I guess so."

"When you lie, you not only hurt those you love, but you hurt yourself."

"How do I hurt myself?" she asked.

"Because you are telling me that we and others can't trust you and if we can't trust you, then you will never have good friends," Darren said.

I think it's true that some children lie and some don't. Some may have active imaginations that play a part in lying; others may simply lie as a protective act to avoid punishment. And others could simply have devious personalities. Whatever the reason, lying is a behavior that can be corrected.

Chloe grew up to be a smart young lady and wise leader of a huge corporation. Her mission statements in her business emphasized honesty. She explained that after her talk with her father about lying, even at that young age, she realized that she wanted to be respected and trusted in life. That she wanted good friends who would cherish her. And from then on, she walked the straight path of honesty.

Perhaps parents should take notice and teach their children the benefits of being honest. It might take a lot of talks and punishments, but if the parents are diligent, they can help mold their children and train them to always act in the highest manner possible. The children will then grow up with a better chance of being a responsible, honest, wise leader.

CONCERN BUILDS TRUST

The term *concern* can be defined in many different ways. For purposes of the present discussion, *concern* is interest for others. In this sense, concern is characterized by a caring for others—their well-being, feelings, thoughts, and ideas. Such concern usually develops as a result of relationships with others. The way Darren showed his love for his daughter, Chloe, is a good example of concern for his daughter's welfare. This can be carried over in business, as well.

When a leader has genuine concern for employees, the employees are inclined to trust the leader. Why? Because the employees believe that the leader—their boss—is honestly looking out for their best interests, their wellbeing. As such, the employees are not suspicious of what the leader does, but feel secure in the leader's motives. Wise leaders genuinely care about the interests of their staffs in business or organizations, and avoid doing anything that jeopardizes those interests. According to

Biblical teaching, leaders should focus more on the interests of their staffs than on their own interests.[171]

Wise leaders attempt to build feelings of mutual concern among all people throughout their businesses and organizations.[172] Biblical thought implies that people in all departments and divisions of a business should have concern for those individuals in all other departments and divisions. When such mutual concern exists, people see themselves as part of a team. When one thinks of working together as a team to accomplish mutual goals, this brings about greater success.

This mutual concern leads to a great organizational benefit.

Businesses that are characterized by mutual concern tend to have strong interpersonal relationships that increase the probability of business success. This is because people appreciate the concern that their leaders, peers, and subordinates show them and will often go out of their way to help those who show this concern. The Bible makes this point by illustrating that an individual so appreciates concern that another shows that he prays that God's blessings be showered upon the individual showing such concern.[173]

YOU AND YOUR CHASE

Trust is a precious commodity, particularly in the workplace, and of course, in life. If you don't have trust in the workplace, you probably don't have it in other areas of your life. Employees

---

[171] Philippians 2:3-4, (*New International Version*): 3 Do nothing out of selfish ambition or vain conceit. Rather, in humility value others above yourselves, 4 not looking to your own interests but each of you to the interests of the others.

[172] Corinthians 12:25, (*New International Version*): So that there should be no division in the body, but that its parts should have equal concern for each other.

[173] 1 Samuel 23:21, (*New International Version*): Saul replied, "The Lord bless you for your concern for me."

prefer to work for managers and companies that they can trust. Managers prefer to hire employees they can trust.

Once trust has been lost, it can be a difficult and arduous process to build it back up. It will take time and consistent effort both on the part of leaders and company owners to earn back the trust of their employees.

Show that you trust your staff by communicating with them any concerns you have. Encourage the staff to do the best they can and to come to you if they need help.

Your employees need to care about your company. They need to feel like they belong—like they are part of something important. It's up to you to make them feel that way. From small tasks to large decisions, your employees need to see that you and the company are worthy of their trust. People trust others who consistently perform as expected, without arbitrary decisions or actions.

Put honesty first in all aspects of your business. If your employees have questions about any issue, answer them honestly and be upfront about any future challenges the company may be facing. Don't hedge questions or obfuscate the truth.

To build trust in the workplace you have to be trustworthy, and this means being honest at all costs. People respect others who can own up to their mistakes and work to correct their errors.

Set new companywide goals. Part of building honesty is working towards a betterment of the company and its employees. Show your staff that you are working towards a brighter future and putting the past behind you. Include them in meetings to brainstorm about the company's vision and heart. Build teamwork. Build community and build trust. This will help build their confidence in your efforts and encourage them to be a part of the change for the better.

The following are some practical steps that you can take as a wise leader to help you build trust. As you read these steps, remember that each of them will help those that you interact with to feel more comfortable in predicting how you will act in the future. To help you build trust, you should:

1. *Keep your word.* What you commit to doing, your word, has to be as valuable and unbreakable as a diamond. If you say that you are going to do something, make sure that you do it. If you make a promise, make sure that you keep it. Don't make promises you can't keep. People cannot tolerate those who do not keep their word. But if you're someone who keeps your word, then people will trust you and respect you.

   The Bible says that even God loves the company of those that keep their word.[174]

2. *Use tact.* Tact is the ability to speak or act without offending others by being sensitive to what is fitting and suitable in dealing with others. A person who is tactful knows how to discuss problems in a logical, objective way without offending anybody. *Offending* means irritating or annoying another.

   Anymore, we are one world. Our economy is global and we all interact often with people from other cultures and countries. It is common in today's global business world for businesspeople to work hard to build trust with customers from other countries and cultures. Many such businesspeople fail at developing this trust because they do not possess the tact to deal with people from other countries. But it is something they can learn.

   When visiting potential business partners in Japan, for example, many U.S. businesspeople do not adequately understand the Japanese culture. They unknowingly offend their potential Japanese partners by innocently walking into a house with shoes on, sitting before someone offers

---

[174] Proverbs 12:22, (*The Message*): God can't stomach liars; he loves the company of those who keep their word.

them a seat, pointing at people. By performing such actions, U.S. businesspeople unknowingly offend their Japanese business colleagues and make it hard for these colleagues to trust them.

The previous example illustrates how, if businesspeople are not sensitive to the customs and values of foreigners, they will offend them. Due to this lack of tact, it will be difficult to develop trust with them and win them over as business colleagues. All one needs to do is study the culture beforehand so she can better understand these people.

Biblical teachings essentially illustrate this/same principle. Paul tells us that when preaching to the Jews, he essentially acted as a Jew, having respect for their ceremonies and customs in order to win them over to Christ.[175]

Wise leaders always follow this same principle, showing respect for the values and customs (and religions and political alignments) of others as a foundation for building trust. Wise leaders respect such values and customs in an effort to minimize their alienation, for alienation makes it difficult if not impossible to win them as trusted business colleagues.

3. *Build a reputation of being trustworthy.* A *reputation* is the set of beliefs that others hold regarding someone. In reality, a reputation is actually given to you by others. You *earn* your reputation, whether it's good or bad. Trustworthy, as discussed earlier, means that an individual is deserving of being trusted. A reputation of being trusted, therefore, is a belief that an individual is deserving of being trusted.

---

[175] 1 Corinthians 9:19-20, (*New International Version*): 19 Though I am free and belong to no one, I have made myself a slave to everyone, to win as many as possible. 20 To the Jews I became like a Jew, to win the Jews.

Wise leaders understand that they build reputations as trustworthy through their actions.[176]

If what wise leaders do is pure and morally correct, they will become known as being trustworthy no matter what country they live in, or what organization or business they run.

It can take a long time and much effort to gain a reputation for being trustworthy. It doesn't happen overnight. Trust has to be *won*. The key is to demonstrate fairness and moral correctness in all that you do every day. Wise leaders understand that they need to not only learn God's Word, but also apply it in their business lives.[177] Show that you are reliable, honest and trustworthy by honoring your word. Serve others in the organization, treating them respectfully and fairly. As others see you acting this way over time, your reputation for trustworthiness will grow.

But why would wise leaders focus on building a reputation of being trustworthy? The answer is simple and clear. If a business leader has a reputation for being trustworthy, others in the organization will trust him or her more quickly, thereby enabling the organization to gain the benefits of a *high-trust* organization more quickly. And doesn't every business leader want that?

---

[176] Proverbs 20:11, (*New International Version*): Even small children are known by their actions, so is their conduct really pure and upright?

[177] James 1:22, (*New International Version*): Do not merely listen to the word, and so deceive yourselves. Do what it says.

RUN THE WISDOM MARATHON

Do you not know that in a race all the runners run, but only one gets the prize? Run in such a way as to get the prize.

1 Corinthians 9:24 (NIV)

This book has taken you on a journey. It's not over. It's a lifelong journey, not a quick and easy one that ends with reading the last page. Think of this journey, in a very real sense, as just *starting* after you read the last page. It is comprised of an intertwining path of concepts and Biblical thought about becoming wiser—to know what's right and wrong in solving difficult problems in your business, and ultimately, in your life.

Do you think you're ready to continue your journey—to run the *Wisdom Marathon?* To actually put what you've been reading into action? To *chase wisdom?* To take up the call to success by moving forward and marathoning through all the topics we've discussed in this book?

This is not a fast race, not a sprint. It takes motivation, training, discipline, persistence and perseverance to *chase wisdom.* It's slow and methodical, but with the right training, study of life and Biblical thought, of God's Word, as well as your own mindset, you can do it. This marathon is comprised of all the vital steps to becoming wiser in business, and ultimately, in life.

To start on your *Wisdom Marathon,* take the different disciplines, activities, and information you've studied in this book and commit to running this chase, a long-term effort focused on becoming better and wiser in business and life. As the introductory verse at the beginning of the chapter recommends, run the race as you must in order to win—run this race slowly and methodically, pacing yourself over your lifetime. No matter how old you are, you can always become wiser.

Understanding the concept of *Running the Wisdom Marathon* begins by exploring the following real-life workplace adventure experienced by Matthew.

THE NO INSTANT WISDOM ADVENTURE

I was working early one morning in my office at Rollins College, preparing PowerPoint slides for a lecture on leadership that I was to give in class the following day. As I was beginning work on one of the slides, I heard a knock at the door. Looking up, I said, "Come in!"

It was nice to see my son, Matthew, walk through the door. At that time, he was only nineteen years old. He was always a breath of fresh air in my sometimes-stuffy office. Tall with brown hair and blue eyes and a joyful smile, he inherited his mother's good looks. Today, he seemed a little puzzled.

I immediately stopped what I was doing.

"Hey, what's up?" I asked nonchalantly. "Want some coffee?" I motioned towards the coffee pot in the corner. "It's still good. I only made it about an hour ago."

"No, thanks, Dad. I've already had some coffee. Had my usual Starbuck's before I came over. Just thought I'd drop by for a visit if you have time."

"Sure, here, have a seat. What's on your mind?" I motioned at the chair in front of my desk and I sat down alongside it and took a sip of coffee. Even though it was a little strong, it still tasted good.

"I had lunch with Michael yesterday," Matthew said. Michael was a friend of our family's, close to retirement at about seventy years of age, and a partner in one of the premier advertising agencies in Orlando.

"Nice!" I said. "How's Michael doing? How'd the lunch go?"

"Michael's doing great, as always," Matthew said. "He's one of the most positive men I've ever known. And, what's interesting is that every time I brought up a challenge or problem that I was facing at work, Michael had real practical insights about how to deal with my situation—like some kind of business guru. He had these really cool ideas about how to handle disgruntled employees, how to increase customer satisfaction with my services, and even how to create partnerships with other firms as a vehicle for growing the company. All things that I needed to hear."

According to Matthew, the luncheon conversation went really well but as Matthew left, he felt a new challenge. Matthew said, "Driving back to the office from lunch, I couldn't help but think over the things Michael said. You know that I admire Michael for who he is and what he knows. For some strange reason, I suddenly felt like I had a new challenge in life. How could I ever know as much as Michael? How would I ever have as much insight about business operations as Michael does? I want to know what Michael knows, and the sooner the better."

"Matthew," I said encouragingly, "it takes time. Michael is much older than you. He's had a lifetime of experiences to gain knowledge and wisdom. And he's a man who studies the Bible and goes to church. He studies and believes in God's Word.

"He's had more time to grow and develop in business and life. It's only natural. You'll grow in wisdom as you gain more experiences and spend personal reflection time on personal improvement and Biblical principles. You're doing a great job with your business and every experience you have is a tool for becoming wiser about your business. Remember that.

"Be patient. Someday, you will give some sage advice to a young businessman like yourself and you will remember Michael. All of a sudden, it will dawn on you. You have grown in wisdom!"

Don't forget: Every business and personal relationship and experience is an opportunity for you to grow in wisdom and transform your life.

INITIAL REFLECTIONS ON NO INSTANT WISDOM

Unless God-given, there's no such thing as becoming wise *instantly*. It just won't happen, as I explained to my son, Matthew. Think about becoming wiser as a lifetime, never-ending endeavor. Focus on becoming wiser in business as a lifetime challenge. It *should* be a lifetime commitment. And as you traverse these roads, don't forget to enjoy the journey because it's in the journey where you will find those nuggets of wisdom.

Many of us become so busy, we seldom think about wisdom. We want to be wise, but we avoid doing the things that will help us to become wiser like reading the Bible and studying God's Word. We say, "I don't have time for that!" Instead, some of you might find yourselves coming home after a long day at work and then plopping down on the couch, watching TV for hours and hours instead of studying God's Word.

The *Wisdom Marathon* consists of sound guidelines for becoming wiser over a lifetime. These guidelines include defining problems, referring to Biblical insights and experiences related to solving the problems, praying about these insights, taking action related to those insights to solve the problems, talking to someone you respect and admire like Matthew did with our old friend, Michael, and conscientiously reflecting to accumulate insights for future use about solving such problems.

In essence, this book is not really about *my* teaching you something. Rather, it is about *your teaching yourself* through the steps I've offered and through the *Wisdom Marathon*. It is not about *my* answering questions about wisdom. It is about *your* asking and *answering* questions yourself. You are the marathoner. You are the finish line.

Why should you commit to running the *Wisdom Marathon*? The answer is simple. If you are successful in winning and possessing wisdom, this wisdom will become more valuable to you than silver or gold. It will become more precious than jewels or anything else in this world that people see as valuable.[178]

How can wisdom be this valuable? This answer is simple. Possessing wisdom is a businessperson's key to making the best decisions possible.

As a result, wisdom is the key to achieving business success by employing God's Word in all that you do. If you think this is overstating the value of wisdom, you don't really understand wisdom. Wisdom is also valuable because knowing how to use Biblically based knowledge and acting in harmony with Jesus' teachings gives us a feeling of self-respect and an inner peace.

THINK OF YOURSELF AS A MARATHONER

You most likely know what a traditional fitness marathon is. It's a very long race involving a designated track that requires both speed and endurance from a runner. People know about the dedication and training it takes to complete a marathon, which is a long-distance running event covering 26 miles and 385 yards.

---

[178] Proverbs 3:13-18, (*New International Version*): 13 Blessed are those who find wisdom, those who gain understanding, 14 for she is more profitable than silver and yields better returns than gold. 15 She is more precious than rubies; nothing you desire can compare with her. 16 Long life is in her right hand; in her left hand are riches and honor. 17 Her ways are pleasant ways, and all her paths are peace. 18 She is a tree of life to those who take hold of her; those who hold her fast will be blessed.

Although the marathon is actually one of the original Olympic events and included in Olympic games since 1896, the actual distance of the race was not standardized until 1921.

Many of my friends are marathon runners, and they take it very seriously with their exercise and training programs, and their dietary protocols. But, do you know what it takes to run the *Wisdom Marathon*? Similar ideas, but a different focus and objective.

As you're already aware, wisdom is defined as insight about right and wrong in solving problems. As you also know, the emphasis in this book has been on gaining this wisdom and additional insight primarily from the Bible–God's Word. Our focus has been on using Biblical knowledge and understanding to better manage problems as a leader in business, and ultimately, in life.

You have learned how to use Biblical thought, i.e., God's Word and guidelines to better develop the ability to discern what's right and wrong and thereby make the best possible decisions to solve problems. The Bible is one of the best roadmaps there is, and still rings true for us as a people and society in the 21st century. That's because truth is truth.

This chapter provides additional tools you'll need for running your own *Wisdom Marathon,* which will help you throughout life. You'll become more efficient, more disciplined, more heartfelt, and ultimately, wiser. And this will help you become more successful in your business.

In attempting to gain more and more wisdom, think of yourself more as a *Wisdom Marathon runner* than a sprinter. As mentioned earlier, gaining wisdom is indeed a marathon and not a sprint!

The sprinter starts as quickly as possible and uses maximum energy to be the first to pass perhaps one hundred yards. You'll burn out fast if you do this.

On the other hand, the marathon runner runs a race carefully and thoughtfully, sometimes conserving energy, knowing that the distance to pass is more like 26 miles with peaks and valleys along the way.

Your efforts to become wiser should not focus on attaining quick, short-term results over a month or so. Just as you wouldn't expect to build a massive savings account in a short time (unless you win the lottery or inherit a lot of money), rather, you build it over months and years. It is the same with building wisdom. Focus on becoming wiser and wiser over an entire lifetime. View building your wisdom as a never-ending project, not just a special project that lasts only a few days, months or even a year.

Wisdom can be built bit by bit, but it takes time, discipline, and commitment. It can be done if you stay focused. Don't get discouraged. Keep at it. Remember Benjamin Franklin's advice: "*Small strokes fell great oaks.*"

When we are centered in God's Word, when we act in accordance with God's wishes—*over time*—we access and express the truest wisdom.

THE WISDOM MARATHON TRACK

To win a race, a marathoner must know the route that the race takes. He must know where the hills are, the curves, the rough spots. Even if a marathoner runs a well-planned race, he or she could lose the race by making a wrong turn and not following the racetrack, or by using too much energy before reaching the highest hills.

I have included your own track to follow when running the *Wisdom Marathon*. The following *Figure A* illustrates the steps on this track. To help you succeed in running the *Wisdom Marathon*, look at this track carefully. It's rather simple, but effective. Make a copy of it and put it on your bulletin board for easy reference. Study it. Commit it to memory. Make it a part of you. It may look complicated at first glance, but in reality it's very simple. You want to make all the correct turns during your race.

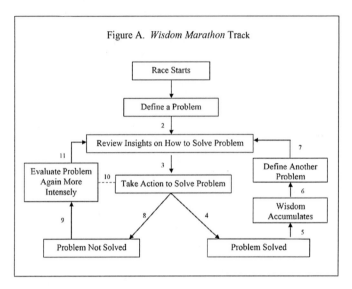

Take a look at your *Wisdom Marathon Track*. The arrows are numbered on the map as an aid to help clarify discussion of the track.

THE RACE STARTS

Step 1: Define a Problem. Start running your *Wisdom Marathon* by defining a problem that you are facing. Keep in mind that some of these numbers will overlap on the *Wisdom Marathon Track*. They are not necessarily exact and you can experiment and move the numbers around to best fit your circumstances. The *Wisdom Marathon Track* is merely a tool to give you an idea of how to structure your race.

That being said, if you do not define what your problem is, your *Wisdom Marathon* is doomed from the very beginning. (Insights about how to define a problem are discussed later in this chapter.)

Step 2: Review Insights on How to Solve the Problem. Once you've defined a problem, the next stage of the *Wisdom Marathon* is to review various thoughts, ideas, and insights about how to solve the problem.

This is the stage of the *Wisdom Marathon* in which your training in studying and understanding God's Word really pays off. Use your mind like a small supercomputer that matches a problem to relevant passages in God's Word, in the Bible. This book will help you as I've listed numerous Biblical quotes and analyses that pertain to business and life situations.

Step 3: Take Action to Solve the Problem. After you define a problem, and review insights on how to solve the problem, then it's time to take action based on your insights. These insights come from studying God's Word. Determine your action as carefully as possible and then focus on implementing it without making any mistakes. When you have a problem, nothing gets solved if you don't act on resolving it. Without proper implementation, the valuable insights you've gained about how to best solve your problem will become worthless. And it might cause you even more problems in the long run. So, you simply must be very careful about your actions and act with wisdom.

Step 4: Problem Solved. The best result of your taking action to solve your problem is that the problem is solved. If this happens, you can move on to the next step on the *Wisdom Marathon Track.*

Step 5: Wisdom Accumulates. Wisdom accumulates after you solve a problem. You put this knowledge and experience in your brain's computer files, where you can retrieve it for further use when other problems arise.

Step 6: Define Another Problem. No one has just one problem in business or in life. There will always be multiple problems to challenge you. This is the way we all grow and develop as human beings. So, define another problem.

Step 7: Review Insight on How to Solve Problem. Again, just as you did with the first problem, define the problem, and repeat the next step, which is the box entitled, *Take Action to Solve Problem.*

You can solve problem after problem. If the problem goes away as a result of your action, then that's great! If not, you need to reassess the problem, and take alternate steps. Keep experimenting until you find the best solution.

Step 8: Problem Not Solved. You'll notice this section on the *Wisdom Marathon Track* that draws attention to your *not solving* a problem. If your action did not solve the problem, then you need to study the problem further, which takes you to Step 9 on the *Wisdom Marathon Track.*

Step 9: Evaluate Problem Again More Intensely. You need to reassess the problem and situation. You will also need to do more studying of God's Word, more reading of the Bible, and more praying and contemplation, to fully understand your problem, and to gain more insights about what action to take. You might want to talk to a mentor or someone you respect at this juncture. That mentor could help you by offering ideas and suggestions to solve your problem.

Step 10: Take Action to Solve Problem. After more intense evaluation and study of your problem, then you should be ready to take action to solve the problem. If you're not ready to solve the problem, however, Step 11 takes you back to Step 2 to start the process again.

The whole point is to get to the *Problem Solved* and *Wisdom Accumulates* boxes on the *Wisdom Marathon Track.* As a result of solving problems successfully, your wisdom accumulates and grows.

You can use this accumulated wisdom—your experiences–when similar problems occur in the future. Or, perhaps you'd like to share your wisdom with others who may be facing similar problems. Just like attorneys look at past cases to determine what was done to solve problems and win cases, you can look at your and others' past experiences to help you solve your problems.

Too many people think that running the *Wisdom Marathon* is over once one problem is solved. That is wrong! Nothing could be further from the truth. It's a continual race just the way your lifelong mission is. This particular marathon lasts a lifetime!

Take the time to reflect on your problem-solving experiences to see what you can glean for future use. Don't just think about how the problem was solved, but how you could have solved it better. How could you have improved?

The value of using God's Word to handle problems is unquestionable.[179] However, using God's Word may not be as straightforward as it seems. God's Word speaks differently to different people, and even differently to the same person at different times. It's because God always gives us what we need when we read His Word. The meaning that's meant just for you can be the "silver lining" between the words, and may not be apparent to everyone. As your wisdom grows, so will your understanding of God's Word.

You have read about Matthew's *No Instant Wisdom Adventure*, and you know that you can't attain wisdom instantly. It's a journey. As you experience your own adventures with friends or in the workplace, don't forget to enjoy the journey because it's in the journey where you will "train" and where you will find those golden nuggets of wisdom.

---

[179] 2 Timothy 3:16-17, (*New International Version*): 16 All Scripture is God-breathed and is useful for teaching, rebuking, correcting and training in righteousness, 17 so that the servant of God may be thoroughly equipped for every good work.

When training for a physical fitness marathon, the runners learn many lessons about their bodies and nutritional needs. In the same way, when you train for your *Wisdom Marathon,* you will learn what kinds of spiritual nutrition you need, as in the Bible, and what kinds of mental exercises will better prepare you for your race.

You might be enjoying a lazy Saturday afternoon watching basketball on TV and ask, "Why should I even commit to running the *Wisdom Marathon?*" (There's nothing wrong with enjoying a lazy Saturday afternoon; just don't get too lazy and undisciplined, or you'll never reach that finish line!) The answer is simple. If you are successful in winning and possessing wisdom, this wisdom will become more valuable to you than silver or gold. It will become more precious than jewels or anything else in this world that people see as valuable.[180]

THE REAL BUSINESS WORLD

The real business world is difficult. Complex. Challenging. We are faced with economic challenges, personality and employee challenges, financial challenges, and more.

And all the while, our goal should be to become wiser because in doing so, we'll manage our businesses better and more than likely be more successful.

Not all the steps of becoming wiser in business are linear. Some steps are circular and overlap with others and not all business leaders seek to achieve the same results. But the steps in the *Wisdom Marathon Track* can be used in any business or life endeavor.

---

[180] Proverbs 3:13-14, (*New International Version*): 13 Blessed are those who find wisdom, those who gain understanding, 14 for she is more profitable than silver and yields better returns than gold.

You may feel that in many ways, our discussion of the *Wisdom Marathon* oversimplifies how to become wiser. Anyone in business knows that you don't often have the luxury of focusing on simply one problem at a time. There are always problems and as a result, you'll probably be thinking about solving multiple problems at the same time. This creates the added complexity of having to review multiple insights on how to solve these problems, while taking action to address the problems, monitoring to see if the problems are solved, and then acting accordingly.

But that's why I designed a *Wisdom Marathon Track* that is somewhat like a circle. You solve one problem, then define another. If you don't solve that problem, re-evaluate and study the problem and how you can best solve it. Then, move on. Over and over again, you define problems and solve them. As a result, you become wiser and wiser.

Always, you are going to have to cope with added complexities in your business life. But, relish this added complexity as a meaningful challenge to becoming wiser. We are here in this life to learn and grow. And this life is filled with problems, uncertainty, and hard lessons. If you stick with it and stay focused on God's Word, you will be amazed at the rewards in both business and personal life. Stay focused on acquiring this wisdom throughout your life, for God readily gives it to us through His spoken Word.[181]

To help deal with the complexity of becoming wiser, you fortunately have a clear, concise source of knowledge upon which you can build your wisdom. Don't forget that God's Word is this source. The Bible is filled with plainspoken, straightforward

---

[181] Proverbs 2:6-8, (*The Message*): And here's why: God gives out Wisdom free, is plainspoken in Knowledge and Understanding. He's a rich mine of Common Sense for those who live well, a personal bodyguard to the candid and sincere. He keeps his eye on all who live honestly, and pays special attention to his loyally committed ones.

knowledge about solving life problems. Of course, since business is part of your life, God's Word is also plainspoken knowledge about handling important business problems.

DEFINING PROBLEMS: A DOCTOR'S VISIT

For the purpose of this discussion, I'd like to illustrate a problem and how to define and solve it. You can do something similar in regard to your own problems. For example, think about the last time you visited a doctor's office and were not feeling well. To determine if you actually had a health problem, the doctor immediately began collecting information—a list of your symptoms. The doctor noted and summarized your signs of health—both good and bad. Among other measurements, the doctor probably took your temperature and blood pressure, and asked if you had been experiencing any dizziness.

From these symptoms, the doctor could conclude if there indeed was a problem, an illness. Suppose the doctor concluded that you had strep throat, which could be a serious problem keeping you from good health. If the doctor gathered and interpreted your symptoms properly, accurately defined your illness, and implemented the right treatment, the problem, in this case, the illness, would be eliminated and your symptoms would eventually vanish.

I've not always been so fortunate with doctors' visits. At times, as probably some of you have experienced, I've had a doctor gather symptoms and then misinterpret them. As a result, the problem, the *illness* wasn't defined accurately. The doctor gave me a prescription for medicine, but the medicine did not help me recover. As a result, I stayed sick and the symptoms continued.

In one particular case, I had to go back to the doctor a number of times. Because the doctor couldn't identify the illness or problem correctly, the problem was not solved. She had to start over and over again to try to identify my illness. I had to continue diagnoses to eventually find the solution to my health problem. This happens in business, as well.

DEFINING PROBLEMS IN BUSINESS

The point is clear. To run the *Wisdom Marathon* successfully, you must be able to accurately define a problem. Without knowing exactly what your problem is, you cannot determine right or wrong actions for solving it. If you define a problem inaccurately, anything that you do to try to solve that problem is wasted time and effort. What you do in such a circumstance may even make the problem worse. You simply cannot consider how to attack a problem properly if you do not have a clear definition of the problem.

Let's think about a practical business situation involving symptoms, problem identification, and problem solution that might exist in your company. Let's say that one of the acceptable norms that you set for your company is that employees should always be honest. Honesty is a highly prized trait and a valuable standard.[182] It epitomizes a person's spiritual backbone.

Imagine that one day you see that an employee has submitted a request for a travel expense reimbursement that includes an extra day of expenses. You're a business leader and you have instilled a code of ethics at your company. You immediately interpret this filed expense report as a sign of dishonesty, a violation of your code of honesty. As a result, you conclude that a problem of dishonesty exists in your organization. You want to act wisely in this situation, so you begin to analyze various right and wrong actions you could take to eliminate this problem of dishonesty. But, stop!

Before trying to remedy any problem, remember that properly concluding that a particular problem even *exists* can be very

---

[182] Proverbs 16:13, (*New International Version*): Kings take pleasure in honest lips; they value a man who speaks the truth.

tricky. You may have *improperly* interpreted the expense report as a sign of dishonesty. Interpreting signs can be confusing. Jesus himself acknowledged both the existence of reading signs and the challenge of interpreting them properly.[183]

Make sure that the expense report provides enough data to determine that a dishonesty problem exists. You may need more data. Perhaps the employee stayed an extra day on the trip, tracked expenses for this day, didn't intend to submit them to you for reimbursement, but the expenses were submitted because of a computer glitch. On the other hand, maybe you uncover other incidents of dishonesty initiated by this employee.

Be careful if indeed this submission is dishonest, but is the only evidence of the employee's dishonesty that you can find. Do not ignore this even though you believe it's only a small incident. Generally, whoever is dishonest in small matters will be dishonest in larger ones.[184]

If you're right in concluding that a dishonesty problem exists and your action eliminates it, the organization can benefit in many ways. As an example, the source of the dishonesty will be eliminated, other employees will know that dishonesty is not tolerated, and the longevity of your company will be enhanced by making sure that costs are real costs and not fabrications.

If you're wrong in concluding that a dishonesty problem exists and still take action to solve the problem, the organization could be damaged in many ways. For example, you might lose the trust of your employees and honest employees might leave the

---

[183] Matthew 16:2-3, 4, (*New International Version*): 2 He replied, "When evening comes, you say, 'It will be fair weather, for the sky is red,' 3 and in the morning, 'Today it will be stormy, for the sky is red and overcast.' You know how to interpret the appearance of the sky, but you cannot interpret the signs of the times."

[184] Luke 16:10, (*New Living Translation*): If you are faithful in little things, you will be faithful in large ones. But if you are dishonest in little things, you won't be honest with greater responsibilities.

company because they feel insulted. Ultimately, you might lose respect as a leader. Don't take action unless you're sure. One of the pioneers who settled this country, Davey Crockett, is often quoted as saying, "Be sure you're right and then go ahead."

There's plenty of sage, old wisdom in that advice.

WISDOM'S WELLSPRING

Respect for God's Word is the wellspring of wisdom. Always remember that wisdom is based upon a true respect for God's Word—for Biblical thought.[185] It's worth repeating—the importance of knowing and understanding God's Word cannot be overestimated. It is broad and far-reaching, equipping all who know it to do good works of all kinds. Albert Einstein once said that he wanted to know God's thoughts because everything else was just detail. Even with all that Einstein knew, he realized if he didn't understand God's Word, he didn't understand much at all.

Respect God's Word as the *standard* for determining the right and wrong ways to handle issues. Wisdom requires that you consider the *bigger picture*. True wisdom knows the difference between doing what is morally correct and avoiding what is morally incorrect. It knows that you consider all people linked to a problem and take action to solve the problem in a morally appropriate fashion. This is action that is in alignment with, and consistent with, God's Word.

True wisdom is not egotistical. You never take action intended to manipulate people into doing things for your own personal benefit. Unfortunately, many people do this. They focus on power and control instead of true wisdom in their everyday business practices. Wisdom is not a tool you use to achieve personal ambition. That's egotistical. Good always comes from taking action based upon what you know is right no matter how it affects you personally. That's the essence of wisdom.

---

[185] Proverbs 9:10, (*New International Version*): The fear of the LORD is the beginning of wisdom, and knowledge of the Holy One is understanding.

WISDOM MARATHONERS DO

Never think of wisdom as simply a mental exercise for considering right and wrong in solving problems. It's much deeper than that. Instead, think of wisdom as one of your main tools for taking action to solve problems. God's Word is your foundation for wisdom, but God's Word is not meant simply to be internalized. God's Word is meant as a guide for what's right and wrong to *do*.

It's all about action. Think of a person who says they are going to go on a diet, exercise and lose weight. That person can talk about it all he or she wants. But unless that person *acts*, he or she will never lose any weight. Likewise, if a guy wants to build muscles, but never lifts weight, it doesn't matter how much he talks about it. He has to actually work the muscles and lift weights to create the strength he wants to achieve. It's about action!

Put God's Word into action. *Walk the talk.*

The wise are doers, not simply thinkers.[186] Be a doer. You show your wisdom through the good life you lead.[187] You set yourself apart from others by your shining examples and moral compass. As someone who is wise, you illustrate a strong spiritual backbone at every step of the *Wisdom Marathon*. You are a *Wisdom Marathoner.*

As examples for others in business and life, the wise take sound, humble action. There is no ego involved, no dishonesty.

---

[186] James 1:22-24, (*New International Version*): 22 Do not merely listen to the Word, and so deceive yourselves. Do what it says. 23 Anyone who listens to the Word but does not do what it says is like a man who looks at his face in a mirror. 24 And, after looking at himself, goes away and immediately forgets what he looks like.

[187] James 3:13-14, (*New International Version*): 13 Who is wise and understanding among you? Let him show it by his good life, by deeds done in the humility that comes from wisdom. 14 But if you harbor bitter envy and selfish ambition in your hearts, do not boast about it or deny the truth.

The wise don't lie. They focus on the truth for that is the only way to live.

GENERAL DAVID PETRAEUS: FOOLISH BEHAVIOR CAN RUIN A WISE REPUTATION

It would be remiss if I didn't mention that some people travel along in life and continually run *Wisdom Marathon*, thus building reputations for being wise. Then, something happens. They make bad decisions or use poor judgment and behave foolishly in some way and tear down all they have worked so hard to build.

General David Petraeus is an interesting example of this. Petraeus, the top U.S. and NATO Commander in the Afghanistan War, saw a serious problem in the summer of 2010. The problem was that an event planned by Pastor Terry Jones in Gainesville, Florida, was increasing the danger to Petraeus' troops on the battlefield in Afghanistan.

The event was a planned Quran burning by Pastor Terry Jones, the leader of the Dove World Outreach Center. The Center was actually an evangelical Christian church that promoted an anti-Islam philosophy. Jones and his church had developed plans to burn copies of the Quran to commemorate the September 11, 2001 terrorist attacks on the World Trade Center in New York City. The Quran is to a Muslim what the Bible is to a Christian.

Petreaus knew that Muslims considered the Quran to be their holy book and that destroying it on purpose would be a huge sign of disrespect and incite further action against his troops. News coverage of the planned event was being beamed across the world and already causing the Muslim reaction that Petreaus feared.

After Petraeus thought about this situation, he took action. He knew that he had to stop Jones's planned Quran burning and media coverage surrounding it. He addressed his problem directly and quickly. In an effort to minimize the publicity around the Jones situation, he quickly e-mailed The Associated Press saying, "Images of the burning of a Quran would undoubtedly be used by extremists in Afghanistan—and around the world—to inflame public opinion and incite violence." He was urging The Associated Press to lighten its coverage of the Jones's situation.

Next, from Afghanistan, he phoned Jones to try to convince him to abandon his plans because of the possible resulting added danger that carrying out his plans would cause for U.S. troops. Although reports of the contents of the conversation are sketchy, reports of the length of the conversation are pretty clear. The conversation was short. Certainly, Petraeus surely stated his case clearly and concisely with powerful emphasis on the serious negative impact of Jones's plan. He was succinct and didn't *dilute* the meaning of his message by using too many words.[188]

Petraeus's actions along with the actions of others resulted in Jones abandoning his planned Quran burning. Although some criticized Petraeus for the action he took, most agreed that Petraeus had significant impact on Jones's decisions to cancel his plans. And this was a good thing.

It's obvious how very wise Petreaus's actions were in this situation. He defined the planned Quran burning as a problem, a factor that could further endanger his troops. Recognizing how powerful sensibly chosen words can be[189], he sent his carefully-crafted message to The Associated Press to try to minimize the impact of Jones's publicity related to this situation.

In addition, Petraeus initiated a conversation with Jones as an attempt to get the plan canceled, again using very carefully chosen words. As a result of his actions, Petraeus was able to avoid a very harmful situation for all parties involved.

Petraeus defined the problem, reviewed his own insights on how to solve the problem, and took action to solve the problem.

---

[188] Ecclesiastes 6:11, (*New International Version*): The more the words, the less the meaning, and how does that profit anyone?

[189] Proverbs 13:3 (*The Message*): Careful words make for a careful life; careless talk may ruin everything.

Problem was solved. He adhered very well to the *Wisdom Marathon Track.*

In 2011, General Petraeus was named the Director of the CIA. Just 14 months later, in November 2012, he resigned after he confessed to "extremely poor judgment" in cheating on his wife of 37 years with his biographer, Paula Broadwell. The FBI launched an investigation into Broadwell, who allegedly hacked into the former general's email, according to NBC News.

At the end of 2012, Barbara Walters revealed that General David Petraeus had been chosen as her pick for Most Fascinating Person of The Year. Walters said that Petraeus had been chosen as the Most Fascinating Person of the Year just two years prior as a result of his outstanding military service. In 2012, he was selected due to the scandal. Walters went on to discuss military honor and how Petraeus's actions caused him to fall far from grace. She questioned the contradictions in his character and his career and reminded us that *no one, however powerful, is free of human frailty or immune to reversals of fortune.*

I don't think anyone could have said it better. Wise men sometimes fall from grace. No matter who you are, temptations can interfere with a person's wisdom and decision-making. However, if a person stays true to God's Word, and keeps his thoughts and prayers on God, then he or she will always have the right tools to stay firm on the *Wisdom Marathon Track* and not be deterred. It just takes one mistake to fall from being *wise* to *foolish.*

WISDOM MARATHONERS FOCUS ON THEMSELVES

There are some excellent books on the market that can help you study how to *chase wisdom* while embarking on your own *Wisdom Marathon.* One of the bestselling books of all time is called *The Purpose Driven Life.* Written by Rick Warren, this book begins with a now famous one-sentence paragraph: "It's not about you." Warren is making the point that the purpose of *your life* is far greater than you becoming *personally fulfilled*, having peace of mind, or even being happy. Instead, you were born as part of God's Plan and your purpose is to help fulfill that plan. I take no issue with these thoughts.

You need to think about your wisdom a little differently, however. It *is* all about you. Let me explain. You need to be your own project. The project is becoming wiser, achieving greater wisdom. Focus on yourself. This doesn't mean that you should start being selfish. The point is to take time to focus on your own thinking and decision-making, your study of God's Word. This may be uncomfortable sometimes. Oftentimes in life, when we're struggling and searching, we may feel restless and bad about ourselves. We may want to take the focus off ourselves because if we look too closely, we won't like what we see.

But think back to the example of a marathon runner. That runner won't be able to finish a marathon race if he or she doesn't focus on his or her training. The dietary and exercise regimen that will help the marathoner complete the race. This focus on oneself is crucial to success.

Often, in society, we are discouraged from questioning or sorting through the lies in society, in materialism, in the way we should think or behave. Generally, if we want to be seen as normal, we are simply expected to go along with the norm. Kind of like zombies who are hypnotized by mass media.

We just plod along and do what everyone else is doing. What society is telling us to do. And frequently, we go along with lies among our employees or peers. It's easier than standing out and bucking the system. A true leader—a wise business leader—stands out because he or she does not simply go along with the norm without a good reason.

By focusing on yourself, praying, contemplating on God's Word, and *digging deeper,* you will uncover the truths, and as you apply these truths in life, you will become wiser.

Do you consider yourself wise? Why or why not? What can you do to become wiser?

WISDOM MARATHONER: STAY FOCUSED!

My father was a good man, a hardworking man who I loved and respected very much. I still do even though he is no longer with us. I have a very vivid boyhood memory of my father practicing his trade as a carpenter. One of his tools was a saw—not an electric saw—but a hand saw that he would push and pull back and forth across the wood to cut it. The saw was about 26 inches long and had about eight cutting teeth per inch—208 teeth overall. It took a lot of strength to push and pull this saw.

Since using this saw was such an important part of my father's work life, he would spend what seemed like hours meticulously sharpening his saw. He would place the saw in a vice and carefully use a special file to make sure each tooth was perfectly honed. He wanted the saw to be just right because he knew that if this tool wasn't as sharp as possible, his on-the-job productivity would suffer.

In thinking about becoming wiser, think of wisdom as your old-fashioned saw. In each and every day of your business life you will have to sharpen your saw—wisdom. If not, it will become rusty and eventually, unusable altogether.

Stay focused on sharpening your wisdom. You will continually need this wisdom to make sound decisions, interact with employees, and establish organizational and business policies. Every time that you face a difficult problem, you'll notice that your wisdom tool, your *saw,* is sharp and ready to use.

The key word is *focus.*

YOU AND YOUR CHASE

You've read Matthew's *No Instant Wisdom Adventure* and learned how it isn't normal for a young man to be as wise as an older, accomplished businessman.

Becoming wiser is usually a long-term, never-ending project the way your life's mission is a lifelong project. It's a continual *Wisdom Marathon*. Wisdom is not instant and doesn't happen overnight-unless, of course, you ask God for it and He simply grants it to you..

You've also read about General David Petraeus and learned that just because you've gained a certain amount of wisdom in life, that does not mean that you can't fall from grace. It can happen. One bad decision is all it takes. You now know it's more important than ever to use the tools I have provided to help ensure you always make wise decisions.

Throughout this book, I have provided you with tools and steps that you can take in *chasing wisdom in business and life*, in *growing* your wisdom. The steps are simple: define your problems, review and contemplate on Biblical insights, on God's Word, and use your experiences as tools to traverse the *Wisdom Marathon Track*, and to gain insights on solving problems.

Take the time to define problems carefully and don't expect that you'll solve a problem simply because you take action aimed at solving it. Be patient. You may have to try several different things to solve your problems. And, you may need to redefine a problem over and over again, or improve the actions aimed at solving it in order to get the results you desire. This is a lifelong *Wisdom Marathon*, right? Defining and solving problems is a lifelong activity.

Remember that respect for God's Word is the wellspring of wisdom. If you do not respect the Word of God and put it into practice, into action, you're not really serious about becoming wiser. Know and appreciate that God's Word gives you insights about doing good and right things in your business life, as well as your personal life. If you're smart in business, you're more likely to be smart in your personal life.

The way to reach the endpoint of wisdom is action. Knowing what you should do is of no value if you don't do it. Taking action is how you make impact in the business world, and the world in general.

If you follow the steps of the *Wisdom Marathon Track* properly, you're more prepared to take worthwhile action and achieve your goal of solving problems.

Don't be afraid of taking action. Don't be afraid to make mistakes. You can learn from those mistakes. (*General Petraeus can certainly learn from his mistake and start rebuilding his reputation. It may take a while, but he can do it!*) Taking *wise* action, action that reflects God's Word, will always be of value. It will give you that spiritual backbone that sets you apart from others.

And finally, focus on yourself. This is not the same thing as selfishness. You are your own project and as such, you need to always be thinking about how you can improve. This is staying focused. Don't lose sight of your *self-improvement project* to become wiser. If becoming wiser is not in the forefront of your mind, then the emphasis on self-improvement that you need to maximize your wisdom over time will simply fade away.

You now have valuable tools to change your life. You have met my sons Brian and Matthew and heard some of their stories involving lessons and problems as they continually *chase wisdom in business*, and strive to grow wiser every day. You've met numerous heroes and some "non-heroes" throughout this journey, as well. You've met people who have tried and failed, and others who have tried and succeeded. Everyone you've met has employed a bit of wisdom—*or lack of*—in their lives to achieve their outcomes.

You now know what wisdom is and how to get started on your own *Wisdom Marathon Track*. You know how to *bridle the tongue* to keep you from doing or saying something you will regret, which could be a deterrent in your business. You now know that anger can harm your relationships in business and ultimately, your personal life. And you understand how anger backlash can totally derail your business.

You now know that pride, when it becomes a part of ego, can be a deterrent to your success. When used in the right way, it can serve as a positive force in helping you create a good, successful business environment.

You now know that implementing justice is important in your business decisions. You know that fools exist in our world and often will go along with others and their bad behavior because they want to be accepted by their peers. You know that to be a truly wise business leader, you can't allow the fools of this world to usurp your business morals and ethics.

You know that the wise understand how to handle both discipline and self-discipline, which are important for both you and your employees in crafting an environment that is conducive to business success.

You know that good listening is a skill that is crucial to success. Crucial to knowing and understanding yourself and others. Crucial to *chasing wisdom* throughout life. And you know that trust is necessary in business if you're going to succeed. If you can't trust any of your employees, how can you possibly succeed?

And finally, you know that if a business doesn't have the right heart, it won't be as successful as it could be. A business without right heart is just a mechanical *thing*. Sure, it might have some degree of success, but does it shine? Will it stand up to the true test of time and economics? Will it thrive?

All of these issues are incorporated into your actual *Wisdom Marathon* in life. To your *chasing wisdom*. You've got your wisdom *fitness* tools at your fingertips and you're ready to get moving!

As I leave you, why don't you start on your *Wisdom Marathon* right now? As my sons Brian and Matthew have done, you might enjoy sharing and/or writing down your stories—the successes and nonsuccesses—and studying them on your journey. If you'd like to share them with me, please feel free to email me at scerto@ rollins.edu.

I would love to hear about your journey and how you're running your marathon! It's never too soon (or too late) to get started on the different disciplines and activities needed to complete your *Wisdom Marathon*. It is never too late to study and implement Biblical thought—God's Word—as your vehicle to wisdom.

In your pursuit to be a wise leader, don't worry about achieving all that you can today, or even tomorrow. Know that it's a process. A journey. Enjoy the journey, and maybe somewhere, someday, I'll meet you on the *chase*. Somewhere on the *Wisdom Marathon Track*.

I truly hope so.

EPILOGUE: COMMIT TO THE CHASE

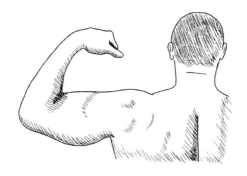

Be diligent in these matters; give yourself wholly to them,
so that everyone may see your progress.

1 Timothy 4:15 (*New International Version*)

Make no mistake about it—*this is a pep talk!* A talk to help you
feel strong, courageous, and enthusiastic about *chasing wisdom in
business and life.* A talk you might hear from a coach, mentor, or
tutor. A talk that you might hear from your boss, a friend, or even
your parents.

Commit to becoming wiser and wiser! Go ahead. The time
is now. Take the actions involved in building discipline, being
honest, and creating community in your business world (and
personal life), and you will succeed.

This entire book has been about *chasing wisdom in business
and life* with steps on *how* to become wiser. The main focus has
been on using Biblical thought—*God's Word*—to become more
and more insightful about what is right and wrong in solving
problems and in making wise decisions. As you become more
and more insightful, you'll become wiser, and more and more
proficient at handling difficult problems. Your success as a leader
will grow—don't doubt me on this one!

Chase, but be realistic in your chase. Although you chase wisdom all your life, never really expect to achieve the pinnacle of true mastership, as Jesus did. That's okay. What's important is the journey—the *Wisdom Marathon*—and your dedication to keep running, growing, experiencing, and learning how to be wise.

UNDERSTAND YOUR COMMITMENT

Commitment is hard...*very hard!* You can't just say you're committed to the chase. You have to *be* committed, so be committed to *chase wisdom*. If you don't *commit to the chase*, you'll go nowhere. An uncommitted bodybuilder will never achieve a desirable body shape and uncommitted chasers of wisdom will never be as wise as they can be.

Think about becoming wiser every day. Run at least part of the *Wisdom Marathon Track* every day. Think daily about applying every thought in this book to help you become wiser.

We can all see that the bodybuilder at the beginning of the *Epilogue* stayed committed to his bodybuilding routine. You can do the same. Show everyone that you're a *wisdom-building* bodybuilder and that you're committed to becoming wiser through the wise decisions that you make and actions you take!

As the Bible verse at the beginning of the Epilogue implies, you must be completely dedicated to becoming wiser. If you are, those around you will see the difference in you as your wisdom grows. You will not only become wiser through this dedication, but you will become a role model for others on how to become wiser. You must not only think about being wise, you must *do* wise things.

Think of *commitment* as being bound—emotionally, intellectually, or both—to a particular course of action. Commitment starts with a choice. When committed to *chasing wisdom in business and life*, you choose to do whatever is necessary to make the chase successful.

The choice in itself is not enough however. The choice must be sustained by dedication and perseverance. You must stay dedicated to, and persevere in, your choice to chase wisdom.

WHY COMMIT TO THE CHASE?

Without true commitment to become wiser, you will never be pleased with how wise you are. Most people have been inspired at one time or another and most have had good ideas about something in business or life. But, not everyone acts on those good ideas. Pursue those ideas! Commit to achieving something!

Don't let your thoughts about becoming wiser be just another bright idea that you don't act upon and gain nothing from.

When you first have a spark of an idea, it is like a tiny ember that is glowing, ready to burst into fire. If you put kindling on the embers, it will grow into a beautiful, warm fire. That is your bright idea. Put kindling on it and build a fire!

Your new ideas about becoming wiser can lead to a good start and a new bright beginning. However, starting is not enough. Excellent ideas are no better than terrible ones if we do not follow through on them. And like a runner who wants to complete a marathon, the idea is a good one, but unless you train for it, you won't succeed. In business, you need to constantly train to be wiser and wiser as you learn more on your journey in business and in life throughout the years.

Many people have good ideas and dreams, but not everyone follows through and realizes their dreams. The people who do are often the ones who create and invent things that change the world, and that can change business models. Anyone who has a dream must commit to that dream and pursue it with determination and persistence. Are you that person? Can you overcome obstacles in your path and achieve all that you're dreaming? Get started! Start running your *Wisdom Marathon Track* now!

Vince Lombardi (1913-1970), ESPN's Coach of the Century, once said, "The difference between a successful person and others is not a lack of strength, not a lack of knowledge, but rather, a lack of will."

Similarly, Victor Hugo (1802–1885), a famous French poet, playwright, and human activist, wrote, "People do not lack strength; they lack will." Here, "will" refers to commitment, to determination.

Be committed to chasing wisdom in business and life! Be committed to running the *Wisdom Marathon Track*. There is great power in deciding to follow through on gaining wisdom and achieving your dreams.

Do not operate aimlessly or whimsically but understand that commitment and determination can move mountains and understand that embracing God's Word will help move those mountains. Therein lies the worth of your commitment … Wisdom.

Abraham Lincoln once said, "Determine that the thing can and shall be done and then we shall find the way." Moving from impossible to possible requires commitment. Committed people never doubt that what they're trying to accomplish, they indeed will accomplish.

The popular Nike ad, "Just Do It" is a great example of this. Instead of just saying you're going to run that marathon, just do it! You can achieve your dreams and become wiser during the process. Don't let others stop you!

So, I encourage you to set out on your wisdom adventures in life and in business. I wish you well. Try it! If you shoot for the moon, you may hit a star. What a treat!Don't be afraid to dream big dreams. I've always wondered why people limit their dreams to, "I want to sell one hundred copies of my book." They should say, "I want to sell millions of copies of my book!" There are no limits to dreaming. We put our own limits on ourselves when we dream for less.

We can run the *Wisdom Marathon Track* and *chase wisdom in business and in life* because we're in charge of our lives. We can commit to becoming the masters of our lives through the guidance that we receive through Biblical insights—through God's Word. When you understand this and put your commitment into action, you can truly gain wisdom beyond your wildest dreams. Beyond your ever-imagined goals!

And why would you want to commit to gaining wisdom beyond some ever-imagined goals? Because what you can gain from being wise can also go beyond some ever-imagined goal.

WISDOM BUILT ON FAITH AND TRUST IN GOD

To commit to chasing wisdom in business and life, you must have faith. Faith is belief and trust in God. It's committing yourself to God and studying and living God's Word. Unfortunately, many people are too busy for God these days. Even people who think they are wise tend to leave out God in their planning and as such, become fools.

It doesn't matter how smart someone is or how many college degrees a person has. A person's education or intelligence does not measure how wise a person is. Wisdom comes only from God or knowing God's Word.

Be proactive. Study and learn what the Bible teaches us to do in managing problems in both business and life, and remember, wisdom for you can be born from God's Word. Jesus promised wisdom to all who seek Him, and it will be provided to all who trust Him. Seek God.

COMMIT NOW...

When is a good time to commit to chasing wisdom? The following lyrics from the recent hit song by Tobymac entitled "City on Our Knees" gives us the answer:

If you gotta start somewhere
Why not here?

If you gotta start sometime
Why not now?
Here and now! Start now on your journey to *chasing wisdom in business and in life*. Start on your own *Wisdom Marathon Track*. It's simple, friends! Commit now to learning what insights the Bible offers for managing your problems in business and life. If you want wisdom in business in the truest sense, start asking the right One right now. Ask God. What do you have to lose? Commit now and start reaping the advantages of growing in wisdom. Don't wait. You will miss out on far too much if you delay!

As you venture out in the world to become wiser in business and in life, remember to enjoy the journey—all the hardships, trials, setbacks and successes. Be grateful for all of it because it will all teach you, and therein, are the lessons of wisdom. Remember, you can start becoming wiser every day. Blessings your way!

BIBLIOGRAPHY

Active Listening. www.wikipedia.com (accessed).

Ash, Mary Kay. The Mary Kay Way: Timeless Principles from America's Greatest Woman Entrepreneur. New York, New York: John Wiley & Sons, 2008.

Bellinger, William H. Psalms: Reading and Studying the Book of Praises. Ada, Michigan: Baker

Academic, 1990.

Blackaby, Henry. Spiritual Leadership: Moving People On to God's Agenda. Nashville, Tennessee: B&H Publishing Group, 2011.

Bounty Rewards Program, New Orleans Saints. 2012. www. profootballweekly.com (accessed).

Carl R. Rogers. www.brittanica.com, www.wikipedia.com (accessed).

Certo, Samuel C., Certo, S. Trevis. Modern Management: Concepts and Skills. New York, New York: Pearson Publishing, 2012.

Chick-fil-A. www.wikipedia.com (accessed).

CNL Financial Group. www.investingbusinessweek.com (accessed).

Cousins, Don. Experiencing LeaderShift: Letting Go of Leadership Heresies. Colorado Springs, Colorado: David C. Cook, 2008.

DeMoss, Mark. The Little Red Book of Wisdom. Nashville, Tennessee: Thomas Nelson, 2011.

Duhigg, Charles. The Power of Habit: Why We Do What We Do in Life and Business. New York, New York: Random House, 2012.

Elliott, Matthew. Feel: The Power of Listening to Your Heart By. Carol Stream, Illinois: Tyndale House Publishers, Inc., 2008.

Elwell, Walter A., Robert W. Yarbrough. Encountering the New Testament: A Historical and Theological Survey. Ada, Michigan: Baker Academic, 2013.

Erickson, Millard J. Introducing Christian Doctrine. Ada, Michigan: Baker Academic, 2nd Edition, 2001.

Feeding the Bears, Colorado Division of Wildlife. 2011. www. HuffingtonPost.com (accessed).

Figueira, Thomas J., Brennan, T. Corey, Stemberg, Rachel Hall. Wisdom From The Ancients: Enduring Business Lessons From Alexander The Great, Julius Caesar, And The Illustrious Leaders Of Ancient Greece And Rome. New York New York: Basic Books, 2001.

Forni, Pier M. The Civility Solution: What to Do When People are Rude. New York, New York: St. Martin's Press, 2008.

Garrett, Ginger. Desired: The Untold Story of Samson and Delilah (Lost Loves of the Bible). Colorado Springs, Colorado: David C. Cook, 2011.

Hall, Stephen S. Wisdom: From Philosophy to Neuroscience. New York, New York: Vintage Books, 2011.

Henry, Matthew. Matthew Henry's Concise Commentary on the Whole Bible. Nashville, Tennessee: Thomas Nelson Publishers, 1997.

Holy Bible: New International Version. Grand Rapids, Michigan: Zondervan, 2005.

Inamori, Kazuo. A Compass to Fulfillment: Passion and Spirituality in Life and Business. New York, New York: McGraw-Hill, 2010.

Isaacson, Walter. Steve Jobs. New York, New York: Simon & Schuster, 2011.

Isaacson, Walter. Einstein: His Life and Universe. New York, New York: Simon & Schuster, 2008.

John Mackey of Whole Foods Market on Creating High Trust Organizations. YouTube video (accessed).

Katzenbach, Jon R., Douglas K. Smith The Wisdom of Teams: Creating the High-Performance Organization. New York, New York: HarperCollins Publishers, 2003.

Lerner, Ralph. Playing the Fool: Subversive Laughter in Troubled Times. Chicago, Illinois: University of Chicago Press, 2009.

Life Application Bible, New International Version. Grand Rapids, Michigan: Zondervan, 1988.

Millman, Dan. The Four Purposes of Life: Finding Meaning and Direction in a Changing World. Tiburon, California: HJ Kramer/New World Library, 2011.

Millman, Dan. No Ordinary Moments: A Peaceful Warrior's Guide to Daily Life. Tiburon, California: HJ Kramer, Inc., 1992.

Millman, Dan. The Life You Were Born to Live: A Guide to Finding Your Life Purpose. Tiburon, California: HJ Kramer, Inc., 1993.

Millman, Dan, Childers, Doug. Divine Interventions: True Stories of Mystery and Miracles That Change Lives. Emmaus, Pennsylvania: Rodale Press, 1999.

Peterson, Eugene H. The Message. Colorado Springs, Colorado: Navpress, 2002.

Petraeus's Next Battle. 2011. www.thedailybeast.com (accessed).

Pherson, Marnie L. Trust Your Heart: Building Relationships That Build Your Business. www.BooksByMarnie.com, 2012.

Ramsey, Dave. EntreLeadership: 20 Years of Practical Business Wisdom from the Trenches. Brentwood, Tennessee: Howard Books, 2011.

Silvious, Jan. Foolproofing Your Life: How to Deal Effectively with the Impossible People in Your Life. Colorado Springs, Colorado: WaterBrook Press, 1998.

Scazzero, Peter. Emotionally Healthy Spirituality: Unleash a Revolution in Your Life In Christ. Nashville, Tennessee: Thomas Nelson, 2006.

Sternberg, Robert (Ed), Jordan, Jennifer (Ed). A Handbook of Wisdom: Psychological Perspectives. New York, New York: Cambridge University Press, 2005.

Sternberg, Robert J. Wisdom: Its Nature, Origins, and Development. New York, New York: Cambridge University Press, 1990.

Szollose, Brad. Liquid Leadership. Austin, Texas: Greenleaf Book Group Press, 2011.

Taco Bell. 2011. www.Foxnews.com (accessed).

The Holman Illustrated Study Bible. Nashville, Tennessee: Holman Bible Publishers, 2006.

The Mike Slater Show Blog. www.http://mikeslaterradio.com (accessed).

Underwood, Jim. More Than a Pink Cadillac: Mary Kay Inc.'s Nine Leadership Keys to Success. New York, New York: McGraw-Hill, 2003.

Vaden, Rory. Take the Stairs: 7 Steps to Achieving True Success. New York, New York: The Penguin Group, USA, 2012.

Warren, Rick. The Purpose Driven Life: What On Earth Am I Here For? Grand Rapids, Michigan: Zondervan, 2012.

www.biblegateway.com (accessed).

www.motivatingquotes.com/discipline (accessed).

www.rockefellerfoundation.com (accessed).

www.twitter.com/wiseleaders.

www.wikipedia.com (accessed).